D0897886

The Question of Class in Contemporary Latin American Cinema

The Question of Class in Contemporary Latin American Cinema

María Mercedes Vázquez Vázquez

LEXINGTON BOOKS
Lanham • Boulder • New York • London

Published by Lexington Books
An imprint of The Rowman & Littlefield Publishing Group, Inc.
4501 Forbes Boulevard, Suite 200, Lanham, Maryland 20706
www.rowman.com

6 Tinworth Street, London SE11 5AL, United Kingdom

British Library Cataloguing in Publication Information Available

Library of Congress Cataloging-in-Publication Data Available

ISBN 978-1-4985-5302-5 (cloth : alk. Paper)
ISBN 978-1-4985-5303-2 (electronic)

♾™ The paper used in this publication meets the minimum requirements of American National Standard for Information Sciences—Permanence of Paper for Printed Library Materials, ANSI/NISO Z39.48-1992.

Printed in the United States of America

To William Lau

Contents

List of Figures

Acknowledgments

My scholarly preoccupations with Latin American cinema and class started to coalesce into a book project as a result of my teaching and research at HKU for over two decades. Latin American Studies has as yet no institutional presence at HKU and, therefore, the book's eventual completion was almost entirely at my expense bar the occasional financial support for conference attendance, for which I am indebted. This limiting condition might initially appear as a handicap, but it has instead turned out to be an advantage for two main reasons. First, a basic premise of this book is that the site of enunciation conditions a filmmaker's approach to class and my own position as a researcher as well as class affiliation has inevitably influenced my approach in researching the subject matter. This awareness has led me to adopt novel, creative, and somewhat unusual perspectives in the study of class on the screen and to carefully re-examine existing ones that had been fashionably discarded as outmoded by others. Second, much of the time I had to rely on the assistance of some wonderfully generous film researchers, institutional representatives, producers, and filmmakers around the world. Without their help, this book would not have been possible.

The unflinching support I received from Gina Marchetti reinforced my belief that this project was necessary and this kept me going during difficult times. I will always feel indebted to this demanding film scholar for enabling me to pursue a research career in Latin American Cinema in Hong Kong. The professors and visiting scholars at HKU's School of Humanities and School of Modern Languages and Cultures create a thriving research-intensive community that has also been instrumental in shaping my global approach to the study of cinema. I am particularly indebted to the generosity of Julia Lesage and her late *compañero* Chuck Kleinhans, two inspiring models for a "socially-minded" and activist scholar, and to Aaron Magnan-Park and

Esther C. M. Yau for their incisive criticism. Lúcia Nagib and the anonymous reviewer of this work offered invaluable critical insights that allowed me to sharpen and develop my arguments, and Barbara Weinstein provided helpful advice. Naturally the responsibility for any mistakes lies with the author.

I am fortunate to have warm and hard-working colleagues in the Spanish Program with a healthy sense of humor and collegiality. Special thanks go out to my Director Rocío Blasco for her flexibility in allowing me to gradually incorporate my research into the Spanish Program and to explore and innovate beyond the confines of the restricted field of Spanish as a Foreign Language.

People I met at institutions and conferences made some very hard-to-get films and other texts available to me, kept me updated in film developments and film scholarship, and challenged my preconceptions. The Cinemateca de Cuba and ICAIC in Cuba, Fundación Villa del Cine, Fundación Cinemateca Nacional and Amazonia Films in Venezuela, ENERC's library in Argentina, the Library of Congress in the United States, and the Library of the University of Hong Kong provided me with the necessary data. From these institutions, special thanks are reserved for Manuel Herrera, Pablo Pacheco, Alicia García, Luciano Castillo, Marisol Rodríguez, David García, Blanca Rey, Víctor Luckert, Lorena Almarza, Edgar Márquez, Maite Galán, and Diana Tsui. Edmundo Aray furnished me with important historical documents and Ricardo Azuaga was an excellent host at Universidad Central de Venezuela. Fellow presenters at conferences such as Clara Kriger, Antonio Isea, Michelle Farrell and Belkis Suárez, and colleagues who have provided feedback to some chapters in this volume such as Claudia Sandberg, Carolina Rocha, and Naomi Pueo Wood also deserve my sincere gratitude.

My friends Carol Michelena and Ares di Fazio, thank you for the initial discussions on cinema and politics that sparked my curiosity and for opening my eyes to the almost insurmountable difficulties that people who fight against hegemonic worldviews face. Ana Dubraska in Venezuela, Óscar Ruiz de la Tejera in Cuba, and Federico Marengo and Silvina Pezzetta in Argentina provided me with much needed logistical support and the conversations with them incited reflection about my investigation, and especially about my position as a researcher on Latin American cinema based in Asia. My dearest friends Pily Galán from Venezuela and Francisco Puñal from Cuba/Spain are proof that human and virtual networks based on commitment to the study of film and generous friendship are indispensable for effective research (much like those networks in film co-productions).

My conversations with filmmakers, actors, and producers such as Román Chalbaud, Dayana Gauthier, Efterpi Charalambidis, Ignacio Huang, Juan Martín Hsu, Rodrigo Moreno, Sebastián Borensztein, Benjamín Naishtat, Andrés Rodríguez, Rafael Gil, Alejandro Brugués, Esteban Insausti, Luis

Alberto Lamata, Liliane Blaser, and Chow Keung helped me touch base and experience different perspectives from the practice.

I would also like to thank the editors Jessica Thwaite and Nicolette Amstutz for their patience and careful edition, and to Nicolette in particular for her belief in my project throughout these years.

My families in Venezuela and Spain have borne with me all the sacrifices that come with the commitment to writing a book. In their histories rests my profoundest motivation to study these cinemas. I owe a debt of gratitude to my children who grew up with a mother always glued to a computer screen, or visiting a cinema, or leaving for a self-funded research trip to Latin America even when they were as little as two years old. There are no words to compensate for the time that this book stole from them. Last but not least, this book is dedicated to William.

Portions of this book have appeared in *Jump Cut* (first part of chapter 1) and *Brazil in Twenty-First Century Popular Media: Culture, Politics, and Nationalism on the World Stage* (chapter 3).

Introduction

The success of the family comedy *Nosotros los Nobles* (2013),[1] which portrays the fictional fall into poverty of a wealthy family and closely references another highly popular film about the rich and the poor, *Nosotros los pobres* (1948), confirms Mexican audiences' continued interest in films with a strong focus on class across more than six decades. Indeed, the resounding success of a class-inflected narrative like *Nosotros los Nobles* does not constitute an isolated case in Latin America in the twenty-first century although framing class relations as "class antagonism" no longer is the most popular approach to this theme, as the 2013 comedy clearly illustrates.[2]

The present volume is the result of my interest in class on contemporary Latin American cinema starting from 2007, when a strong research focus on class was uncommon. This book endeavors to identify the particular nature of the class ideologies of a selection of Latin American films during the period 2003–2015. Attraction to class issues has experienced a worldwide resurgence since the onset of the global financial crisis in 2008. Concerns about the accumulation of wealth by the 1 percent, the growth of inequality, and the pernicious effects of neoliberalism have occupied much of the press and academic publications while terms widely used in the 1960s and later abandoned, such as *the people* and *populism*, have made a comeback worldwide. The growing precariousness of living and working conditions in developed and developing countries due to the effects of unbridled neoliberalism has contributed to the gradual reawakening of the interest in class outside and within academia. This volume is a response to this renewed interest and seeks to examine the aesthetics and politics of class in a selection of twenty-first-century Latin American films produced in five nations, namely Venezuela, Cuba, Mexico, Brazil, and Argentina, with the aim of understanding the relationship of certain cinema practices to the socio-political transformations taking place in these countries in the first fifteen years of the new millennium, bearing in mind the difficulties of theorizing "about the relationship of texts . . . to specific socio-historical moments and struggles."[3]

A close examination of selected texts from these nations under the lens of class allows for the identification of characteristic cinematic developments, bearing in mind that there is no contemporary continental movement and that the diversity of the cinemas of these five nations in the new millennium poses a great challenge to the present endeavor. An overarching approach as the one adopted in the present study goes against contemporary scholarly trends tending toward more specific studies but is necessary due to the nature of this intellectual inquiry for several reasons. First, the resurgence of discourses on social contradictions in Latin America was motivated by a major shift to the left of the political spectrum in the years 1998–2015 labeled the "Turn-to-the-Left" (or "Pink Tide") and the more recent "Right Turn,"[4] both of them construed as pan-continental political transformations. These phenomena were concomitant with the rise of the middle classes,[5] and the growing influence of China on the Latin American economy. This book is thus concerned with films produced between 2003 and 2015, a period when the Turn-to-the-Left was fully-fledged in Venezuela, Brazil, and Argentina while Mexico and Cuba continued with their long-established neoliberal and socialist programs respectively.

Second, the examination of how class plays out on the screen in the first years of the new millennium in comparison to earlier practices and ideologies is likewise timely because conceptions, uses and connotations of the term 'class' have evolved, and new terms have been added to its semantic field. Class is a key concept in sociology, cultural, and film studies that has not always been consistently defined,[6] or even defined at all. A close reading of its application to the study of Latin American cinema shows that the tenets of class analysis have been changing considerably following a period from the end of the 1950s to the beginning of the 1980s when class played a prominent role in film practice and theory. Recent discussions of class in Latin American cinema include, among others, disquisitions about new textual politics or depoliticization in texts shot with impassive cameras, demonstrations of the abandonment of *el pueblo* (the people) as the privileged historical subject,[7] and the terminological shift toward "neoliberal," "precarious," and "populist" cinemas. A further consideration for the need of the multinational approach adopted here is based on the belief that some film analyses of contemporary politics made on the basis of studies focusing on global art from the best-studied cinemas have led to generalizations and assumptions that become complicated when expanding the range of films to less studied cinemas and filmmakers.

The book's methodology combines the study of the formal resolution of class in texts with the interpretation of class-based articulations of production, distribution and reception (the latter to a lesser extent). The close textual analysis of films within the methodological framework of comparative literature combined with the analysis of national and transnational funding schemes, cultural policies, and reception, exposes class dynamics which remain obscure or inconclusive when using other methods that focus solely on extratextual media dynamics. Although this book is eclectic in its theoretical framework, a Marxist method of film interpretation is widely used for its capacity to identify "the specific elements . . . which are the material keys to [aesthetic] intention and response, and, more generally, the specific elements which socially and historically determine and signify aesthetic and other situations."[8]

I am aware of the scholarly skepticism toward a homogenizing application of the umbrella term "Latin American Cinema." In the present study, the thematization of existing differences and commonalities between the five cinemas is conducted with respect for their specificity. The methodology employed here builds upon the method used by Ruby B. Rich in her work—Rich identifies the transition from collectivity to subjectivity in Latin American filmmaking by contrasting Brazilian, Cuban, Mexican, and Argentine texts, a finding that would have had much less significance had she focused on a single national cinema.[9] Likewise, my research on a certain aspect—class—in five cinemas runs against the tendency to "concentrate on one or two Latin American countries" in academic literature on Latin American film[10] and follows the trend to combine Spanish-speaking and Portuguese-speaking cinemas that has been gaining prominence in recent years.[11] Furthermore, this comparative methodology has also been advocated by the research group RICiLa (Red de Investigadores sobre Cine Latinoamericano) a network of researchers of Latin American cinema created in 2011 to promote comparative film studies in Latin America in line with the earlier efforts by film scholars Paulo Antonio Paranaguá, Julianne Burton-Carvajal, and Zuzana M. Pick.[12]

A NEW CLASS LENS

In the 1990s, Chuck Kleinhans remarked that, although the term "class" in film studies was "often evoked as a term," it "ha[d] yet to be elaborated adequately as a critical concept."[13] Being a main component of Latin American film scholarship up to the 1980s, the interest in class gradually diminished in subsequent decades. In addition to Kleinhans, several other prominent scholars showed alarm at the silencing of class in research. Stuart Hall posited the need to reconceptualize class, not necessarily to regain a dominant explanatory position in the study of social and cultural formations to the detriment of other categories such as gender or ethnicity but to occupy a new, decentered position.[14]

Around the same time, David E. James noted that the struggle to empower women and people of color had resulted in "advances in the relevant constituencies in society at large" and a subsequent theoretical development of race and gender. By contrast, the absence of the working class from academia (the class consciousness of working-class women and people of color entering academia had been "systematically inhibited" and there was no critical mass of working-class-identified subjects in academia) prevented the formulation of "any single systematic or comprehensive theory of the way class could inform the study of cinema."[15] The wealth of publications on gender and/or race looking into Latin American cinema published in the twenty-first century by researchers like Leslie L. Marsh, Parvati Nair, and Julián Daniel Gutiérrez-Albilla, Tatiana Signorelli Heise, David William Foster, Gustavo Subero, Lisa Shaw, and Stephanie Dennison confirm that these are thriving subfields of research in Latin American film scholarship in our century.[16] A book by the telling title *Redirecting the Gaze: Gender, Theory and Cinema in the Third World* (edited by Diana Robin and Ira Jaffe) signals the turn to this new sensibility by advocating a shift from the "totalizing" and Marxist-inflected discourses of Third Cinema to a focus on gender.[17]

None the less, the experience that societies are constituted in social classes is perhaps more acute now than ever, and this social experience is immanent in contemporary cinema. Even though there are no recent monographs on class in the five Latin American cinemas object of this study except for Matthew B. Karush's *Culture of Class: Radio and Cinema in the Making of a Divided Argentina, 1920–1946*, class concerns are important in some recent studies on the effects of neoliberalism and social crises on cinema, among others. This volume attempts to redress the imbalance in the attention paid to gender/race, on the one hand, and class, on the other, by offering a unique insight into contemporary Latin American cinematic figurations of class.

Historically, Latin American cinema is best known worldwide for the continental movements known as *Nuevo Cine Latinoamericano* (New Latin American Cinema, NLAC), *Tercer Cine* (Third Cinema, term coined in Argentina), and *Cinema Novo* (in Brazil). I will use NLAC as a shorthand form to represent all of these terms henceforth when I refer to their shared characteristics, without the intention of conflating them. The 1960s and 1970s were the golden age of these socially-committed film movements whose practice and interrelated theorization in the form of manifestoes and a book written by filmmakers influenced cinemas worldwide and contributed significantly to Film Theory.[18] These movements were part of a wide range of alternative practices[19] but one of the most characteristic features of NLAC is its explicit celebration of class struggle, as NLAC specialist Zuzana Pick reminds us,[20] which explains why references to NLAC in this book are understandably frequent. As NLAC is a Marxist-inflected practice, before outlining some new ways of explaining class, I will briefly summarize this theory.

The concepts of class commonly used in film and cultural studies originate in Western sociology and political theory. As is often deployed in film studies, class designates "a group of people sharing common relations to the means of production"[21] but this is not a term exempt from controversy and has been evolving within and outside film practice and film studies for decades. Being the main and earlier scientific tradition to use class as a key concept for understanding social relations in spite of the fact that "Marx himself never systematically developed a theory of class,"[22] Marxism deserves priority in this discussion. The Marxist conceptualization of class has been evolving since the mid-nineteenth century to accommodate changes in society, but its major characteristics are its relational character, its egalitarian agenda, its basis on the mode of production, and its characteristic use of exploitation for describing relationships within the capitalist mode of production. What matter most for Marxist class analysis are "class relations" (i.e., relations between those who own the means of production, the bourgeoisie, and those who do not, the proletariat)[23] and "class structure."[24]

Marxism deeply influenced NLAC and hence some of its most representative films employ dialectic Marxist film techniques like Sara Gómez's *De cierta manera* (*One Way or Another*, 1977), Sergio Giral's *El otro Francisco* (*The Other Francisco*, 1974) and Fernando Solanas and Octavio Getino's *La hora de los hornos* (*The Hour of Furnaces*, 1968). The movement was widely appreciated at international film festivals for embracing a social concern with a modernist aesthetics that differed from both art-house cinema from Europe and socialist realism from the USSR. Although Marxist theory in its classic or neo-Marxist forms still informs an important sector of film and cultural studies scholarship,[25] since the collapse of state communism in Eastern Europe and the USSR, and the perceived failure of Marxism in Cuba and Venezuela, this theory is often regarded as unviable and discredited. Ignacio M. Sánchez Prado's research is a case in point. Writing about political cinema, the Mexican film scholar claims that,

The construction of an entirely new set of institutions of cinema in Mexico, with complex networks interconnecting the State, private investment, and individual filmmakers, requires an understanding of political film in a new way. "Third Cinema" represents an *idealistic* paradigm for approaching film as an instrument of direct social change or, at least, as a testimonial of the voices that had been silenced by years of repression and marginalization.[26] (emphasis added)

Sánchez Prado posits the inadequacy of Third Cinema (discussed by him as some kind of monolithic whole) for contemporary Mexican political cinema and instead proposes a reading of the latter that recognizes the affective and ideological engagements of specific groups contributing to the box office, that is, the Mexican middle class who shares "the political and cultural ideals brought about by neoliberalism."[27] In sum, through the study of a wide range of genres, Sánchez Prado documents the rise of the middle class as an essential audience evolution influencing the politics of contemporary Mexican cinema. This finding leads him to observe that instead of "taking a clearly contoured ideological position, like directors in the 'Third Cinema' paradigm," films like *Todo el poder* register a social discontent.[28]

Other relevant studies that also seek to adequately describe the politics of current film practice but in Argentine cinema are those of Silvana Díaz and Joanna Page. Díaz interprets the shift in forms of social engagement from the Argentine cinema of the 1960s to that of the 1990s as a transition from cinema being "a tool for social transformation" to "chronicling the political and social changes."[29] In much the same vein, film scholar Joanna Page views some contemporary texts as seemingly depoliticized but still finding a way of being political and commenting on neoliberalism. In her analysis of the superimposition of "primitive" communities and market economies in Martín Rejtman's *Los guantes mágicos* (*The Magic Gloves*, 2003), for instance, Page notes that, "Rejtman's vision is not nostalgic . . . what emerges under his more neutral gaze is not a full-scale critique of capitalism, nor a defense of it, but a dissection, intelligent and often witty, of the relationships between the economic and the social in contemporary Argentina."[30]

Notwithstanding the differences between all these critical analyses and others that describe film's capacity to grasp antagonistic collective discourses of social classes,[31] key terminology used in them appears to function in line with what Page denominates "neutral gaze." *Chronicling* (Kathleen Newman), *reflecting* "on tensions between interdependent social classes" (Leslie L. Marsh), "[more] than representations of social issues, these films are *sensory explorations of realities* yet to be properly understood" (Tiago de Luca), and *registering* (Ignacio M. Sánchez Prado) are some of the expressions used (emphasis mine).[32] Other interrelated arguments for this discussion such as Lúcia Nagib's insight into the evolution of the socialist utopia in Brazilian cinema and Gonzalo Aguilar's contention of the irrelevance of the landmark political subject of *el pueblo* in contemporary Argentine cinema will be engaged in several chapters of this book.

A similar symptom of relative depoliticization (or new politicization) in the portrayal of social problems pervades filmmakers' discourses, as will be observed in the analysis of Carlos Reygadas' *Post Tenebras Lux* in chapter 2 or Juan Martín Hsu's *La salada* in chapter 6, for example. The director David

Pablos, in an interview about his feature *Las elegidas* (a Mexican film about the prostitution of children selected for the *Un Certain Regard* section of Cannes in 2015) claimed that,

> I would not sell my film as a social drama. I mean, it does touch on an essential topic that *needs to be talked about* today, which is women trafficking (a serious problem at a global level), but foremost I was clear about two things when I wrote the script: I was not interested in making a film of denunciation, nor did I want to make a sordid or sensationalist film. Not at all. My intention always was to portray a human drama from an intimate perspective . . . . I think that from this intimate drama, the film encapsulates much greater questions and it is from the personal how it manages *to talk about* something global. But never from a didactic perspective. That would be a serious mistake.[33] (emphasis added)

The contrast between the 1960s and the twenty-first-century's key terms for describing what films about social problems did—"denouncing," the former and "talking/registering," the latter—is a sign of a radical change. None the less, this presumed depoliticization of contemporary narratives and attitudes is not restricted to cinema. In the broader debate whether advertising consti tutes "capitalist realism" in the social mobilization of demand (Schudson) or manipulation of consumers (neo-Marxists), Arjun Appadurai states that "any decisive analysis of the effects of advertising would have to proceed to see the images of advertising in tandem with changing ideas about art, design, lifestyle, and distinction."[34] This is therefore a dilemma pertaining to contemporary art at large.

It is important to note that interpretations elaborated in line with Page's neutral gaze tend to be of films by Argentine or Mexican auteurs active in film festival circuits and not of other commercial or independent films from Brazil, Cuba, or Venezuela. Equally important is to underscore the middle-class background of well-studied Latin American filmmakers, the implications of which occupy several chapters in this book in analyses of the texts' "strategies of containment." Fredric Jameson uses Marx's analysis of petty bourgeois ideology, which is not so much predicated on class affiliation or origins but on the fact that limitations in petty bourgeois minds are driven by the limitations imposed by their material interest and social position. This is made evident in the formal or intellectual strategies of containment.[35]

On a different note, an emerging term in film studies scholarship, "precarious cinemas," denotes film practices that bring new working conditions and interrelated life situations that are perceived as distinct from the conditions of the traditional working class to the screen. The recently published volume *The Precarious in the Cinemas of the Americas*,[36] to which I myself have contributed a chapter, constitutes the first systematic application of this term from the social sciences to the study of film. The editors and contributors in this volume define precariousness, precariety, and other terms in their semantic field in various ways. My own skeptical application of the term borrows from Guy Standing's "the precariat," a word that attempts to describe a group of people working in insecure conditions within a fragmented global class structure. His contention that this group (not a class, in his view) does not correspond to the working class or proletariat has been rightly questioned by some sociologists, as I discuss in chapter 5.[37]

Another innovative application of a term that has regained impressive currency in the last years to the point of becoming "the word of the year" in some newspapers is that of populism. Its application to cinema is nothing new but its use has not been extensive and is practically nonexistent in Latin American cinema. This research posits the idea that populism informs class figurations in some contemporary Venezuelan cinema by challenging social and formal boundaries. For this study, I mainly borrow from Ernesto Laclau's empowering concept of populism as a social logic.

While the newest theoretical stances outlined above capture a new aesthetics and ideology, they are not sufficient to fully explain the enactment of social contradictions (still existing, regardless of filmmakers' interest in them) on films. Ultimately, there is a need for an overarching theoretical framework that provides meaning to the acts of "reflection," "neutral gaze," and "dissection" in contemporary films. In the following paragraphs, I will critique a major aspect of this approach to filming and studying films.

THE SEPARATION OF AESTHETICS AND POLITICS

A common operation found in film festival and global films made in Argentina, Brazil, and Mexico consists in the separation of class issues from the film's aesthetics, which has become an "isolable extra-social phenomenon."[38] Laura Podalsky starts her investigation on the politics of affect and emotion in Latin American cinema by quoting Ivana Bentes' and Carlos Monsiváis' attacks against well-promoted films from Mexico and Brazil for their superficial engagement with socioeconomic issues and preoccupation with style betraying neoliberal values.[39] This phenomenon has to be grasped under the light of the transformations experienced by these film industries toward more reliance on film festival and independent funding starting from the 1990s. International funding schemes privilege certain narratives and often promote an exoticizing view of Latin American societies, although not to say that they fully determine the aesthetics of the films funded. The same influence may be exerted in co-productions and films subject to other sources of funding, including multinational schemes like Ibermedia or state funding.

The theoretical approach followed in this book is based on the basic prem-ise that all cultural texts are social and political, a claim that both Fredric Jameson and Raymond Williams made. Jameson maintains that the division of cultural texts into those that are political and those that are not "is worse than an error: namely, a symptom and a reinforcement of the reification and privatization of contemporary life." Films are, in this sense, "socially sym-bolic acts"; they are not free from the social and the historical, and simply recording that films "reflect" their social background is not sufficient for class film analysis.[40]

Furthermore, Williams views the separation of art as a categorically separate dimension of the material world as characteristic of the "bourgeois aesthetic theory," a separation that attempts to escape the capitalist process of commodification, of transforming all experience into useful instruments. Williams finds problematic a view of art in which art constitutes an *isolated* mediation between subjectivity and universality. The problem that this con-ception poses is similar to the problem encountered by the formalists who tried to isolate "the art-object as a thing in itself," ruled by an exclusive poetic language.[41] The emphasis on the sensorial in much of art-house contemporary filmmaking acts within this attempt of isolation of the aesthetic realm, even when trying to construct a new politics. This trend seems to be an effect of the cultural logic of late capitalism too. Williams' and Jameson's theories allow us to note the ideological operations involved in the (at least, relative) separation of the aesthetics from the politics, which is untenable because cinema forms part of various material and social processes. The comparison of selected texts from film "industries" as diverse as the Cuban, the Brazilian, the Venezuelan, the Mexican, and the Argentine in the following chapters proves this point.

Emphasizing the indissoluble relation between aesthetics and politics, the critical inquiry undertaken here seeks to unveil the contradiction of messages emitted by the varied sign systems embedded in a given artistic process as well as in its general social formation, Jameson's definition of "ideology of form."[42] This term accounts for the heterogeneous synchronic and diachronic processes that leave an imprint on the films.

FILM SELECTION AND CHAPTER OVERVIEW

This is the first volume on Latin American cinema with a focus on class that compares films made by a global elite of filmmakers straddling cinemas as diverse as Hollywood, Netflix and Brazilian cinema (Padilha, Jakubowicz) with those by directors circumscribed to one or two Latin American nations whose works are forgotten by the "implacable market logic"[43] (Charalambidis,

Jabes, Hsu); works by global auteurs (Babenco, Reygadas, Escalante, Yu) are also compared here with features by filmmakers who have devoted an important part of their careers to TV and/or publicity (Daranas, Muylaert). This diversity is necessary because, to perceive figurations of class in texts, "questions of address are as crucial as questions of representation."[44]

Global realities cannot be fully grasped by an individual consciousness. For this consciousness to exist there first needs to be a figuration (that is, a figure situated between reality and our consciousness) of a new reality whereby classes become visible. Before becoming conscious about the constantly changing class relations in our societies, it is necessary to be able to live them experientially, and it is through narratives in film, literature, television, and so on that we are able to work out and experience these new realities.[45] The films in this study have been selected for their capacity to stand as figurations that point to critical and distinctive aspects of how class is rendered in their respective cinemas as well as in the group of cinemas selected in this study as a whole.

The films examined here are not necessarily representative of their national cinemas, but they are representative of key figurations of class relations and class structure in spheres ranging from the intimate through the national to the global. This research is thus structured as a progression from the intimate to the global. It begins with the analysis of how class plays out in romantic relationships, to move on to professional relations in the domestic space, class-based repression in state institutions—the slum and the prison—, class-inflected challenges to the state—populism—, and migratory movements that provoke changes in global class articulations (both migration and immigration).

As mentioned above, the reasons for studying the period 2003–2015 in this book are closely tied to socio-political developments in the five selected countries. The year 2003 saw the rise of Luiz Inácio Lula da Silva and Néstor Kirchner to the Brazilian and Argentine presidencies respectively. The socio-political programs of these two left-leaning charismatic leaders was soon perceived in relation to the "twenty-first socialist" program initiated by Hugo Chávez in Venezuela in 1999, a perception that led to the coinage of the terms "Turn-to-the-Left" and "Pink Tide" in Latin America (broadly, a post-neoliberal or post-liberal period). The time between 2003 and 2015 was also a period of intensification of neoliberalism across the world and in Latin America—particularly in Mexico but similarly in countries governed by the Left. During the same period, Cuba underwent a change of leadership (Raúl Castro assumed power in 2008) and initiated a very slow transition to a more open economy whose effects in society at large and in the filmmaking sector in particular are still negligible.

In spite of the critiques against what Paul Julian Smith calls "the primacy of the fiction feature film" in studies focused on the relationship between media and socio-economics,[46] I have selected fiction cinema because, while television and other so-called "transitory" forms of mass media are useful for an understanding of class dynamics in Latin American societies, the "permanent" and less spontaneous character of feature films makes them more suitable for creating the mythologies of our secular worlds to which Elsaesser refers, in particular "class mythologies." As such, the effects that fiction feature films have on viewers may be more lasting. As Elsaesser explains,

> The cinema, in contradistinction to television, is still our most vivid machine for creating memory. As Godard has said: "cinema creates memory, television fabricates forgetting," which may be no more than saying that the cinema is indeed the space of a certain mythology, the only one in a secular world. It testifies at once to the need for transcendence and to its absence as redemption.[47]

Robert Stam's comparison of a TV News rendition of the Carandiru massacre with the feature fiction film *Carandiru* concludes similarly: the former medium "offers a hasty 'first draft' of history under the pressures of inexorable deadlines," while the latter "offers a more considered and researched 'second draft.'"[48]

Chapter 1 ("Class and Romance in Socialism") explores the cinematic figuration of class conflict in the cinemas of two countries whose governments are committed to building socialism starting from 1959 (Cuba) and 1999 (Venezuela).[49] An initial comparison between two Venezuelan features (*La clase* and *Secuestro express*) provides a glimpse of the heightened political polarization of Venezuelan society and especially, for our purposes, of the association and manipulation of certain visual styles to particular ends. The power of cinema in the struggle for cultural hegemony is equally present in such disparate forms of fiction cinema as the government-sponsored productions of Fundación Villa del Cine (FVC) (*La clase*) and Hollywood-promoted blockbusters (*Secuestro express*). Perhaps due to the importance attached to cinema in the Soviet era, cinema remains one the most valued arts for the governments of Cuba and Venezuela at the same time that, commercial filmmakers like Jonathan Jakubowicz are aware of the power of ideologically charged blockbusters to penetrate every home.

After the initial comparison circumscribed to Venezuela, in the second section of the chapter, a further contrast with a production from a country with such a long tradition and prestige in oppositional cinema as Cuba, Ernesto Daranas' *Los dioses rotos*, permits us to witness the substitution of earlier modes of representation (typical of NLAC) by new modes of socially-committed filmmaking. The melodramatic proposal by Daranas engages both with a national audience avid for commercial cinema and television produced elsewhere (as evidenced by the popularity of the *paquete semanal*, a weekly package full of American entertainment delivered underground to Cuban homes through a hard drive) and a global audience for whom Cuba's imagery must be congruent with their preconceived ideas about the increasing role that prostitution and *santería* play in Cuban society today. Equally important is to note the full support of the Cuban government to the production of *Los dioses rotos*, which adds the socialist commitment and film history components to the latter audience expectations to deliver a film that symbolically captures the tensions and contradictions involved in visually representing class transformations on the island.

In addition to this, taking into account that these are the first features of three filmmakers (José Antonio Varela, Jonathan Jakubowicz and Ernesto Daranas) allows us to observe their shared concerns about the appropriate style for a socially-minded cinema in their respective conjunctures and the results of the different kinds of institutional support they received. Although Daranas had previous experience in television and documentary filmmaking, none of these three filmmakers were well known at the time they produced their first narrative films when compared to established directors also under scrutiny in this volume such as Anna Muylaert, Carlos Reygadas, Héctor Babenco, or José Padilha. In the decade that has passed since the release of their first fiction films, however, these three filmmakers have achieved recognition in their respective countries and have continued filming fiction, which could be interpreted as a success of the institutions, producers, and distributors that had faith in their talent in the first place.

This chapter is thus concerned with variations in the politics of form of three films: a commercial blockbuster with a social agenda whose presumed ideological neutrality is conclusively debunked, a Marxist social drama of twenty-first century revolutionary Venezuela that rejuvenates the much-vilified dichotomy of exploiter and exploited, and a post-Special Period Cuban feature that is closer to commercial cinema than to the Marxist dialectical filmmaking that made the country famous. Ultimately, the combined study of these socially concerned filmmaking styles with one of the most common themes in films about class (social mobility through relationships) sheds light on the strikingly different cultural effects that the divergent historical conjunctures and political economies of Venezuela and Cuba produce. Striving for diversity, it is apt to note that these are two cinemas with very different histories. Venezuelan cinema plays a minor role in Latin America and has not been influential in aesthetic or ideological terms in Latin America or elsewhere. Cuba, on the other hand, is perhaps the fourth most developed industry in Latin America in terms of volume,[50] and is a representative cinema of

NLAC. Indeed, the Film Festival of New Latin American Cinema of Havana is still one of the most important festivals specializing in Latin American Cinema. The dialogue established here between these three features throws into relief how films can act as diametrically opposing figurations of class even when produced in countries whose governments officially attempt to build a classless society.

The Question of Class in Contemporary Latin American Cinema pays particular attention to the formal and thematic imprints of the rising aware-ness of filmmakers' own social class on the films they direct and often script (most of whom belong to the middle and upper-middle classes worldwide). Chapter 2 ("Space Defining Class") brings together two Latin American cin-ematic heavyweights: Brazil and Mexico. It explores the way in which two filmmakers, who are markedly different from the filmmakers in chapter 1 since they have long professional trajectories (Anna Muylaert and Carlos Reygadas) contribute to a cinema that I will refer to as *cine clasemediero* (middle-class cinema). The interrelated practices of space construction and cinematography serve as privileged practices for the interpretation of the interactions between employers and employees thematized in these films. The social segregation exacerbated by the spread of neoliberalism in Mexico and Brazil, the rise of the middle class in Latin America and the Turn-to-the-Left or Lula era in Brazil have left their mark on the screen in the form of subjective points of view, framing of space, and distinct camera movements distinguishable by the social class of the subject filmed, among other signifi-cant aesthetic and thematic choices.

Brazil's international standing increased exponentially in the PT era (Par-tido dos Trabalhadores or Workers Party to which the former presidents Lula da Silva and Dilma Rousseff are affiliated) although a reverse trend toward negative economic growth and a formidable political crisis has been unfold-ing since 2015. Mexico's successive governments since 1994, alternately ruled by the center "revolutionary" PRI and the center-right PAN parties until the historical election results of July 1, 2018, steadily implemented neoliberal policies in the country that have not yielded the expected posi-tive results for the country as a whole yet. In fact, the success of the leftist leader Manuel López Obrador in 2018 can be viewed as a failure of previous neoliberal governments. In chapter 2, the analysis of Anne Muylaert's *Que horas ela volta?* alongside *Post Tenebras Lux*, by the Mexican global auteur Carlos Reygadas, demonstrates the existence of a middle-class filmmaking sensibility that surpasses these national differences. There exist many differ-ences between *Que horas ela volta?*, a drama with touches of comedy that generally follows a chronological order, uses continuity editing, and adopts other techniques typical of mainstream cinema widely, and an experimental film like *Post Tenebras Lux*, which promotes viewer disorientation due to its seemingly unjustified change of settings and languages, among other unconventional characteristics. The films, however, come closer when examining the limitations and, I will argue, liberation, in relation to the filmmakers' positions toward the treatment of their subject matter to better correspond to the filmmakers' social position and material interests. In this regard, Doreen Massey' relational concept of space becomes useful for its capacity to view the filmic space's political potentiality as constructing and being constructed by social class relations: in the same way that space constructs class, class constructs space.

Brazilian cinema is also the object of my attention in the subsequent chapter, "Class and the State." Chapter 3 delves into the ways in which films as diverse as the art-house *Carandiru* by Héctor Babenco, and the blockbusters *Tropa de elite* and *Tropa de elite 2* reinforce stereotyping perceptions about the lower classes in the same way as some standard measures by public Brazilian institutions perpetuate the segregation and criminalization of the underprivileged. Being successful productions that managed to attract such a wide audience and temporarily challenge Hollywood's hegemony in Brazil, these films invite us to question the extent to which a "cosmetics of hunger" (Ivana Bentes' celebrated term for capturing the impoverishment of Glauber Rocha's "aesthetics of hunger" for a revolutionary cinema in contemporary Brazilian blockbusters depicting violence in the slums like *Cidade de Deus*) is required for the films' wide appeal.

The aestheticized violence in *Tropa de elite* and *Tropa de elite 2* reinforces mass media's common association of poverty and crime in a way that is in keeping with other well-known Latin American features such as *Cidade de Deus* and *Amores perros*, and therefore in this book these two films were selected for being the Brazilian version of this subcontinental mode of representing the underprivileged. The State is viewed as participant in class differentiation and/or struggle insofar as it reproduces or constructs class ideologies through the actions of Repressive State Apparatuses like the police and the prison and Ideological State Apparatuses such as cultural institutions.[51]

Studying these blockbusters by Padilha with Babenco's art-house feature in chapter 3 allows for the examination of commonalities concerning class even when differences in circulation due to the choices of distribution channels and exhibition venues, the intended target audience and the response of critics and scholars are significant. These variations, as Hopenhayn has argued, are fundamental in the articulation between culture and politics, an articulation that is occurring with greater frequency in the field of the cultural industries and is shaped more by the conditions of circulation than by modes of production.[52]

These important differences notwithstanding, the three films contradicted official self-congratulatory messages and served as reminders of the nation's challenges when Brazil's standing in supra-national organizations from the Global South was rising. Their attention to collective social problems also distances them from a prevailing interest in "the micropolitics of emotion" identified as a marker of contemporary Latin American cinema by Paul A. Schroeder Rodríguez, although they are part of a trend toward genre cinema.[53] However, on querying the films' critical geography of class similarities in the failure of the three features to clearly articulate an indictment of institutional and systematic repression are found. In this sense, chapter 3 expands Ismail Xavier's criticism of the narrow perspective of *Tropa de elite* and its skewed moral mission and Babenco's idiosyncratic depiction of institutional repression in overcrowded prisons.[54]

Chapter 4, "The Return of the People," is one of the first contributions to the growing scholarship on Latin American cinematic populism. Unlike in the previous chapters, classes do not appear in the films in this chapter as pre-constituted entities but as being constructed by the equivalence of demands unsatisfied by the State. The State's strong institutional presence in the previous chapter turns into the State's absence and negligence as precondi tions for the reawakening of a collective class dynamics that Ernesto Laclau would denominate populist. The variety of forms that this emerging mode of socially-committed filmmaking adopts is exemplified here with productions by two first-time filmmakers (of which there are a relatively large number in a country where the democratization of the filmmaking scene like Venezuela is an official policy), Hernán Jabes and Efterpi Charalambidis.

Chapter 5 ("The Globalization of Class on Screen") widens the lens and turns to migration originating in Latin America to present another major aesthetics of class figuration in Latin American cinema that I refer to as "engaged visuality," Amat Escalante's wonderful style for filming one of the major migratory movements in the world today: the Mexican exodus to the United States. This term (engaged visuality) captures two main aspects pertaining to filming social inequality in the twenty-first century: the filmmaker's commitment with his reality and the need to engage with global filmmaking trends whereby aestheticism has replaced a seemingly more didactic style that was typical of some, but not all, NLAC productions.

The film closely analyzed in this chapter, *Los bastardos*, is the second feature by Amat Escalante, a global auteur that, like his mentor, Carlos Reygadas (whose work is examined in chapter 2) relies heavily on film festivals for international projection, rather than solely focusing on national audiences. These conditions of circulation will therefore be taken into account. The last two chapters present two different alternatives to the narrative logic of postmodernism, Escalante's engaged visuality and Yu Lik-wai's magic realism (in Jameson's application of the term for film analysis).

Lastly, chapter 6, "Class and Race," delves into cinematic figurations of a trans(national) or borderless class system[55] and immigration to Latin America. The selected films *La salada* and *Plastic City* deal with the ways in which Latin American social classes are being affected by global changes of class and migratory movements (as one of the characters in *Plastic City* says, Vietnamese and Chinese workers are being paid slave wages to maintain low prices in goods sold in Latin America). Indeed, one of the major flows of people and objects in the world today is happening from Asia to Latin America. The presence of Asians in Latin America is certainly not new and Asians have contributed to the construction of the Latin American nations to an extent that is yet to be fully recognized[56] but the films under focus in this concluding chapter push the boundaries even further. Juan Martín Hsu's *La salada* and Yu Lik-wai's *Plastic City* are films whose primary concern are global flows of objects ("unauthorized" goods) and people migrating from Bolivia (intra-continental migration), Taiwan, Japan, China, and Korea (inter-continental migration) to Latin America. The films' capacity to expand the definition of Latin American cinema to include films made by Asian filmmakers in Latin America, although important, is of less relevance here than the question of the extent to which these figurations of global class transformations intertwine class and race.

The two films in this last chapter were produced in neighboring countries: Argentina and Brazil. The long-running preoccupation of this book with the appropriate contemporary aesthetics for a politics of class emerges in this chapter in the comparison between a film that is a conscious product of New Argentine Cinema (a diverse group of films perceived by critics and scholars as a movement appearing in the 1990s where what Joanne Page identifies as "a neutral gaze" in the filming of social problems predominates) and a global co-production between Brazil, Hong Kong, and Japan, shot in Brazil by a Chinese director. Not only are the films in this chapter representative of figurations of the human and material flows characteristic of globalization but the films themselves are embodiments of globalization given that some members of both film crews are foreign or of non-mainstream ethnic origin. The films' generic heterogeneities invite speculation on the use of genre for class ideological purposes.

The films in these six chapters cover the main aspects of class construction in spheres ranging from the intimate to the global that have received considerable attention from filmmakers. The slow but ongoing democratization of the Latin American screen requires the study of works by first-time filmmakers that produce films not necessarily aligned with international film festival circuits and global filmmaking trends in combination with more studied films that are in line with global trends and attuned to global film distribution circuits. The themes covered in these films do not necessarily represent all the major topics regarding class in the profilmic reality of (at least) the five countries included in this volume, but this might be due to the filmmakers' and producers' preference for some themes that concern them as members of a certain class over others. For instance, in Brazil and Mexico, the struggle for land has become increasingly visible in the form of displacement of working-class residents or lumpenproletariat from favelas and the proliferation of gated communities. The social interactions between the middle classes and the working class or the lumpenproletariat are disproportionately figured in the cinemas of Mexico and Brazil as invasions of rich dwellings by the underprivileged rather than as encroachments of middle-class communities in public and poor areas.

To ensure a balance in the study of class figurations on the screen, *The Question of Class in Contemporary Latin American Cinema* includes both films that have been widely circulated in specialized and/or commercial circuits and those that have enjoyed a more limited exhibition because this heterogeneity is essential for understanding the impact of certain articulations of class in contemporary Latin American filmmaking. To allow for a broad view of the subject and explore how different modes of production impinge on the narratives, the films chosen for analysis are as varied in their conception (from global and national film art to genre cinema) as the makers of the films in critical acclaim and experience. Moreover, these films are the visible results of both established and emerging film production strategies in the region of diverse nature, including the creation of a new state producer in Venezuela in 2006, the increasing reliance on international film festivals in the case of Mexican cinema, and a novel experimentation in Asian-Latin American co-production in Brazil. These multifarious processes allow us to study the implications of different funding schemes on the class politics of the texts.

NOTES

1. The popular success of *Nosotros los Nobles* (*The Noble Family*, directed by Gary Alazraki) was such that Netflix hired Alazraki to take charge of its first Spanish-language original series aimed at Latin American and Latino audiences. Angelique Flores, "Netflix Takes another Step to Reach Latino Audiences," *Home Media Magazine* 36, no. 14 (May 12, 2014): 13.

2. In contrast to this contemporary attitude toward class representation, "class antagonism" was "[t]he most recurrent theme" in the cinema of the 1960s and 1970s, according to Teshome Gabriel. Teshome Gabriel, *Third Cinema in the Third World* (Michigan: UMI Research Press, 1982), 15.

3. Ana M. López, "*The Battle of Chile*: Documentary, Political Process, and Representation," in *The Social Documentary in Latin America*, ed. Julianne Burton (Pittsburgh: University of Pittsburgh Press, 1990), 270.

4. See, for instance, Jon Beasley-Murray, Maxwell A. Cameron, and Eric Hershberg, "America's Left Turns: An Introduction," *Third World Quarterly* 30, no. 2 (2009): 319–30; John D. French, "Understanding the Politics of Latin America' s Plural Lefts (Chávez/Lula): Social Democracy, Populism and Convergence on the Path to a Post-Neoliberal World," *Third World Quarterly* 30, no. 2 (2009): 349–70; Joshua Frens-String and Alejandro Velasco, "Right Turn," *NACLA Report on the Americas* 48, no. 4 (2016): 301–02; Jens Andermann, "Turn of the Tide? Cultural Critique and the New Right," *Journal of Latin American Cultural Studies* 27, no. 1 (2018): 1–3; and Jorge Castañeda, "Latin America's Left Turn," *Foreign Affairs* 85, no. 3 (2006): 28–43.

5. Some of the numerous studies on this development are The World Bank, "New World Bank Report Finds 50 Percent Increase in Middle Class in Latin America and the Caribbean over Last Decade," (November 13, 2012); Luis de la Calle and Luis Rubio, "Clasemedieros," *Nexos* (May 2010); Jorge Castañeda, *Mañana Forever?: Mexico and the Mexicans* (New York: Vintage, 2011), 35, 43, 46; Marcelo Neri, *A nova classe média. O lado brilhante da base da pirâmide* (São Paulo: Saraiva, 2011). Leslie L. Marsh has paid close attention to this change in her research on Brazilian cinema. Leslie L. Marsh, "Reordering (Social) Sensibilities: Balancing Realisms in Neighbouring Sounds," *Studies in Spanish & Latin American Cinemas* 12, no. 2 (2015): 139–57.

6. For a discussion of this term, see Jeff Manza, "Class," in *Oxford Bibliographies in Sociology*, ed. Lynette Spillman (Oxford University Press, 2014), http://www.oxfordbibliographies.com.

7. Gonzalo Aguilar, *Más allá del pueblo. Imágenes, indicios y políticas del cine* (Buenos Aires: Fondo de Cultura Económica, 2015), 10.

8. Raymond Williams, *Marxism and Literature* (Oxford: Oxford University Press, 2009), 157.

9. Ruby B. Rich, "An/Other View of New Latin American Cinema," in *Feminisms in the Cinema*, eds. Laura Pietropaolo and Ada Testaferri (Bloomington: Indiana University Press, 1995).

10. Libia Villazana, *Transnational Financial Structures in the Cinema of Latin America: Programa Ibermedia in Study* (Germany: VDM Verlag, 2009), 9.

11. Lisa Shaw and Stephanie Dennison, for instance, present some linguistic and historical reasons for distinguishing Brazilian cinema from other Latin American cinemas in their *Brazilian National Cinema* (London: Routledge, 2007) but the approach to combine Spanish-language and Portuguese-language cinemas is gaining prominence. See, for instance, Denise Mota da Silva, *Vizinhos distantes. Circulação cinematográfica no Mercosul* (São Paulo: Annablume, 2007); Cacilda Rêgo and Carolina Rocha, eds., *New Trends in Argentine and Brazilian Cinema* (Bristol: Intellect, 2011); and Jens Andermann and Álvaro Fernández Bravo, eds., *New Argentine and Brazilian Cinema: Reality Effects* (New York: Palgrave Macmillan, 2013).

12. The respected film scholars Suzana Pick and Alberto Elena described the benefits of searching for transnational connections when conducting research at separate

symposia. Ana Laura Lusnich, Suzana Pick, and Juan Antonio García Borrero, "Presentacion [sic] RICILA," I Simposio Iberoamericano de estudios comparados sobre cine (CIyNE UBA, Biblioteca Nacional de Argentina, December 5–6, 2011); Alberto Elena, "América Latina y Bollywood: La posibilidad de un encuentro," II Simposio Iberoamericano de estudios comparados sobre cine y audiovisual: perspectivas interdisciplinarias. Debates del cine y la historia (Biblioteca Nacional de Argentina. December 5–7, 2012).

13. Chuck Kleinhans, "Class in Action," in *The Hidden Foundation: Cinema and the Question of Class*, eds. David E. James and Rick Berg (Minneapolis: University of Minnesota Press, 1996), 254.

14. Stuart Hall, "Cultural Studies and the Politics of Internationalization: An Interview with Stuart Hall by Kuan-Hsing Chen," in *Stuart Hall*, eds. David Morley and Kuan-Hsing Chen (London: Routledge, 1996), 401. Having originated in the Marxist tradition, Hall's intellectual trajectory involved a continued critical dialogue with Marxism that enriched this tradition, although a shift from classical Marxism to Foucauldian discourse has been observed in cultural studies work influenced by this author. See more on this in David Morley and Kuan-Hsing Chen, eds., *Stuart Hall: Critical Dialogues in Cultural Studies* (London: Routledge, 1996), 4. In *New Times* (1989), for example, Hall goes as far as acknowledging the "leading role" played by consumption and the prevalence of consumer differentiation over older categories like social class as determined by the Registrar General ("The Meaning of New Times," in *Stuart Hall*, 224).

15. James and Berg, eds., *The Hidden Foundation*, 2, 5.

16. An example that confirms this imbalance in scholarly attention is Ana Peluffo's analysis of Lucrecia Martel's *The Swamp*. Peluffo acknowledges the urgent need to address class in this film that had been mainly studied under the focus of gender despite the fact that labor relations in this film correspond to "an almost feudal society." Ana Peluffo, "Staging Class, Gender and Ethnicity in Lucrecia Martel's *La ciénaga/The Swamp*," in *New Trends in Argentine and Brazilian Cinema*, eds. Cacilda Rêgo and Carolina Rocha (Bristol: Intellect, 2011), 211–23.

17. Diana Robin and Ira Jaffe, eds., *Redirecting the Gaze: Gender, Theory and Cinema in the Third World* (Albany: State University of New York, 1999,) 2.

18. Although NLAC tends to be seen as a past tradition, there are scholars who defend the contemporary relevance of Third Cinema theory "as theory," a view that runs counter to the trend to deny its grandeur by other scholars like David Bordwell and Noël Carroll, as Anthony Guneratne regrets. Guneratne observes three causes for the neglect of Third Cinema theory: the Eurocentrism of film theory, the unproductive critical generalization about Third World cinema, and the inexistence of a closely argued body of criticism in this tradition. Anthony R. Guneratne and Wimal Dissanayake, eds., *Rethinking Third Cinema* (New York: Routledge, 2003), 2, 10.

19. Robert Stam classifies some of these alternative practices such as magic realism in "Beyond Third Cinema: The Aesthetics of Hybridity," in *Rethinking Third Cinema*, eds. Anthony R. Guneratne and Wimal Dissanayake (New York: Routledge, 2003), 32.

20. Zuzana M. Pick, *The New Latin American Cinema: A Continental Project* (Austin: University of Texas Press, 1993), 24.

21. "Class," Marxists Internet Archive, Encyclopedia. Glossary of Terms. Marxists Internet Archive (MIA), n.d.

22. James and Berg, eds., *The Hidden Foundation*, 5.

23. Erik Olin Wright, ed., *Approaches to Class Analysis* (N.p.: Cambridge University Press, 2005).

24. Erik Olin Wright, "Class, State and Ideology: An Introduction to Social Science in the Marxist Tradition," *Course Materials of Sociology 621* (Madison: Department of Sociology, University of Wisconsin, 2013), 19.

25. Such scholars include Eric Olin Wright, Étienne Balibar, Fredric Jameson, Raymond Williams, and Slavoj Žižek, among others.

26. Ignacio M. Sánchez Prado, *Screening Neoliberalism: Transforming Mexican Cinema 1988–2012* (Nashville: Vanderbilt University Press, 2014), 107.

27. Sánchez Prado, *Screening Neoliberalism*, 108, 109.

28. Sánchez Prado, *Screening Neoliberalism*, 140.

29. Catherine Leen, "City of Fear: Reimagining Buenos Aires in Contemporary Argentine Cinema," *Bulletin of Latin American Research* 27, no. 4 (2008): 477.

30. Joanna Page, *Crisis and Capitalism in Contemporary Argentine Cinema* (Durham: Duke University Press, 2009), 80.

31. I am borrowing here from Fredric Jameson, who, within a Marxist method of cultural interpretation, views our object of study (the films) as "the smallest intelligible unit of the essentially antagonistic collective discourses of social classes." Fredric Jameson, *The Political Unconscious: Narrative as a Socially Symbolic Act* (London: Routledge, 2002), 61.

32. Kathleen Newman, "A Different Mexican Postcard: Fernando Eimbcke's *Lake Tahoe* (2008)," *Studies in Spanish & Latin American Cinemas* 12, no. 2 (2015): 159–74; Leslie L. Marsh, "Reordering (Social) Sensibilities: Balancing Realisms in *Neighbouring Sounds*," *Studies in Spanish & Latin American Cinemas* 12, no. 2 (2015): 139; Tiago de Luca, *Realism of the Senses in World Cinema: The Experience of Physical Reality* (London: I.B. Tauris, 2014), 240; Sánchez Prado, *Screening Neoliberalism*, 140.

33. Cynthia García Calvo, "David Pablos, director de 'Las elegidas,'" *LatAmcinema.com* May 7, 2015.

34. Arjun Appadurai, *The Future as Cultural Fact: Essays on the Global Condition* (London: Verso, 2013), 58.

35. Jameson, *The Political Unconscious*, 37.

36. Constanza Burucúa and Carolina Sitnisky, *The Precarious in the Cinemas of the Americas*, (Cham: Palgrave Macmillan, 2018).

37. Guy Standing, *A Precariat Charter: From Denizens to Citizens* (London: Bloomsbury, 2014), 11.

38. Raymond Williams, *Marxism and Literature* (Oxford: Oxford University Press, 2009), 153.

39. Laura Podalsky, *The Politics of Affect and Emotion in Contemporary Latin American Cinema: Argentina, Brazil, Cuba and Mexico* (New York: Palgrave Macmillan, 2011), 2–3.

40. Jameson, *The Political Unconscious*, 4, 5, 66.

41. Williams, *Marxism and Literature*, 153.

42. Jameson, *The Political Unconscious*, 84.

43. Ambrosio Fornet uses this reason as one of the causes for the NLAC's failure. See Ann Marie Stock, ed., *Framing Latin American Cinema: Contemporary Critical Perspectives* (Minneapolis: University of Minnesota Press, 1997), xii.

44. Robert Stam, "The Carandiru Massacre: Across the Mediatic Spectrum," in *New Argentine and Brazilian Cinema*, eds. Jens Andermann and Álvaro Fernández Bravo (New York: Palgrave Macmillan, 2013), 147.

45. As Jameson puts it, "the classes have to be able to become in some sense characters in their own right." Fredric Jameson, "Class and Allegory in Contemporary Mass Culture: Dog Day Afternoon as a Political Film," *College English* 38, no. 8 (1977): 845.

46. Paul Julian Smith, "Transnational Cinemas: The Cases of Mexico, Argentina and Brazil," in *Theorizing World Cinema*, eds. Lúcia Nagib, Chris Perriam, and Rajinder Dudrah (London: I.B. Tauris, 2012), 66

47. Thomas Elsaesser, *European Cinema: Face to Face with Hollywood* (Amsterdam: Amsterdam University Press, 2005), 52. See also the documentary *Godard on Television* (Michel Royer, 1999).

48. Stam, "The Carandiru Massacre," 143.

49. Hugo Chávez was elected in 1998 but started to govern in 1999.

50. The application of the term "film industry" in Latin America is necessarily controversial due to the lack of continuity and specialization but its use here indicates that cinema is viewed as a total system and not just a compendium of texts. The allocation of the fourth position to Cuban cinema was made by García Canclini in his article "Will There Be Latin American Cinema in the Year 2000?," but small cinemas in Latin America often shift positions in this ranking. Néstor García Canclini, "Will There Be Latin American Cinema in the Year 2000? Visual Culture in a Postnational Era," in *Framing Latin American Cinema: Contemporary Critical Perspectives*, ed. Ann Marie Stock (Minneapolis: University of Minnesota Press, 1997), 252.

51. For a definition of the terms, see Louis Althusser, *On the Reproduction of Capitalism: Ideology and Ideological State Apparatuses* (London: Verso, 2014).

52. Martín Hopenhayn, "¿Integrarse o subordinarse? Nuevos cruces entre política y cultura," in *Cultura, Política y Sociedad. Perspectivas latinoamericanas*, ed. Daniel Mato (Buenos Aires: CLACSO, 2005), 30.

53. Paul A. Schroeder Rodríguez, "After New Latin American Cinema," *Cinema Journal* 51, no. 2 (2012): 108.

54. Ismail Xavier, "Ways of Listening in a Visual Medium: The Documentary Movement in Brazil," *NLR* 73 (January–February 2012), 116.

55. See David Harvey, "Introduction," in *The Communist Manifesto*, eds. Karl Marx and Friedrich Engels (London: Pluto Press, 2008), 1–30; Geoffrey P. Faux, *The Global Class War: How America's Bipartisan Elite Lost Our Future—and What It Will Take to Win It Back* (Hoboken, NJ: Wiley, 2006); Steve Derné, *Globalization on the Ground: Media and the Transformation of Culture, Class, and Gender in India* (Los Angeles: Sage, 2008).

56. See, for instance, Kathleen López, "In Search of Legitimacy: Chinese Immigrants and Latin American Nation Building," in *Immigration and National Identities in Latin America*, eds. Nicola Foote and Michael Goebel (Gainesville: The University Press of Florida, 2014), 182–204.

Chapter 1

Class and Romance in Socialism[*]

The Contrasting Politics of La clase and Secuestro express and The Fallen Gods of Cuban Cinema

Upward social mobility through cross-class romance is a staple in dramas and comedies concerned with intimate relationships in cinemas around the world, and Latin America is no exception, as the popularity of melodramas across the region shows.[1] This section examines three case studies where romantic relationships appear entwined to socio-political developments in two socialist countries (Venezuela and Cuba) between 1989 and the first years of the twenty-first century. As with Cuban cinema produced since 1959, the politics of class has exerted a powerful effect in twenty-first-century Venezuelan film production, ranging from social dramas (*Pelo malo*, *Bad Hair*, Mariana Rondón, 2014; *Desde allá*, *From Afar*, Lorenzo Vigas, 2015) to musical documentaries (*Tocar y luchar*, *To Play and To Fight*, Alberto Arvelo, 2006) and comedies (*Comando X*, José Antonio Varela, 2008). The personal is clearly political in these features. In a similar fashion to the way in which the classic Cuban films *De cierta manera* (*One Way or Another*, Sara Gómez, 1977) and *Lucía* (Humberto Solás, 1968) demonstrated how social and personal relations necessarily underwent interwoven transformations in the process toward the establishment of a new socialist society, the Venezuelan films *La clase* (*The Class*, José Antonio Varela, 2007) and *Secuestro express* (*Express Kidnapping*, Jonathan Jakubowicz, 2005), and the contemporary Cuban film *Los dioses rotos* (*Fallen Gods*, Ernesto Daranas, 2008) illustrate the currency of the potential of cinematic romantic relationships to stand as allegories of social change. In these films, what Michael Chanan observed regarding earlier Cuban cinema, namely that, "when narrating apparently private stories,

[*] The first section of chapter 1 is an updated version of the article "*Secuestro express* and *La clase*: Politics of Realism in Contemporary Venezuelan Filmmaking," published in *Jump Cut* 52, http://www.ejumpcut.org.

they turn on metaphors of the inextricable links between the personal and the political, the individual and the national, the private and the historical,"[2] still holds true. In the particular case of Venezuela, Farruco Sesto, the minister of the Popular Power for Culture when *La clase* and *Secuestro express* were released maintains that, "posing a dichotomy between politics and culture may represent an act of intellectual dishonesty. There is no such dichotomy. There is no such contradiction. We have the responsibility to do politics and contribute to raising awareness and developing the power of the people to create, precisely from the cultural front."[3]

Set in 1980s Caracas, *La clase*, meaning "the (social) class," tells the story of a young woman who is torn between her working-class boyfriend and a new love interest from a middle-class background whom she met at the orchestra. Social unrest (the *Caracazo* riots of 1989) will later serve as *La clase*'s climax and a decisive moment in the protagonist's personal life. While *La clase* is set at the end of the 1980s, it clearly reflects on events unfolding in Venezuela during the first years of the twenty-first century. To fully understand *La clase*, a film made from the perspective of the anonymous working class and produced by the epoch-making state producer Fundación Villa del Cine (FVC), it would be enlightening to compare it with a Venezuelan crime film partially produced and distributed in Hollywood: *Secuestro express*.

Also set in Caracas, *Secuestro* was released two years before *La clase*, during the tumultuous period of the gradual implementation of a socialist state marked by crises such as the 2002 coup against Hugo Chávez and the oil strike of 2002-2003 aimed at destabilizing his government. This film deals with the express kidnapping (a common form of abduction to extract money from victims) of an upper-middle-class couple by three *malandros* (thugs). While being held captive, the female protagonist ends up rejecting her fiancée and developing a close relationship with one of her kidnappers, who will save her from rape and death. As will be demonstrated in the following analysis, the two Venezuelan films present opposing ideological agendas. The former film embraces the socialist vision of the Bolivarian government whereas *Secuestro express* constitutes a seemingly nonpartisan filmmaking practice while depicting the Venezuelan society in a way that sparked off an acrimonious dispute between director Jakubowicz and the Venezuelan government.

Following the comparison between these two features, the contrast with the Cuban film *Los dioses rotos* further allows us to observe differences in the aesthetics and politics of films produced in socialist countries that are developing in opposing directions (gradually opening to the market in Cuba and intensifying state control of the economy in Venezuela). *Los dioses rotos* deals with the rather unlikely and complicated romance between two prostitutes (a female and a male prostitute), a pimp, and a university researcher in Havana, broadly set around the same historical period as *Secuestro express* (the early 2000s). It is a time following the so-called "periodo especial" in Cuba, a "special period" characterized by extreme privation that Cubans had to endure as a result of the collapse of the socialist bloc in Europe and the ensuing withdraw of Soviet support. Among other effects, this special period brought about a sharp rise in prostitution and inequality on the island, problems that the socialist revolution of 1959 failed to eradicate. Despite being produced by the Cuban state studios ICAIC, *Los dioses rotos* does not shy away from this failure. It employs the attractive visual language of sexual encounters, passionate love, and betrayal to the depiction of social and personal conflicts in the purportedly classless Cuban society, at the same time that it allegorizes social transformations at large in the decaying socialist state where the leadership is increasingly being questioned.

Regarding their production, *Secuestro express* is a commercial feature partially produced and distributed by a US major (Miramax) while *La clase* and *Los dioses rotos* were produced and distributed by the Venezuelan and Cuban state producers, the young FVC and Amazonia Films, and the mythic Cuban Film Institute (ICAIC) respectively. In what follows, I examine the implications of employing these different modes of production and distribution in combination with the (useful methodology of) textual analysis to identify different ideologies of form in these films.

THE CONTRASTING POLITICS OF *LA CLASE* AND *SECUESTRO EXPRESS*

La clase is a 2007 feature about inequality set between the Caracas slums (spaces that the film's director knows well) and middle-class spaces. It is a paradigmatic production of FVC, the state's film production unit created in June 2006 and conforms to the cultural policies put forward by the late president of Venezuela Hugo Chávez from 1999 to 2013 in accordance with his twenty-first century revolutionary and socialist program. Three years after releasing this film, José Antonio Varela became the president of FVC (in 2010). The script is an adaptation of a homonymous novel written by Farruco Sesto Novás. It won awards at the film festivals of Mérida in 2008 and Málaga in 2009, and an honorific mention at the Iberian American Film and Video Festival Cinesul 2008 but is generally unknown outside Venezuela. The plot concerns a young woman called Tita (Carolina Riveros) who must decide between Yuri (Laureano Olivares), the dependable boyfriend from the slums where she "belongs," and Anselmo (Darío Soto), the wealthy boyfriend who can take her away from "hell"—as she calls the barrio where she lives. After a long internal debate and the experience of Caracazo, she chooses to stay with the people from the slum where she belongs.

Venezuelan cinema has a long tradition in the depiction of inequalities, crime, and precarious life in the slums. This extended cinematic empathy with the slum dwellers contrasts markedly with its scant presence in Argentine cinema up to recent times, for instance.[4] The first film projections in Venezuela took place in 1896, as in most Latin American countries, only a few months after the first collective exhibitions in the United States and Europe. From the beginning, many Latin American intellectuals and public leaders expressed an interest in the use of cinema for social improvement, and the attitude of the Venezuelans toward these new technologies included attention to films' potential for moral education.[5] Life in the *barrios* (the Venezuelan term for "shantytown" or "slum") has been a characteristic theme of Venezuelan filmmaking for decades, particularly since the release in 1959 of *Caín adolescente* (*Adolescent Cain*), the first feature film of Venezuela's most prolific filmmaker, Ramón Chalbaud, who has produced more than thirty films so far and whose taste for melodrama has deprived him of the international reputation enjoyed by other Latin American counterparts.[6]

In 1950s Venezuela, filming an "abject" subject such as many of those in Chalbaud's films, an innovative idea at the time, was not exempt from criticism. The early creation of national archetypes (the prostitute, the criminal, and the guerrilla) by Chalbaud and other two influential filmmakers (Clemente de la Cerda, and Mauricio Walerstein) points to cinema's social engagement with the underclass from the end of the 1950s to the mid-1980s as well as its contribution to the construction of an imagined community. These were also, according to Tulio Hernández, the archetypes that attracted the Venezuelan audience to Venezuelan cinema:

> We must not forget that this is the first great dialogue of the Venezuelan people, at least of the contemporary Venezuelan people, with the screen which was up to them closed to them, where they did not exist. I think that it is interesting that the three more prolific directors, the three who created the myth of the 1960s whose works continue to be the most popular at the box-office, the three who provided these three themes who conform to the myth of the cinema in the 1960s. And this still is, up to today, the only relevant, the only worth stressing, the great contribution in terms of the country's collective imaginary.[7]

In his recent historical overview of the representation of the malandro in Venezuelan cinema, Gonzalo Chacón Mora anticipated that the new cinema promoted by the Bolivarian government would introduce changes.[8] While it is true that contemporary state-sponsored productions embrace new forms of social commitment that represent the underprivileged according to a new vision (*una nueva humanidad*), since its establishment in June 2006 under the Ministerio del Poder Popular para la Cultura (Ministry of Popular Power for Culture), FVC's productions strengthened these strong cinematic currents widely developed before 1999 rather than inventing something entirely new. Thus, it must be noted that the interest in these themes is not a fully innovative result of a revolutionary cultural program and, in fact, *Secuestro express* takes part in this tradition too to a certain extent. This is one of the reasons that validates the present comparison whose results show that *La clase*, more than *Secuestro express*, constitutes an innovative contribution to the development of this long-standing tradition in Venezuelan filmmaking.

One of the aspects that better proves this point is the concept of the nation underpinning these two film projects. Burton-Carvajal's idea of film as "a weapon of choice in the (re)definition of the national project" during periods of social transformation is most useful in the Bolivarian Republic of Venezuela.[9] *La clase* is an outcome of the efforts of the Bolivarian government to integrate cinema and community interests. Eighty percent of *La clase* was shot in the barrio of Zumba de Guarenas and some of the film's extras and assistant producers were originally from this slum.[10] This revolutionary mode of production enables the necessary democratization and renewal of the filmmaking sector (which is mostly in the hands of the middle class at continental level) and constitutes a new cinematic vision within a socialist state. This modus operandi has continued after FVC moved from the Ministerio del Poder Popular para la Cultura to the Ministerio del Poder Popular para la Comunicación y la Información (Ministry of Popular Power for Communication and Information) in 2014. One of the reasons for its transfer to this new unit is that "el cine y los medios audiovisuales inciden en la formación de la ciudadanía en el fomento de los valores de una sociedad democrática y en el propio desarrollo social de la nación" (cinema and audiovisual media educate citizens, promote democratic values, and the social development of the nation).[11] Other FVC productions around the time *La clase* was released were documentary features about the omnipresent national petroleum company and the persecution of leftist opponents during democratic periods due to the Cold War, and a series of biopics of independence leaders. The priority of these themes stems from the government's commitment to reassess the nation's history. As Steve Ellner rightly points out, "President Chávez's condemnation of traditional political historiography as 'bourgeois history' based on an 'imported' model . . . and his refusal to vilify Pérez Jiménez have encouraged his followers and even many outside of his movement to rethink the nation's past."[12]

La clase prompts Venezuelan audiences to rethink the history of the Venezuelan class struggle. As mentioned above, the violent clashes seen at the end of the film correspond to the Caracazo. This is a pivotal event in Venezuela's history that is constantly being reassessed[13] and it was extremely inspiring cinematically. The year 1989 marked the beginning of the collapse of socialism in Europe and the sowing of the seeds of Bolivarian socialism. In February, the newly elected president of Venezuela Carlos Andrés Pérez, who governed the country from 1989 to 1993, faced nationwide protest riots known as the Caracazo. These demonstrations were brutally repressed by the army and the police, resulting in a large number of dead and disappeared,[14] although the exact numbers of those killed and wounded by firearms are still unknown.[15] Pérez was re-elected president of Venezuela for a second term for his anti-neoliberal agenda (in his first term, 1974–1979, he had implemented interventionist measures such as the nationalization of the oil industry and the enhancement of job security measures). Surprisingly, once he became president, he received pressure from the International Monetary Fund (IMF) to apply a neoliberal shock treatment to the Venezuelan economy. The reform package known as "el paquete"[16] included privatization of major state companies and decentralization, measures which led to a sharp increase in prices, including hikes of more than 30 percent in public transportation fares. The man who would be elected by a large majority of the population to be president of Venezuela from 1999 until his death in 2013 and who spearheaded the continental turn to the left, Hugo Chávez, was "repulsed by the excessive use of force" of the repressive state apparatus[17] during the Caracazo. Chávez led an unsuccessful coup in 1992–the year that President Carlos Andrés Pérez passed a Privatization Law to sell key national industries–and won the presidential elections in 1998.

Secuestro express belongs to an entirely different mode of filmmaking, more in line with Hollywood crime thrillers like those by Guy Ritchie than Venezuelan cinema. It enjoyed greater commercial success than *La clase* both in Venezuela and internationally, even though it is not "the top grossing movie in Venezuela's box office history," as has been wrongly described,[18] Venezuelan cinema did not start with it,[19] and Jakubowicz is by no means "Venezuela's most celebrated filmmaker and writer," as a well-known commercial database describes him.[20] Involvement from the American film industry in this project provides some light to understanding the reason for the film's success. *Secuestro express* was the first Venezuelan film to be internationally distributed by Hollywood's Miramax, a subsidiary of Walt Disney Motion Pictures Group. The film's producer, Sandra Condito, production vice president of Miramax when the film was made, suggested that Jakubowicz make a film about express kidnappings after learning about his experience of this crime. The film's executive producer, the Venezuelan Elizabeth Avellán, also works in the American film industry, and the film was premiered in Los Angeles.[21] In addition to its production and distribution, *Secuestro*'s success may also come from the way it conforms to the aesthetic conventions of the contemporary Hollywood thriller as well as promoting an image of Latin America in line with the worldwide stereotype of a violent-poor-unstable continent.

Taking all these conditions into account, it was to be expected that accolades such as Best Foreign Film in the British Independent Film Awards 2005 and the Golden Trailer Award in 2006 obtained by Jakubowicz's film were not widely celebrated in the country. The vice president of Venezuela at the time and journalist José Vicente Rangel denounced the feature as a "miserable film, a falsification of the truth with no artistic value,"[22] and Jonathan Jakubowicz has responded criticizing the Bolivarian government on many occasions. With regard to FVC in particular, he calls them "los Villanos del Cine," "the Villains of Cinema" and considers that they "do not make Venezuelan cinema, they do Chavista cinema."[23]

With regard to the vision of the nation inherent in this thriller, in one of *Secuestro's* DVD editions, the menu is set against a background of *bolívar* notes—the prone to fast-rising inflation Venezuelan currency at the center of much criticism against the government. The film starts with a brief shot of a Russian roulette scene, followed by a fast montage of diverse images: a bird's eye view of the high-rises of Caracas and the slums that surround them, graffiti proclaiming the words "I love you Caracas," an image of the Virgin Mary, rich golfers, smart shopping malls, rioting in the streets, police attacking opposition demonstrators, the demonstrators in turn calling for army intervention, another image of the independence hero Simón Bolívar, the much publicized image of a leftist activist called Rafael Cabrices firing his gun from Puente Llaguno, "dangerous" youngsters consuming drugs, tattooing themselves, and fighting at night in the slums.

Among these significant snapshots of Venezuelan society, there is one that merits special attention, that of Simón Bolívar. The identification of the successive Bolivarian governments with Bolívar is such that this socialist state, "doesn't assume Marxism as the guiding ideology of the process, but rather Bolívarianism."[24] The name of the country was officially changed to *República Bolivariana de Venezuela* (The Bolivarian Republic of Venezuela) as early as 1999.[25] Therefore, by associating the image of Bolívar with chaotic scenes in *Secuestro express*, Jakubowicz may wish to imply that Chávez's Bolivarian vision for the country has failed to ensure order and stability. This image of Bolívar contrasts sharply with a majestic image of the same historical figure depicted in a statue in Plaza Bolívar in the film *La clase*. The negative connotation of Bolívar in *Secuestro* is confirmed shortly after the initial montage when a radio host refers to the country as *República Bolivariana de la Marihuana* or Bolivarian Republic of Marijuana, mocking the nation's current denomination.

Another controversial image in this initial montage is an extract of archive footage that shows Chávez supporter Rafael Cabrices shooting from a bridge in April 11, 2002, when the brief coup against President Chávez is about to take place. Documentaries like *The Revolution Will Not Be Televised* (*La revolución no será transmitida*, Kim Bartley and Donnacha O'Briain, 2003) or *Puente Llaguno, claves de una massacre* (*Llaguno Bridge, Keys to a Massacre*, Ángel Palacios, 2004) were produced to interpret this controversial incident.[26] Basically, the opposition claims that Chávez supporters were firing at members of the opposition, and the private media presented it as such, whereas the President's supporters argue that the people on the bridge were in fact protecting themselves from sniper fire. Cabrices died of a heart attack while the legal proceedings to have his image removed from the film were in progress. Situating this image in the middle of a series of images that denote violence could be interpreted as a sign of support for the former interpretation, and this is in fact how the Chávez's government interpreted this inclusion. Such indexes of partiality contradict the claims that the director makes about his impartiality and concur with the film crew's vision of Venezuela as the USA's backyard.[27]

Jakubowicz's deference and attention to the US audience stand in contrast to José Antonio Varela's contribution to a decolonial imaginary (in Walter Mignolo's terminology) in line with the efforts made by Hugo Chávez to fight US hegemony in the continent. The connection between Chávez's political project and Varela's creative concept is explicitly established through Eduardo Galeano's words. In a gesture that attracted international media attention in 2009, Chávez presented to President Barack Obama an history of Latin America by Galeano titled *Open Veins of Latin America: Five Centuries of the Pillage of a Continent,*[28] one of the most read and quoted books about the destructive colonial enterprise in Latin America, probably used by Chávez in 2009 as a reminder of the persistence of imperialist attitudes in USA. *La clase*'s epilogue is precisely a famous quote by this Uruguayan essayist: "Above all, the world is divided in unworthy and the *indignados*. And it is up to each one of us to decide what side we want to or we can take."[29] Looking at these interlocking political and cultural gestures allows us to see the close connection between anticolonial struggles and the experiences of the *damnés*, the wretched of the earth.[30]

Secuestro express has been presented at times as a "class war" thriller where things go horribly wrong but the feature's portrayal of this social conflict is distant from Galeano's account.[31] The film follows a general action-film formula, except for the fact that it introduces class politics into the script and displays a strong commitment to realism from the start. A kind of journalistic or documentary impulse is revealed in the intertitle that opens the film: "An incalculable number of kidnappings happen daily in Latin America. This is the story of just one of them." This kind of introduction, that it's a true story, has a long life in fiction, in which it induces a special kind of audience involvement with the narrative. A related statement in voiceover finishes *Secuestro* in a complementary way: "Half the world is starving, whilst the other half is dying of obesity. There are only two choices left: either we confront *el monstruo* (the beast), or we invite it to dinner," where "we" stands for the middle-class citizens like the kidnapped and the intended audience and "the beast" for the kidnappers. In addition to these statements in the film, the director has commented widely about his efforts to represent a *real problem objectively*. *Secuestro* makes some to wrongly perceive the film as a representation of pure reality, as does Venezuelan scholar Sandra Pinardi in 2007 when she writes, "The documentary nature of the film is emphasized by the fact that many actors do not "perform"; they do not elaborate a representation. Instead, they tell things about themselves and their milieu."[32]

These explicit moral statements in both *Secuestro* and *La clase* were not common in the earlier Venezuelan tradition referred to above, and the two features exhibit other striking similarities. The leads are young women whose future depends heavily on the development of romantic relationships with men. In *La clase*, Tita's choice of future political/social action is strongly linked to her choice of boyfriend. Choosing Yuri implies fighting alongside the poor masses, whereas staying with Anselmo entails immediate access to the middle class. In *Secuestro*, for Carla (Mía Maestro), the developing romantic relationship with one of her kidnappers, Trece (Carlos Julio Molina), saves her from being kidnapped or killed by the other kidnappers and the police. Similarly, both films have scripts that delineate a causal link between inequality and violence but differ in their politics of class, in line with Venezuela's polarization, as will be demonstrated in the subsequent analysis of their aesthetics. In this context, pretending that the film *Secuestro* offers a nonpartisan look at inequality issues in Venezuela is not only inaccurate but misleading. *Secuestro*'s script is clearly written from a bourgeois point of view that proposes a charitable approach to solve problems of inequality.[33] Such an invitation differs strikingly from the lower-class position that predominates in *La clase*'s narrative, and also from *La clase*'s adhesion to a Fanonian perspective on violence applied to situations of extreme social inequality. The thinker Frantz Fanon viewed violence as inherent to colonialism and inevitably used in decolonizing struggles when "throwing it back in the face of those who initiated it."[34]

Different Narrative and Aesthetic Approaches in *La clase* and *Secuestro express*

Aesthetically and narratively, the two films obviously differ in a number of aspects that generally correspond to the conventions of the social drama and action/crime film. *La clase* uses noirish aesthetics for an aspirational narrative of the working class, alternating between three main locations: the barrio of Catia (one of the largest slums in the country known for media activism), the *urbanización* (upper-middle-class condominium) of Anselmo (located in Campo Claro in Sesto's novel but unspecified in the film), and the theater where Tita and Anselmo's orchestra rehearse. It is narrated chronologically with continuity editing except for the last part when the Caracazo breaks out. In this last section, there is a montage of images combining stills and film at different places about the riots and other metaphorical images of slaughtering cows that connects the end with opening references to slaughtering. This montage mainly serves to connect the climax of Tita's internal conflict with the social conflict and to make the film's allegory explicit, as I explain below. This film with a grainy texture was shot in low-key lighting. Scenes in nearly black and white color alternate with others in color, but it is only the red color of the slaughtered cows inserted in this final montage that has a vivid tone.

Secuestro express follows a chronological time as well although it appears more fragmented than *La clase*, employing MTV-style aesthetics (attractive to youth accustomed to music videos and commercials) extensively. It exhibits higher production values than the former film, with aerial establishing shots of Caracas, scenes shot in cars and the casting of well-known actors and singers such as the Argentine Mía Maestro, the Panamanian Rubén Blades, the Venezuelan hip hop artists from the bands Vagos y Maleantes and Tres Dueños, and the singer Edgar José "Dolor" Quijada. In the following paragraphs, I will analyze these differences in more detail mainly focusing on the films' imagery and characterization.

La clase as a Latin American Allegory

La clase opens with images of a slaughterhouse, followed by the appearance of Tita. She is a young violinist who plays in an orchestra of the Sistema Nacional de *Orquestas Juveniles e Infantiles de Venezuela*, the prestigious system of national youth symphonic orchestras, within which orchestras are organized as instruments for social improvement and are a source of Venezuelan national pride. Anselmo plays in the same orchestra and has made an effort to attract her attention. He is a middle-class young man who is ignorant about the living conditions in the barrios and like Tita's boyfriend is dependable. His family does not oppose his relationship with a poor girlfriend like Tita. As her relationship with Anselmo intensifies, Tita gradually leaves Yuri behind. Such a theme, in which a suitor offers the promise of upward mobility, is common in film and literature. One of Tita's friend, Margarita (Zair Montes) is aware of Tita's problems to rehearse at her home and invites her to move to her comfortable home but, just as Tita is about to move there, the Caracazo breaks out and she remains with her people.

Apart from her work at the orchestra, Tita teaches music to small children at a local church. One day, Edwin (Gabriel Rojas), Tita's neighbor, while chased by the police, enters the church and holds Tita and the children hostage. Edwin shoots fearfully and hits a young girl in the arm, the police capture him, and later inform Tita that he was fatally shot while attempting to escape, but Tita believes the police executed him like an animal, a view that the priest (Asdrúbal Meléndez), holds too. The priest, known for helping people in the neighborhood, comforts Edwin's mother, and explicitly discusses the source of inequalities with Tita when she feels confused (another explicit political message that was not characteristic of socially-committed films from previous eras). The priest is an easily recognizable character type in Latin America, and in Venezuela he might have been inspired by priests like Numa Molina and Francisco Wuytack, or the American Reverend Jesse Jackson, a friend of the late Hugo Chávez. Edwin's funeral is portrayed with dignity and Tita explains to the children that they should not call him malandro (an indication toward a new representation of one of the traditional characters in Venezuelan filmmaking).

Filmmakers concerned with questions of class often explore their concerns as much through cityscapes as characterization. Architecture and urban geography speak much about social relations and money. For example, because *La clase* deals with Tita's dilemma of choosing between a rich and poor life, the film's locations show a city divided between the barrio and the urbanización. While the middle-class spaces are mostly interiors, both interior and exterior shooting takes place in the barrio, which the film portrays in more depth. The intersecting or, in Stavros Stavrides' terms, "threshold" space,[35] allows Tita to cross classes through her relationship with Anselmo and Margarita. Graffiti and murals in the barrios of *La clase* are also part of the cityscape and exhibit explicit political messages (unlike in *Secuestro express*). They are in fact, the manifestations of its inhabitants' political awareness and a form of art that is widespread in contemporary Venezuela and practiced by official institutions as well as individuals."[36]

In the urbanización, none of Anselmo's friends or neighbors is shown. Obviously, the barrio residents are represented in much more depth than the upper classes with their two-dimensional idyllic figures. His mother, an artist, is always impeccably dressed in light-colored clothes, even when painting at home, a space decorated with Cubist paintings and modern sculptures (the original novel of which the film is an adaptation mentions artists such as Soto, Jacobo Borges, Feliciano Carballo, and Andrés Pujol). In this film, such a detail is part of a class critique, since "art for art's sake" is a principle against which generally NLAC filmmakers and social realist artists react with skepticism. It is also in line with Pierre Bourdieu's analysis of the middle-class preference for form over content in contrast to working-class attitude to art.[37]

In contrast to the emptiness and isolation of the interiors in the urbanización, the strong sense of community associated with the barrio contributes to its largely positive image: we can see friends of different ethnic back-grounds gathered in the streets, workers eating together, a funeral, a wedding, an offer of food to a neighbor, etc. Although Tita persistently complains about the rough environment of the barrio, she is not subject to much violence herself. Her working-class family members are good natured and do not show signs of having serious problems. The barrio is presented as a lively and complex environment but serious problems such as gang fights or drug dealing are minimized or unrepresented here. Instead, most people living in the slum in the film are working-class citizens (Fig. 1.1). One of them, an African-Venezuelan man (Roger, played by Wilian Cuao) who works with Yuri in construction, is shot dead at the end of the film during the riots while he is taking meat from a refrigerator truck. The scene is filmed in such a way that what is often misrepresented in the media as "looting" by "criminals" appears here as a Fanonian reaction to the violence exerted against the working class by the ruling middle class. Tita's and Yuri's affective relation to Roger invites the audience to identify with him and to understand his actions. Roger has been slaughtered like an animal if we accept the association of images appearing at the end. In this last scene, a surrealist bloody image of a girl who had been assisted by Yuri and Tita earlier on appears, as well as numerous images of slaughtered animals. These are connected to the initial images of a slaughterhouse that were seemingly unrelated to the plot. The story circles back to the same theme but this time the animals are seen dripping blood.

This imagery extends the film's allegory beyond the concrete Venezuelan referent, a common trope that is prominently used in the foundational novel *El matadero* (*The Slaughterhouse*) by Argentine writer Esteban Echeverría

Figure 1.1   Roger and his Coworkers. *Source: La clase.*

as well as in the famous film *Strike*, by the Soviet filmmaker Sergei Eisenstein.[38] In his book, Echeverría contrasts the brutal and ignorant masses of the *federales* with the educated (middle-class) *unitarios*. The workers and supporters of the Rosas' federal regime slaughter a unitario as they had earlier done with a bull. That novel is marked by the identification of the proletariat with the barbarians, claims Jason Wilson, which stands in stark contrast with director José Antonio Varela's sympathetic view of the construction workers. Despite these differences in characterizing the proletariat, this metaphor of the slaughter of dumb animals serves in both texts as a "parable of ongoing Argentine violence,"[39] and it continues to provide effective imagery for representing irrational violence and class struggle in Latin America by extension. In other words, the use of the trope of civilization versus barbarism suggests that *La clase* can be interpreted as an allegory of Latin America as a whole (a continental allegory).[40] In the following paragraphs, I demonstrate that *Secuestro express* takes on a completely different narrative and aesthetic approach.

Secuestro express: The Bourgeois Point of View

Secuestro express was made in a contrasting style reminiscent of blockbusters like the Brazilian *Cidade de Deus* (*City of God*, Fernando Meirelles and Kátia Lund, 2002) and the Mexican *Amores perros* (Alejandro González Iñárritu, 2000). As Ivana Bentes explains, this "transnational aesthetics" is "a post-MTV language," a "new realism, that has as a basis high discharges of adrenaline, per second reactions created by editing and full immersion in the images. This means the same bases of pleasure and efficacy as that of the North American action movies."[41]

This aesthetics is distant from what is traditionally understood as socially-committed filmmaking both in NLAC theory/practice and in the Venezuelan film tradition as outlined above. The film's opening intertitle ("An incalculable number of kidnappings happen daily in Latin America. This is the story of just one of them") seems to suggest otherwise. Immediately after this intertitle, we see extreme close-ups of a dark-skinned man (Niga, played by the rapper Nigga Sibilino or Carlos Madera) talking about a Russian roulette game and a gun aimed at and shot at a victim (Martín, played by Jean Paul Leroux) whose subjective point of view is adopted by the camera. The audience thus views this episode (and, by extension, the whole film) from the middle-class victim's POV. Jakubowicz confirms this identification with the kidnapped in the following comment: "And in a way I felt that the audience should be a part of the victim's point of view."[42]

The first seven minutes of the film show the city, the main characters, and the preparations for the crime. While a wealthy young couple, Martín and Carla (Mía Maestro) are at a party in the country club, a criminal gang specialized in "express" kidnapping is preparing for a job. Speeded-up scenes alternate with stills with schematic descriptions of the characters as if a video game were about to start. Among the kidnappers, Niga is labeled as "Ex Con, Religious, Killer," Budú as "Painter, Rapist, Sentimental Father," Dolor as "Original Gangster, Cab Driver, Hunter of Rich Kids," and Trece as "Middle-class, Romantic." Apart from Trece's characterization (which allows him to play the role of savior), these lower-class characters are scripted throughout the film as sources of violence, not as victims of inequalities. At some point in the film, there is an attempt to complicate this Manichaean characterization, when the couple are taken by these individuals in Martín's car. Inside the car, the assailants beat up Martín at the same time that they make or receive calls from their families. Showing the children of the kidnappers arguably reveals their human side and softens the extremely negative perception that most viewers may have of them up to this point. The screen splits to depict victims' and kidnappers' family members at the same level, visually rendering all of them as somehow equal, but in reality this film fits into the narratives of fear of the lower classes by the middle class and the spectators are clearly interpellated as middle-class subjects.

Another attempt at providing a more complex picture of the characters is the character of Trece. He is important in this narrative because his romantic relationship with Carla points to the possibility of class reconciliation. However, even though Trece and Carla develop a relationship during the short period that they meet and this saves her from several rape attempts (from the kidnappers and the police), the relationship is not pursued due to the film's class ideology according to which class reconciliation is impossible.

From what has been observed so far, both Jakubowicz and Varela are concerned with the consequences of existing inequalities, particularly with the causes of class violence, a term understood differently in each of the features. *Secuestro* is concerned with a particular form of violence that undermines the quality of life of wealthy people, who live in fear of the underprivileged, but the film's chaotic vision of Venezuelan society "results from the lack of a humanist social perspective."[43]

In contrast, the violence that preoccupies the director of *La clase,* José Antonio Varela, is a collective violence that does not imply criminalization of the lower classes. Instead, lower-class riots are represented as a political response to a situation, not exclusively related to financial motives. The focus in *La clase* is not so much on the psychological impact that the social conflict has on the characters, but on the rational dilemma that they have to solve.

The differences found in this comparison between *Secuestro* and *La clase* reveal the bourgeois approach of the former film and the socialist realist approach of the latter. Although *La clase* contains techniques that are not associated to a socialist realist aesthetics, particularly the last scene where quick montage, surrealist associations, polyphonic soundscape, distortions, and freeze-frames provide an emotional effect, it is a socialist realism film according to Georg Lukács' definition because it is "in a position . . . both to portray the totality of a society in its immediacy and to reveal its pattern of development."[44] *Secuestro* lacks the social perspective of *La clase*, it offers a static view of class struggle (the film "talks about" violence, "portrays" violence) whereas *La clase* views class struggle as *a process* and, in this sense, tries to engage the audience in the active construction of a different society outside the cinema theater. This explains that we do not see much beyond the kidnapping in *Secuestro*, whereas in *La clase* the characters' milieu is well defined (we see a number of different environments as we observe the orchestra, the police taking action against youngsters, the sad state of public hospitals, the construction workers, and the riots in the street).

Secuestro can be aesthetically affiliated to sensational entertainment products produced in Latin American and Hollywood. *La clase*, on the other hand, with its class struggle and identity-building themes, is a continuation of NLAC in the twenty-first century. Contemporary critics as well as audiences in developed societies tend to disapprove of films with a focus on class, especially "films with a moral" such as *La clase*, and sometimes such films are labeled as propaganda. It is a liberal commonplace that class concerns do not promote artistic filmmaking. However, as seen in a comparison between *La clase* and *Secuestro*, the high level of class awareness of *La clase* lets it trace out social reality in more depth than *Secuestro*, with its fragmentation and isolation of different parts.[45]

In *Secuestro express* and *La clase* intimate relationships are key for understanding different figurations of class. The following analysis of *Los dioses rotos* deepens our comprehension of this question.

THE FALLEN GODS OF CUBAN CINEMA

Los dioses rotos (2008) is the first fiction feature by one of the most recognized emerging Cuban filmmakers, Ernesto Daranas. Prior to this film's release, he had experience in radio as well as a scriptwriter and director of short documentaries and a film for television. *Los dioses rotos* was produced by ICAIC at a time when the Cuban state was starting to face increasing pressure from filmmakers to provide a legal framework for independent filmmaking in the country. The beginning of the 1990s is key for understanding the recent history of film funding and distribution in Cuba. Between 1959 and 1990, the ICAIC was nearly the sole producer, distributor, and exhibitor in Cuba.[46] It was founded in March 1959, three months after the establishment of the Cuban revolutionary government, in a sign that culture was of paramount importance for the new political elite. Cinema was a tool to legitimize the regime and to create an anti-imperialist and decolonizing cinematic culture and thus compete with the hegemonic images and ideologies of Hollywood.

In 1990, the Cuban government declared a "Special Period in Times of Peace" as a result of the withdrawal of support from the Soviet Union to Cuba during the perestroika, one year before the implosion of the Soviet Union. It brought with it extreme material scarcity for the general population and a crisis in cinema that would eventually gear Cuban filmmakers toward more heterogeneous modes of financing.[47] This included the gradual development of an independent film sector in Cuba, which poses particular difficulties as legislation has yet to be passed.[48] The lack of "a film statute that structures, foments and defends [Cuban] cinema in all of its aspects" is precisely considered by Daranas as the most pressing challenge contemporary Cuban cinema faces.[49] Nevertheless, *Los dioses rotos* obtained a low budget film fund by the Cuban Ministry of Culture, was produced by ICAIC and, even involving the Mexican producer Altavista Films, resources to complete the film were scarce.

With hindsight, we know that *Los dioses rotos* enjoyed less success than Daranas' second feature, *Conducta* (*Behavior*, 2014), but was still particularly well received by the public and press associations. Some of the film's positive reviews include Joel del Río's pronouncement that *Los dioses rotos* was "the main audiovisual event in Cuba in the last few years"[50] and "a befitting way for the Cuban Institute of Cinematographic Art and Industry (ICAIC) to celebrate its 50th anniversary."[51] Its submission to the Oscars category of Best Foreign Language Film by ICAIC in 2010 is another example of the appreciation received. The film does capture the spirit of a period of momentous changes in Cuba in a profound sense, as I will demonstrate.

Changing the Appreciation of Cultural Capital

Cuban society is tightly knit. Politics and culture have been closely interrelated since 1959 and political decisions directly impinge on the development of cinema and narratives themselves. As a result of the status conferred in Cuba to art in general (to cinema and music in particular), and thanks to the human and economic (in relative terms) resources invested in them, the Cuban cinema of the 1960s and 1970s produced some of the classics of world cinema and was lauded by filmmakers and scholars worldwide. Many of them would go on to visit the country to teach, learn, or share ideas, especially at the Festival Internacional del Nuevo Cine Latinoamericano de la Habana, an event held annually since 1979. In its first edition, the presidents of the festival were the Nobel Laureate Gabriel García Márquez and the Cuban mythic documentarist Santiago Álvarez. The EICTV (Escuela Internacional de Cine y Televisión—International Film and Television School) of San Antonio de los Baños, founded by García Márquez, is an initiative to provide aspiring filmmakers of any nationality with a film education venue (its other name is "School of All the Worlds"). Despite Cuba's dire economic situation, this school is still successful today in nurturing global talent and counts among its graduates a number of well-known directors and producers such as Mariela Besuievsky, Carlos Lechuga, Marité Ugás, Mariana Rondón, and Benito Zambrano. The international standing of Cuban cinema and Cuban film institutions contrasts markedly with the scarce knowledge and recognition of Venezuelan cinema outside its borders.

It has become commonplace to observe that one of the most striking characteristics of Cuba for those who have little knowledge of the country is the combination of material scarcity and high levels of literacy, an achievement attributed to the success of the socialist policies employed there. Education is a key feature for understanding Cuba since 1959 and a major interest of Daranas, who graduated in Pedagogy and whose first two fiction films (*Los dioses rotos* and, particularly *Conducta*) deal with education and educators. Moreover, "the educator" was a traditional character of the pre-Special Period cinema that has generally moved offstage to give way to a "more nuanced range of characters,"[52] a trend to which *Los dioses rotos* and *Conducta* are exceptions.

The plot of *Los dioses rotos* concerns a teacher and researcher, Laura (played by Silvia Águila), who intends to write a thesis on the survival of the myth of Yarini in contemporary Cuba. She struggles to have her project accepted by a panel at the University of Havana. Yarini is a real historical figure who became the first myth of the young Cuban republic in 1910.[53] He was a famous pimp from the San Isidro quarter at the turn of the twentieth century who died fighting over a prostitute in a duel with a French competitor. Laura wants to do research on a sensitive topic for the secular and atheist Cuban nation:[54] the persistence of religious rituals around Yarini and the rise of prostitution in socialist Cuba in the twenty-first century. She suspects that a procurer called Rosendo (Héctor Noas) keeps the relic of Yarini and when Laura attempts to gather data from him and sex workers under his protection, Rosendo refuses to collaborate with her. At the same time, Rosendo repeats history by falling in love with a prostitute named Sandra (Annia Bú) who has just come out from jail. In the past, Sandra was emotionally involved with a gigolo named Alberto (Carlos Ever Fonseca), who had been her childhood friend and had betrayed her. At the moment when Sandra is released from jail and promises to be faithful to Rosendo, Alberto returns to Havana, and Sandra struggles with her strong feelings toward Alberto. This romantic triangle soon becomes a foursome when Laura starts to interfere in Rosendo's business and Alberto is commissioned by Rosendo to discourage her. Alberto is an attractive young man who works as a sex worker for a middle-age writer and retired researcher, Isabel (played by the well-known Isabel Santos), and uses his charm to help customers to strike business deals. Making himself attractive to Laura proves to be effortless. The film has all the elements of a passionate drama and makes ample use of erotic scenes and kinetic fight scenes between the rival female lovers.

The theme of romantic relationships between teachers/intellectuals and members of the working class or lumpenproletariat was a staple of revolutionary Cuban films with such memorable examples as *Memorias del subdesarrollo* (*Memories of Underdevelopment*, Tomás Gutiérrez Alea, 1968), *De cierta manera* (*One Way or Another*, Sara Gómez, 1974) and *Hasta cierto punto* (*Up to a Point*, Tomás Gutiérrez Alea, 1983), and it survives on in the recent controversial film *Santa y Andrés* (*Santa & Andres*, Carlos Lechuga, 2016). *Los dioses rotos*, like these features, displays the duality of class and culture "that was—and some argue remains—a fundamental feature of Cuban national identity."[55] Unlike the Venezuelan films seen in the previous section where upward social mobility generally means better material conditions, these Cuban narratives deal with the raising of social awareness as a benefit of engaging in such unequal relationships.

De cierta manera is a good counterpoint to *Los dioses rotos* which combines education and class conflict with an unusual attention to gender and urbanization. It is a hybrid film, a narrative fiction with documentary elements including actors and real characters. In his study of the sociospatial discourse of *De cierta manera*, Michael Chanan concluded that spaces such as the worker's factory and the teacher's school are not used to simply "color" the plot in Gómez's film, as is usual in conventional narrative movies, but spaces are characters in their own right and as such affect the character of the protagonists.[56] The relationship between the female teacher and the male worker evolves dialectically throughout *De cierta manera* in line with sociopolitical developments. Likewise, John Hess considers that "the dialectical relationship between the social and material world, on the one hand, and individual consciousness, on the other, has dominated Cuban cinema from the most optimistic, utopian films of the 1960s to the more conventional and pessimistic films of the 1990s."[57] As we can see in the development of Laura's character, this analysis is still partially valid for the 2008 feature *Los dioses rotos*.

Like the teacher in *De cierta manera*, who struggles to understand both children from underprivileged families and his boyfriend's *ñáñigo*'s affiliation (from the Afro-Cuban religion Abakuá), Laura ventures into the realm of the lower classes. She intends to study a historical figure who subverted the separation between the realms of education, religion and prostitution at the turn of the twentieth century: Alberto Manuel Francisco Yarini Ponce de León. He was a member of the Cuban aristocracy (his father was a highly respected dental surgeon and professor at the University of Havana) with political aspirations who had received a privileged education in the United States but ended up making a living out of prostitution. During his life and until his tragic death in 1910, he was widely supported by the ñáñigos. His end in a fight with a French procurer turned him into a saint revered by followers who, a century after his assassination, still pray to him and leave offerings at his tomb and under a tree (*ceiba*) that grew next to where he passed away.

In *Los dioses rotos*, the blurring of scientific rationalism and belief is visually conveyed as a dissolve in one of the first scenes of the film when Laura leaves the University of Havana, disappointed as her research project has been received with little enthusiasm by a panel of judges. Joining the unjoinable, the Alma Máter (the mother who feeds students with knowledge) is substituted by a Catholic Virgin of Mercy (the patroness of the captive, syncretized in Cuba with the Yoruba deity Obatalá) (Figs. 1.2 and 1.3). At the temple of Nuestra Señora de la Merced located at the quarter of San Isidro in Old Havana, where Yarini lived, Laura interviews one of her research subjects.

The merging of science and devotion points to a devaluation of knowledge, if we accept Marx's critique of religion as the opium of the people (befitting in a socialist country) and the fact that the Cuban revolutionary government has viewed all religions negatively, although since 1991 there has been a

Figure 1.2   Laura Leaving the University of Havana. *Source: Los dioses rotos.*

Figure 1.3   The Alma Máter Merging with the Virgin of Mercy. *Source: Los dioses rotos.*

change in official attitudes toward religion.[58] The film's textual analysis points to the interpretation that merging the Alma Máter with the Virgin of Mercy signifies a profound disillusion with the power of education: a bedrock of socialist Cuba, and therefore an implicit critique of socialist Cuba. In addition to this, this confusion of symbols indicates the revalorization of identifiers mainly associated to the lower classes (the captive whom the Virgin of Mercy protects) who believe in the Virgin's powers, unlike types like Laura.

In this sense, the film partakes in the disillusionment characteristic of narratives produced after the onset of the Special Period[59] and re-evaluations of education in Cuba as indoctrination conducted by socially-minded filmmakers like Ricardo Acosta.[60] This disillusionment and sense of social "decomposition," is obvious in other cultural sectors as well. A musical example of the same phenomenon is the unexpected popularity of the reggaeton "Chupi Chupi" by the singer Osmani Garcia and its infamous accompanying music video of 2012. The lyrics of this popular song make repeated references to fellatio in a highly chauvinistic fashion, something that aroused the disdain of some Cuban intellectuals; this music video was nominated for the Cuban music video contest "Premios Lucas," but was later taken down for its extreme display of vulgarity. The video's success prompted the winner of the Cuban National Prize for Literature in 2012 Leonardo Padura Fuentes to comment:

In the same way that the Mexican narco-corridos evolved from the reality of drug dealing, the Cuban reggaeton reflected the social and economic crisis exploding in Cuba in the 1990s, which became a crisis of values, and for several years placed people in a position where daily life was a fight for survival. The generation that arose from the world in those years grew up in a dark, hot, impoverished atmosphere which we have not managed to escape entirely. These were the years when Cuban migratory attempts were rising . . . ; the years in which the balance between salary and the domestic economy was broken; when the supposed monolithic and egalitarian structure of our society was shattered and people's possibilities start to differ . . . . What is being manifested through the spirit of this reggaeton and similar manifestations is not simply the typical generational impetus to distinguish itself from the preceding generation and find its own place in the world: for its connotations, it is a symptom of decomposition.[61]

Padura's diagnosis serves to better understand *Los dioses rotos*. The loss of distinction (in Bourdieu's terms) by the middle-class Caucasian who possesses cultural capital (Laura) is confirmed by her alignment with the Afro-Cuban prostitute (Sandra), who lacks such capital, in two scenes (when they fight for Alberto and at the end of the film). *Los dioses rotos* represents the disenchantment with the narrative of progress toward a classless society thanks to the Cuban revolution. In this sense, it is successful in pointing toward a contemporary redefinition of class whereby the elites who previously occupied the upper floors in a hierarchical society as represented in the banned film *Alicia en el pueblo de Maravillas* (*Alice in Wondertown*, Daniel Díaz Torres, 1991) are now at the same level as the prostitutes.[62]

Cuban Film in Search of an International Audience

At an aesthetic level, the film avoids both outdated aesthetics such as socialist realism (which had never really taken off in Cuba[63]) and NLAC's dialectical filmmaking as well as innovations in contemporary global cinema (which other Cuban filmmakers like Fernando Pérez or Carlos Lechuga follow). Instead, Daranas opts strongly for the aesthetics of publicity and musical videos with extensive use of freeze-frames, fragmentation, musical synchronization and rhythm, and generally follows dominant modes of Hollywood filmmaking. This style is suitable for the film's emphasis on stereotypical themes of contemporary Cuban culture and society such as the spread of prostitution, the rise of *Santería* and the identification of the island with musical talent, all sources of tourist and foreign attraction. In this sense, the film's conception follows a Special Period aesthetics originated by the necessary introduction of foreign participation in Cuban film production observed by Cristina Venegas.[64] It also reintroduces "an exotic Cuba for foreign consumption" that had been "challenged by the Revolution of 1959."[65]

Los dioses rotos is to a certain extent a brothel melodrama. The sense of timelessness achieved by the cinematography and art direction contributes to establishing a link with one of the most developed film genres in early Latin American cinema.[66] Although *Los dioses rotos* contains documentary elements, particularly the archival footage and the interviews conducted by Laura, the resulting documentary effect is minimal because of the highly emotional tone of the interviews and the effective interweaving of the documentary elements with the passionate relation between Sandra and Alberto. Ernesto Daranas employs eroticism and melodrama in combination with an attractive and carefully crafted soundtrack and a vivid color palette to entice the viewer. This combination of entertainment and social engagement in the particular context of Cuban cinema raises questions about the possible implications that this strategy might have for the figuration of class struggle. The combination of ethnography and entertainment was also observed by Cuban critic Rufo Caballero who praised the film for its capacity to continue the Cuban filmmaking tradition of contributing to the anthropological study of Cuba without preaching and by making good use of sentimentality.[67]

The use of color provides a key for better understanding the film's dominant approach. The director of photography, Rigoberto Senarega, aimed at making Old Havana look "beautiful, dignified, maternal."[68] In his study of color in film Stephen Neal draws from Edward Buscombe's analysis of the ideological use of color in dominant cinema in relationship to realist aesthetics. He calls attention to the fact that one of the reasons for the delay in the use of color in Hollywood in comparison to sound was its incapacity to be instantly accommodated to the realist aesthetics.[69] When color started to be used in Hollywood in the 1930s and 1940s, it was reserved for non-realist genres such as musicals and epics. In the 1950s, when it was more widely used, the artificial connotation gradually disappeared and with the advent of television, color was used in fictional and non-fictional films alike. However, the two basic oppositions soon established in the discourse on color have persisted to this day: nature versus art and spectacle versus realism. If the spectacular mode of color is invoked, the film is not realist and must reflect art. Neale further elaborates on the use of color with regard to the female figure. Within patriarchal ideology, women already occupy "the contradictory spaces of both nature and culture" and they are "socially sanctioned objects of erotic looking."[70] In a large number of scenes in *Los dioses rotos*, color is spectacular and often linked to Sandra (the sex worker). The turquoise and different hues of blue and green dominate her clothes and are important components of the color in many scenes. In *Los dioses rotos*, Daranas' use of color and its association with Sandra point to the film's quality as erotic spectacle.

The film contains explicit sex scenes that are well integrated in the film's narrative. As can be expected from the currency of sex tourism in Cuba, prostitution and explicit sex scenes abound on the screen, a feature of much contemporary Cuban filmmaking. However, the extensive use of sex scenes in a film produced by ICAIC chosen to represent the Cuban filmmaking scene at the Oscars is surprising. This was an attempt by the ICAIC to produce an internationally successful film like the 1994 Academy nominee *Fresa y chocolate* (*Strawberry and Chocolate*, Tomás Gutiérrez Alea and Juan Carlos Tabío, 1993). In addition to this, the film was part of a film series supported by the foreign offices of the Cuban government in places as distant as Chennai (India) and Chillán (Chile), both in 2010.

This analysis sheds light on the transformations of class representation in Cuban cinema as seen in representative films from the 1960s through recent years. *Los dioses rotos* occupies a particular space in this development because it undermines the aristocracy of culture in a country where culture had always been a source of social distinction and, in this sense, it is more innovative than the more recent feature *Santa y Andrés*, where the female farmer is still the one "learning" from the male intellectual. Recent productions like *Habanastation* (*Havanastation*, Ian Padrón, 2011) where the dark face of Cuba's unequal society is exposed in *La Timba* slum show that class differences in Cuban society are increasingly reliant on material conditions.

The formula of *Los dioses rotos* proved to be successful in attracting the public. The film won the Audience Award at the thirtieth International Festival of New Latin American Cinema of Havana held in 2008. It is regarded by Víctor Fowler Calzada as one of the few "important films" produced by the ICAIC between 2005 and 2008 and presents "an in-depth account of the codes of life in Havana's marginal neighbourhoods." In what is becoming a somewhat hackneyed observation, Fowler Calzada also contrasts the allegories of the nation of Cuba's cinematic past with current Cuban films that are "bereft of any ideological discourse."[71] The previous analysis of *Los dioses rotos* unveils such a harsh critique of the Cuban establishment that it is surprising that this film did not only suffer the same fate as *Alicia en el pueblo de Maravillas* but was even nominated for the Oscars.

The previous analyses of Venezuelan and Cuban features show that, aesthetically and historically, Cuban and Venezuelan cinemas are distant. *Secuestro express* aestheticizes violence and propagates an irrational culture of fear, the film *La clase* is progressist in its class politics (conducive to the elimination of exploitation) but exhibits a conservative ideology at the level of form. In contrast to the Fanonian approach of *La clase* where class struggle appears still alive and social advancement is dependent on the struggle of the *damnés*, *Los dioses rotos* exhibits a disillusionment with socialist politics and aesthetics. The traditional social differentiation according to cultural capital in Cuban society is being called into question in contemporary Cuba. For his followers, Yarini was a "god,"[72] but the gods that fall in this film are not only dead historical figures but those who have been, and still are, unable to implement a successful egalitarian agenda in the country.

These stark differences in the way class is viewed in narratives created in nations where social justice occupies a prominent place in the public sphere are due to individual differences and, more importantly, to the specificity of national-historical experience, which imprints its own character on the form. Cuba had been a nominally socialist country for nearly five decades at the time when *Los dioses rotos* was released whereas Venezuela had initiated the Turn-to-the-Left in the continent barely six years before *Secuestro express* and eight years before *La clase*'s premiere. The following chapter delves into domestic space and neighborhood to look at how the filmmakers' own social position conditions his/her construction of space in two internationally successful features from Mexico (a country where neoliberalism has been fully defended by successive governments of different political sign throughout the twenty-first century) and Brazil (another representative of the Turn-to-the-Left up to 2016).

NOTES

1. Class is a crucial factor in the romantic relationships of most successful melodramas. See, for instance, Pérez's description of *Doña Bárbara* (Fernando de Fuentes, 1943) and *Aventurera* (Alberto Gout, 1950) in Gilberto Pérez, "Melodrama of the Spirited Woman: Aventurera," in *Latin American Melodrama: Passion, Pathos and Entertainment*, ed. Darlene J. Sadlier (Urbana: University of Illinois Press, 2009), 19–32.

2. Michael Chanan, *Cuban Cinema* (Minneapolis: University of Minnesota Press, 2004), 14.

3. Farruco Sesto, "Conversaciones," *Con Farruco*, February 21, 2010. https://co nfarruco.blogspot.com/2010/02/conversaciones-210210.html. My translation. Unless otherwise noted, all translations in this volume are mine.

4. The lumpen dramas were a taboo topic up to the 1990s, according to Timothy Barnard, but the Argentine cinema has been gradually changing in this regard, particularly after the crisis of 2001. Timothy Barnard, "Popular Cinema and Populist Politics," in vol. 2 of *New Latin American Cinema*, ed. Michael T. Martin (Detroit: Wayne State University Press, 1997), 453.

5. Yolanda Sueiro Villanueva, *Inicios de la exhibición cinematográfica en Caracas, (1896–1905)* (Caracas: Fondo Editorial Humanidades y Educación, UCV, 2007), 66.

6. This is Julienne Burton-Carvajal's view on the director. Julienne Burton-Carvajal, "South American Cinema," in *World Cinema: Critical Approaches*, eds. John Hill and Pamela Church Gibson (New York: Oxford University Press, 2000), 197. More recently, as the Venezuelan filmmaking sector has become dangerously embroiled in disputes between those in favor of and those against the Bolivarian government, Chalbaud was publicly attacked by some students of Universidad de los Andes (ULA) during the celebration of an event in his honor at the Mérida Film

Festival in 2017 for allegedly supporting the government, but remains one of the foremost directors of this Latin American nation nevertheless.

7. This classification was presented in the course of a discussion organized by Alfredo Roffé on tendencies in the New Venezuelan Cinema produced between 1973 and 1993. José Miguel Acosta et al., *Panorama histórico del cine en Venezuela* (Caracas: Fundación Cinemateca Nacional, 1997), 65.

8. Gonzalo Chacón Mora, "Imagining the Malandro: Anti-politics and the Representation of the Malandro in Venezuelan Cinema," paper, *The Aesthetics of Politics and the Politics of Aesthetics in Contemporary Venezuela* (September 19–20, 2014, University of Cambridge).

9. Julienne Burton-Carvajal, "South American Cinema," 195. In addition to the three filmmakers mentioned above, other figures focusing on socially-engaged practices across the decades from direction through film pedagogy to scriptwriting include César Bolívar, Luis Alberto Lamata, Carlos Azpúrua, José Ignacio Cabrujas, Liliane Blaser and Luis Cerasa, to name a few who are well-known in diverse roles in the Venezuelan filmmaking community.

10. Tania González, "Una nueva visión comunitaria del cine en Venezuela," *Aló Presidente*, July 22, 2007. http://alopresidente.gob.ve/info/6/240/una_nueva_visiue n.html.

11. Gaceta Oficial de la República Bolivariana de Venezuela, 40.357, Decree 791, February 17, 2014,

12. Steve Ellner, *Rethinking Venezuelan Politics: Class, Conflict, and the Chávez Phenomenon* (Colorado: Lynne Rienner, 2008), 20.

13. After seventeen years of socialist governments and in a year of extreme economic problems (2016), the filmmaker Carlos Oteyza released the documentary *CAP: dos intentos* (*CAP: Two Attempts*, 2016), a documentary reassessing Carlos Andrés Pérez's government and advocating for a liberal model of government. Not surprisingly, the film was successful among Venezuelan audiences tired of the socialist agenda (more than 46,000 tickets sold in the first weeks of its release, a large number of receipts at a time when electricity shortages and the rise of insecurity had taken their toll on cinemas).

14. José Antonio Mayobre, "Venezuela and the Media: The New Paradigm," in *Latin Politics, Global Media*, eds. Elisabeth Fox and Silvio Waisbord (Austin: University of Texas Press, 2002), 181.

15. Ellner, *Rethinking Venezuelan Politics*, 95.

16. There are scenes in *La clase* where we can see a graffiti reading "Abajo el paquete" (Down with the reform package).

17. Ellner, *Rethinking Venezuelan Politics*, 96.

18. "Secuestro express 2005," *IMDB database*. In reality, the top grossing films in Venezuelan filmmaking history are *Homicio culposo* (César Bolívar, 1983) and *Papita, maní, tostón* (Luis Carlos Hueck, 2013). *Secuestro express* has been likened to *Cidade de Deus* by many reviewers, such as Nigel Fountain, "Rage in the Ranchos," *The Guardian*, June 2, 2006, https://www.theguardian.com/film/2006/jun/02/1.

19. See the references to Jakubowicz in the following interview by Ángel Ricardo Gómez, "Entrevista Philippe Toledano. La parte débil del cine local es el guión," *El Universal* (Venezuela), October 6, 2008, http://www.eluniversal.com.

20. "Jakubowicz," Biography, *IMDB database*.

21. Jakubowicz's strong connections in Hollywood have allowed him to work, more recently, with an actor of such high international profile as Robert de Niro in his second feature (*Hands of Stone*, 2016).

22. Juan Forero, "Venezuelan Filmmaker Finds His Kidnapping Tale Resonates with the Masses," *New York Times*, Movies, October 6, 2005.

23. Robert Andrés Gómez, "Jonathan Jakubowicz. Por las calles de Hollywood," *El Universal*, April 28, 2008, http://www.eluniversal.com. *Chavistas* is the noun used by some to denote President Hugo Chávez's followers.

24. President Hugo Chávez's interest in Bolívar emerged while he was a student at the military academy, where he formed Bolivarian societies that culminated in the creation of the MBR 200 (Bolivarian Revolutionary Movement 200) in 1982. In 1997, the MBR 200's national assembly decided to create a political party that brought Chávez to the presidency in 1998. Hugo Chávez Frías and Marta Harnecker, *Understanding the Venezuelan Revolution: Hugo Chávez Talks to Marta Harnecker* (New York: Monthly Review, 2005), 9.

25. FVC's first release is perfectly in line with this ideology: the medium-length feature film *Bolívar eterno, ciudadano de la libertad* (*Eternal Bolívar, Citizen of Freedom*, Efterpi Charalambidis, 2006).

26. See Rod Stoneman, *Chávez: The Revolution Will Not Be Televised. A Case Study of Politics and the Media* (London: Wallflower Press, 2008); and Mike Wayne, Mike and Deirdre O'Neill, "Form, Politics and Culture: A Case Study of *The Take, The Revolution Will Not Be Televised* and *Listen to Venezuela*," in *Neoliberalism and Global Cinema*, eds. Jyostna Kapur and Keith B. Wagner (New York: Routledge, 2011), 113–32.

27. Jakubowicz comments that, "You need the gang members and you need the opposite gang and you need a little bit of everyone. And we shot this also in the centre of the political guerrilla and we shot at the centre of the opposition like movement, and you know, everybody was thinking and suspecting that we were from the other side but we were always clear that we had a social message and we were not into politics." *Secuestro express: The Film and the Facts*, DVD extras.

28. For more information, see Richard Gott, "Chávez's Perfect Gift to Obama," *The Guardian*, Opinion, April 20, 2009; Andrew Clark, "Chávez Creates Overnight Bestseller with Book Gift to Obama," *The Guardian*, Americas, April 19, 2009.

29. Original quote: "El mundo se divide sobre todo entre los indignos y los indignados. Y ya sabrá cada quién de qué lado quiere o puede estar." My translation is based on the following definitions by María Moliner: "Indigno: Merecedor de desprecio (deserving contempt); Indignación: Enfado violento provocado en alguien por una acción injusta o reprobable. Indignado: Acometido de indignación." It is the meaning used by the well-known Spanish mass movement established in 2011 the "indignados." María Moliner, *Diccionario de uso del español* (Madrid: Gredos, 1994).

30. This is a connection that Pheng Cheah highlights in his commentary on Walter Mignolo's decolonial thinking, to which, I argue, films like *La clase* contribute. "The Limits of Thinking in Decolonial Strategies," *Townsend Center for the Humanities*

Newsletter (November 2006), http://townsendcenter.berkeley.edu/publications/li mits-thinking-decolonial-strategies.

31. This is the term used by Alice O'Keeffe in "The Chavista War on Cinema," *Newstatesman*, May 26, 2006; Belkis Suárez Faillace prefers to describe the film in terms of "class struggle" ("La ciudad de Caracas amor a muerte y Secuestro Express," paper, LASA-Venezuela, May 26–22, 2008).

32. Sandra Pinardi, "Una política sin sujeto, una práctica del silencio," *Objeto Visual. Cuadernos de Investigación de la Cinemateca Nacional de Venezuela. Lecturas y miradas del cine venezolano* 13 (2007): 16.

33. The same view is shared by Boyd Williamson, "Blood, Guts, and Counter-Revolution," *Popmatters*, February 28, 2007.

34. Tracey Nicholls, "Frantz Fanon (1925–1961)," *Internet Encyclopedia of Philosophy*, http://www.iep.utm.edu/fanon/.

35. Stavros Stavrides states that, "Instead of thinking of social identities as bounded regions, one can consider them interdependent and communicating areas. In an effort to describe urban space as a process rather than a series of physical entities, we can discover practices that oppose a dominant will to fix spatial meanings and uses." Stavros Stavrides, "Heterotopias and the Experience of Porous Urban Space," in *Loose Space: Possibility and Diversity in Urban Life*, eds. Karen A. Franck and Quentin Stevens (London: Routledge, 2007), 174.

36. In her study of the urban social movements of the barrios of Caracas, Sujatha Fernandes contends that "popular fiestas and murals have been important vehicles in post-neoliberal imaginings of urban space and cultural identity, particularly given new geographies of exclusion." Sujatha Fernandes, *Who Can Stop the Drums?: Urban Social Movements in Chávez's Venezuela* (Durham: Duke University Press, 2010), 114.

37. Pierre Bourdieu, *Distinction. A Social Critique of the Judgement of Taste* (London: Routledge, 2010).

38. Echeverría's short story was written in 1839 but could not be published until 1871 due to political censorship.

39. Jason Wilson, "Writing for the Future: Echeverría's 'El Matadero' and Its Secret Rewriting by Jorge Luis Borges and Adolfo Bioy Casares as 'La fiesta del monstruo,'" *Forum for Modern Language Studies* 43, no. 1 (2007): 80.

40. Other representative texts of this tradition are the 1845 novel *Facundo: Civilización y barbarie* (*Facundo: Civilization and Barbarism*) by Domingo Faustino Sarmiento, and the 1929 Venezuelan novel by Rómulo Gallegos *Doña Bárbara*, one of the canonical texts of Latin American literature.

41. Ivana Bentes, "The Aesthetics of Violence in Brazilian Film," in *City of God in Several Voices: Brazilian Social Cinema as Action*, ed. Else R. P. Vieira (Nottingham: CCCP, 2005), 84.

42. Chapter "La película y la realidad" of *Secuestro express'* DVD extras.

43. Georg Lukács, *The Meaning of Contemporary Realism* (London: Merlin Press, 1963), 72.

44. Lukács, *The Meaning of Contemporary Realism*, 99.

45. For further discussion, see Roland Barthes, *Writing Degree Zero* (New York: Hill and Wang, 1977) and Esther C. M. Yau, "Compromised Liberation: The Politics of Class in Chinese Cinema of the Early 1950s," in *The Hidden Foundation: Cinema and the Question of Class*, eds. David E. James and Rick Berg (Minneapolis: University of Minnesota Press, 1996).

46. Michelle Leigh Farrell, "Narrating Precariousness in Cuba beyond Havana and the ICAIC: The Case of Televisión Serrana's Ariagna Fajardo and *¿A dónde vamos?*," in *The Precarious in the Cinemas of the Americas*, eds. Constanza Burucúa and Carolina Sitnisky (Cham: Palgrave Macmillan, 2018), 102.

47. Chanan, *Cuban Cinema*, 444; Cristina Venegas, "Filmmaking with Foreigners," in *Cuba and the Special Period: Culture and Ideology in the 1990's*, ed. Ariana Hernández-Reguant (New York: Palgrave Macmillan, 2009).

48. Filmmakers and scholars have tried to grasp the meaning of "independent filmmaking" in Cuba in the last few years and the new direction that the ICAIC must take for Cuban cinema to survive. The blog *Cine cubano, la pupila insomne* by Juan Antonio García Borrero contains detailed and informed discussions on filmmakers' initiatives to pressure the Cuban government to pass needed film legislation. https://cinecubanolapupilainsomne.wordpress.com/. See also Michelle Farrell, "Redefining Cuban Film and the Imagined Community: A Close-up on Nuevo realizador Aram Vidal," *Delaware Review of Latin American Studies* 15, no. 2 (2014), http://udspace.udel.edu/handle/19716/19748.

49. Andrew S. Vargas, "Ernesto Daranas, Director of Smash Hit 'Conducta' on Making Films in Cuba," *Remezcla*, April 4, 2014.

50. Del Río is a Cuban teacher at EICTV and a film scholar. Joel del Río, "Los dioses rotos, el mayor acontecimiento audiovisual en Cuba de los últimos tiempos," *Juventud Rebelde*, March 1, 2009.

51. Joel del Río, "New Cuban Movie Has the Island Buzzing." *Green Left Weekly*, July 4, 2009.

52. Venegas, "Filmmaking with Foreigners," 41.

53. Mayra Beers, "Murder in San Isidro: Crime and Culture during the Second Cuban Republic," *Cuban Studies* 34 (2003): 120.

54. Kevin M. Delgado, "Spiritual Capital: Foreign Patronage and the Trafficking of Santería," in *Cuba and the Special Period: Culture and Ideology in the 1990's*, ed. Ariana Hernández-Reguant (New York: Palgrave Macmillan, 2009), 54.

55. Beers, "Murder in San Isidro," 97.

56. Chanan, *Cuban Cinema*, 351.

57. John Hess, "No Mas Habermas, or … Rethinking Cuban Cinema in the 1990s," *Screen* 40, no. 2 (1999): 207.

58. In addition to Delgado's analysis in "Spiritual Capital" (54–55), the reflections on religion by the Cuban leader Fidel Castro in his dialogue with Brazilian liberation theologist Frei Betto and the recent visits of Catholic religious leaders to the island provide a complicated view of official attitudes toward religion but, generally, religion remains negatively connoted when compared to education.

59. Cristina Venegas interprets this disillusionment and fatigue in connection to a separation of State and self in Special Period narratives but *Los dioses rotos* does not focus on the self. See Venegas, "Filmmaking with Foreigners," 40.

60. Casa de América, "Ricardo Acosta, El silencio de los otros," video, June 26, 2018, https://www.youtube.com/watch?v=WPi3KRg5ro0.

61. Leornardo Padura Fuentes, "Fin de año a golpe de reguetón," *Cubadebate*, December 18, 2012.

62. This socio-political satire banned by the Cuban government presents a hierarchical social classification of Cuban society that is far from the official narrative of a classless socialist world.

63. Chanan, *Cuban Cinema*, 332.

64. Venegas, "Filmmaking with Foreigners," 41.

65. Luis Duno-Gottberg, "The Role of the State in Cuba and Venezuela," in *The Routledge Companion to Latin American Cinema*, eds. Marvin D'Lugo, Ana M. López and Laura Podalsky (London: Routledge, 2018), 49.

66. With regard to these aspects, critic Rolando Pérez Betancourt writes, "Although this is a contemporary story, the art direction, the set design and the excellent camera work are set to weave a virtually out of time atmosphere." Rolando Pérez Betancourt, "Los dioses rotos del cubano Ernesto Daranas," *Portal del cine y el audiovisual latinoamericano y caribeño*, http://www.cinelatinoamericano.org.

67. "*Fallen Gods*: Press Kit," ICAIC, 2008, 7.

68. Y. P. Fernández, "Entrevista con Rigoberto Senarega, director de fotografía. Entregar más que oficio, espíritu," *La Jiribilla*, January 31–February 6, 2009.

69. Edward Duscombe, "Sound and Color," *Jump Cut* 17 (1978): 23–25.

70. Stephen Neale, *Cinema and Technology: Image, Sound, Colour.* (London: McMillan, 1985), 152.

71. Víctor Fowler Calzada, "Cuban Film: What's New," *ReVista: Harvard Review of Latin America* (Fall 2009), https://revista.drclas.harvard.edu/book/cuban-film.

72. Beers, "Murder in San Isidro," 117.

Chapter 2

Space Defining Class

Middle-class Cinemas: Post-Tenebras Lux *and* Que horas ela volta?

The first decade of the twenty-first century witnessed an unprecedented rise of the middle classes in Mexico and Brazil that is due to neoliberal developments in both countries and, in Brazil, also owes to the legacy of the "Lula era" and the Turn-to-the-Left.[1] This transformation toward *países clasemedlleros* (middle-class countries), in Calle and Rubio's terms,[2] is reflected in the cinemas of Mexico and Brazil, which increasingly create "a sympathetic portrait of the contemporary middle class in Mexico"[3] and record "the lives and inhabited spaces of the upper middle class" in Brazil.[4] In recent years, film scholars and filmmakers have identified a shift toward a predominantly middle-class audience and new articulations of textual politics in Mexican and Brazilian cinemas, even though Brazil was one of the countries of the Turn-to-the-Left.[5] Moreover, the use of cinematic space exposes these widespread and ongoing class transformations in the twenty-first century. As film scholars Cacilda Rêgo and Carolina Rocha note with regard to contemporary Latin American cinema, "space in neoliberal times redefines social relations."[6] Other recent studies have applied notions of place and urban space to examine shifting class relations in contemporary Brazilian films.[7]

This chapter identifies a middle-class perspective through *strategies of containment* in the use of filmic space and cinematography. Fredric Jameson uses the term *strategies of containment* to denote the artistic and theoretical limitations to which petty-bourgeois intellectuals are constrained due to their social position.[8] A predominantly middle-class profession in Latin America,[9] in the past, socially engaged middle-class directors demonstrated a predilection for revolutionary narratives of the poor. In the twenty-first-century however, filmmakers have increasingly turned their gaze toward their own class. Rather than perceiving·it as a *limitation*, this new awareness is better understood as a *liberation* that embodies the filmmakers' acknowledgement of their own constraints and interests. This perception was already occasionally present in Latin American literature. Jorge Luis Borges, an upper-middle class writer, illustrates it clearly in his 1970s short story "Juan Muraña," where he wrote:

> Then, abruptly, Trápani said to me, "Someone lent me your Carriego book, where you're talking about hoodlums all the time. Tell me, Borges, what in the world can you know about hoodlums?" He stared at me with a kind of wonder.
> "I've done research," I answered.
> Not letting me go on, he said, "Research is the word, all right. Personally, I have no use for research—I know these people inside out."[10]

I will take this disjunction into account to examine figurations of conflict between the working class and the middle class in the Mexican drama *Post Tenebras Lux* (Carlos Reygadas, 2012) and the Brazilian *Que horas ela volta?* (*The Second Mother,* Anna Muylaert, 2015), two feature films particularly well suited to illustrate this new sensibility. Though both films contain a skeptical leaning toward middle-class philanthropic attitudes, the cinematography, and framing of space unveil a middle-class point of view. Seen through this lense, directors Carlos Reygadas and Anna Muylaert are part of a group of Mexican and Brazilian filmmakers including Kleber Mendonça Filho, Beto Brant, Gary Alazraki, Alfonso Cuarón, or Fernando Sariñana, who situate their own class concerns at the center of their narratives. Mendonça Filho underlined this attitude when he noted that it was absurd to film in spaces that members of the middle-class are unfamiliar with.[11]

The correlation between the growth of the middle classes in Brazil and Mexico and a cinematic production geared toward narratives set in middle-class milieus thematizing an interaction between social classes as employers and employees justifies labeling this cinema as *cine clasemediero* (middle-class cinema). *Cine clasemediero* reflects spatial developments linked to the effects of neoliberalism in Mexico and Brazil, such as spatial segregation and class lines that limit opportunities for social interaction in public spaces.[12] Another equally common urban development associated with neoliberalism that has severely affected the lower classes is the displacement of the urban poor from city centers in order to make space for middle-class residential developments.[13] While this phenomenon has barely caught the attention of filmmakers,[14] despite being linked to class conflict in both Mexico and Brazil, and indeed worldwide,[15] narratives where house cleaners work for the middle class (*Que horas ela volta?*) or stories in which middle-class individuals fear the invasion of their private space by the lower classes (*Post Tenebras Lux*) abound.

Before proceeding to a close analysis of the spatial dynamics in these two films, a discussion of the notion of space is required. Fredric Jameson's definition of space associated with class fits the conceptual framework of the present analysis since, for Jameson, "the land is not only an object of struggle between the classes, between rich and poor, it defines their very existence and the separation between them."[16] Doreen Massey has critiqued static notions of space such as Jameson's. She views space as a relational notion intimately entwined with time and unavoidably political.[17] Not only does space construct relationships, but also "these relationships themselves . . . *create/define* space and time."[18] The scholar convincingly argues that space and time cannot be viewed as separate entities but are inextricably interwoven and that "the spatial is integral to the production of history, and thus to the possibility of politics."[19] Massey's conceptualization can shed new light on the politics of contemporary films, which will be the point of departure for my analysis of *Post Tenebras Lux*.

POLITICAL SPACES AND FRAGMENTATION
IN *POST TENEBRAS LUX*

The dominance of spatial explorations in "the narrative discourses of contemporary Mexican cinema" is a trend that Miriam Haddu already identified in the Mexican cinema of the 1990s.[20] Vinicius Navarro, on the other hand, identifies space as a key for understanding cinema's "concern with social inequality" and the consequent revitalization of Brazilian political cinema.[21] Yet with regard to Reygadas, studies seem to neglect that in his texts space is intricately interwoven with social and political issues. Ignacio M. Sánchez Prado, for instance, observes that the "re-signification of cinematic spaces" in Reygadas' films works toward "the deliberate undermining of the marks of the national,"[22] and Cynthia Tompkins' analysis highlights the filmmaker's concentration on "feelings and states of mind" in narratives that stress "ideological differences."[23] Reygadas himself seems to confirm this view. In describing his approach to *Post Tenebras Lux*, he noted that "reason [would] intervene as little as possible, like an expressionist painting where you try to express what you are feeling through the painting rather than depict what something looks like."[24] This fits with Tiago de Luca's contention that Carlos Reygadas' films are best understood within Rancière's "aesthetic regime" of art.[25] As de Luca argues,

> More than representations of social issues, these films are sensory explorations of realities yet to be properly understood. Averse to didacticism and univocal messages, they reveal the bewildering complexity of local and global events while producing unexpected configurations of the sensible that contravene the logic of the world.[26]

Without contradicting these approaches to Reygadas' multilayered texts, the following analysis expands on the politics of Reygadas' *Post Tenebras Lux* in line with Doreen Massey's conception of and Vinicius Navarro's approach to space.

Arguably because of its disregard for a structured narrative, the use of computer-generated images and the familyvideo look of some of the scenes, *Post Tenebras Lux* had a mixed reception. Released in 2012, it was selected for the Cannes Film festival where it won the prestigious Best Director Award despite being booed by the audience when it was screened. The main plot of Reygadas' film deals with the daily life of a family of four: Juan (Adolfo Jiménez Castro), his wife Natalia (Nathalia Acevedo), and their two children, living in a house in rural Mexico. A secondary plotline concerns the relationship between Juan and his employees "el Jarro" (José Alberto Sánchez) and especially "el Siete" (Willebaldo Torres), who had been previously employed by Juan. Juan attempts to befriend el Siete by helping to reunite him with his battered wife and children, but el Siete shoots Juan when the former is caught stealing. Juan dies as a result of this attack, something that, together with other traumatic personal problems, will drive el Siete toward self-decapitation.

The film displays a preference for patterns of incoherence and disconti- nuity, whether temporally—the ages of the two children vary in different scenes without any apparent reason and Juan is present at a Christmas dinner that would have logically happened several years after his death—or narra- tively—there are scenes of a rugby match and a bird hunt that are unrelated to the plot. Most scenes are set in Mexico, where the characters speak Spanish, but there are also scenes in the UK (the rugby match), where the characters speak English, and in France (a swingers' sauna), where French is spoken. Underscoring this disjointed style, *Post Tenebras Lux* does not contain estab- lishing shots or exterior images aimed at providing spatial orientation to the viewer. The main space, Juan's home, is located in a mountainous rural envi- ronment, but the landscape shots do not help orientate the audience. Spaces seem disconnected, or only possibly connected through the logic of dreams and the blurred edges of the camera lens support this surrealistic effect. The first sequences are consecutively set in an improvised soccer field with graz- ing cattle in the mountains, Juan's upper-middle-class home surrounded by a similar landscape, a forest with a woodcutter, el Siete, going about his work, the middle-class home of Juan again, a shack covered with a corrugated metal roof where Alcoholics Anonymous members meet, and the aforementioned rugby field.

Juan's middle-class home is in reality Reygadas' own residence in the sub- urbs of Mexico City, but in the film there is no reference to any urban center or neighboring communities that would allow the viewer to locate the area.

Just a few details suggest that this house with an open design, which allows easy access from the outside, is, in fact, a gated community. In *Post Tenebras Lux* only Juan's employee el Jarro and some dogs oversee the house. This scenario induces a certain fear of invasion that is a common trope in other Mexican films. Yet the absence of fences or security cameras contrasts markedly with other contemporary films set in gated communities where we see security devices and overtly conspicuous security staff.[27] In this sense, Juan and Natalia's home temporarily serves as a heterotopia: a "counter-site" that is "outside of all places."[28] More specifically, it is a "heterotopia of compensation" for the insecurity of urban centers in the way that its "role is to create a space that is other, another real space, as perfect, as meticulous, as well arranged as ours is messy, ill constructed, and jumbled."[29] The invasion of Juan's residence by el Siete, however, will prove that his heterotopic home is not immune to attacks from the outside.

The disorienting effect in Reygadas' film that is produced by insufficient spatial mapping is aggravated through a compartmentalization of space that appears to separate social classes from each other. The scenes in interiors around a bed, a table, a courtyard, or a lectern are generally recorded as shots with a static camera, which makes them seem photographic. This is the case in one early scene when the children wake up. The camera remains static, focused on Rut, while the mother, out of frame, picks up toys, and talks to her daughter. In her study of Reygadas' first feature, *Japón*, Laura Podalsky explains that this use of space does not correspond to that of "a 'container' through which the human subject moves; indeed, off-screen sounds often remind the viewer of the limits of the frame."[30] In some cases, Alexis Zabé, the cinematographer of *Post Tenebras Lux*, uses a wide shot which allows us to situate the characters within a particular space, but often, particularly when the characters in front of the camera are from the lower classes, information about the locations in which they move is limited. The medium shots and close-ups used in lower-class settings reduce the field of vision and fragment bodies. There are a number of scenes which document this approach. When Juan and his family are at a village party, there are such shots of people eating at tables. Sometimes, the camera appears static and the characters face the camera. This also occurs when the alcoholics share their substance abuse experiences with each other. The medium and extreme close-ups of these lower-class characters prevent us from seeing them in totality (Figure 2.1).

In contrast with this use of the camera, that produces the effect of lower-class characters "performing" while being scrutinized, the upper-class Christmas party and swingers' sauna, and a rugby match are recorded with long shots. In the Christmas party scene, for instance, a hand-held camera travels through the rooms among different characters, which reflects Reygadas' familiarity and comfort with this more upper-class setting. Conversations

Figure 2.1   Alcoholics Sharing their Experiences. *Source: Post Tenebras Lux.*

between members of this same social class are fluid and rich in detail, whereas the lower-class characters in the film appear mainly in exchanges between Juan and the locals and do not interact among themselves often, suggesting that Reygadas shoots from a middle-class perspective and primarily for a middle-class audience.

This choice of cinematography reflects Reygadas' distrust of collectivism. Reygadas claims to see characters as individuals, not as members of a social class. In a 2010 interview, the director stated that, for him, "community is nothing but the sum of individuals" and that "declaring . . . a social truth will turn it into dogma and therefore will prevent it from being experienced as real."[31] This claim ought to be understood in the context of a general distrust for Marxist ideology and, in cinematic terms, a distancing from the left-wing ideology of New Latin American cinema and Cinema Novo. Reygadas' ideas conform to a wider trend in line with what Leslie L. Marsh observes in the Brazilian Film *O som ao redor* (*Neighbouring Sounds*, Mendonça Filho, 2012), namely "the contemporary urban experience of being distanced, isolated, and disconnected from one's surroundings."[32] However, in *Post Tenebras Lux*, the produced spatial limitation and bodily fragmentation seem more apparent in depictions of members of the lower classes.

This shift from political filmmaking of previous times, and a focus that has shifted from community to isolated individual, is undoubtedly related to the effects of neoliberalism, such as the disintegration of unions, the fragmentation of society, and the precarization of the labor force. Neo-liberalism is, as David Harvey observes, "in the first instance a theory of political economic practices that proposes that human well-being can best be advanced by liberating individual entrepreneurial freedoms and skills within an institutional framework characterized by strong private property rights, free markets, and free trade."[33] The inability of filmmakers to map the whole social environment is related to the rejection of "totalities" described by Jean-François Lyotard[34] and has been identified by Fredric Jameson as the "cultural logic of late capitalism."[35] This is a reflection of the way neoliberalism has infringed on societies culturally and socially, replacing class solidarity with individualist desires.

The framing in the climactic scene when el Siete shoots Juan conveys a somewhat ambivalent social message. Juan and Natalia en route to the airport with their children suddenly remember that Natalia has left the baby stroller behind. They decide that Juan is to return home to collect it while Natalia and the children wait at a restaurant. Upon arriving at his house, Juan discovers his friend and former employee's intrusion. From a distance the audience hears how el Siete shoots Juan, through a static long shot that obscures the men's faces, the weapon, and the wound inflicted on Juan. Juan does not turn el Siete over to the police for his crime and will eventually die, but Reygadas' condescending gesture to avoid criminalizing lower-class characters like el Siete is barely enough to muffle the echoes of the common narratives of fear middle-class characters have of members of lower social classes.

POLITICAL SPACES IN *QUE HORAS ELA VOLTA?*

Anna Muylaert's *Que horas ela volta?* was sold to more than twenty-two countries. In France alone, it was shown in 122 theaters, nearly reaching the box-office success of *Cidade de Deus* there.[36] This interest in narratives about class conflict in Latin America, however, was not so evident in Latin American theaters.

As in *Post Tenebras Lux*, the middle-class domestic space is the setting and theme in *Que horas ela volta?* The narrative takes place for the most part in the Morumbi district of São Paulo, a middle-class neighborhood that is a referent for the living spaces of its affluent urban middle class. *Que horas ela volta?* depicts the relationship of two mothers from different social backgrounds, a fashion/television celebrity, Bárbara (Karine Teles), and her domestic helper, Val (played by the Brazilian star Regina Casé), with their children.[37] Bárbara is married to Carlos (Lourenço Mutarelli), a member of the Brazilian rentier class (living on income from inherited properties) who is also a frustrated artist. One day Val receives a call from her estranged daughter Jéssica (Camila Márdila), to tell her that she is coming to São Paulo to take university entrance exams. Because of a conflict with Jéssica's father, Val has not seen her daughter for more than a decade and the relationship between them is distant. Nevertheless, Val picks up Jéssica from the airport and arranges for her to stay at her employer's home and because the daughter does not abide by the implicit rules established in Bárbara and Carlos' household (that confine her to a lower social status), a series of conflicts arise. Ultimately, Jéssica moves to a rented apartment in the much poorer district of Embu-Guaçú. She passes her first exam, and her mother, socially and emotionally transformed by her daughter, quits her job to finally take care of her daughter and her (newly discovered) grandson.

Que horas ela volta? initially invites a reading through the prism of affect. "Que horas ela volta?"—What time does [mother] come back?—is the question uttered by countless children the world over indicating resentment of the absence of the mother from home. Affect and social mobility are key terms for understanding *Que horas ela volta?*[38] Leslie L. Marsh notes that in Anna Muylaert's films, "domestic space frequently becomes the context for examining issues such as motherhood and cross-class relationships,"[39] but focuses exclusively on gender, rather than space.

I argue that in *Que horas ela volta?* space has centrality as a marker for the division of social classes. Unlike *Post Tenebras Lux*, however, space does not generally appear fragmented. For instance, when Val walks the dog we get a glimpse of the Morumbi neighborhood through a traveling shot, one of the few exterior scenes. The first scene of the film is set in an emblematic part of the house that is charged with class overtones: the swimming pool. The pool is reserved for Carlos, Bárbara, and Fabinho, that is to say, as a place of pleasure that is restricted to the upper-middle class and off-limits for Val and Jéssica. As the family's house cleaner, Val would never dare to enter such a place, as she conforms to the rigid class separation that keeps her out. It is not until later when her daughter plays in the pool and challenges her mother that she contemplates and eventually uses this space for her own enjoyment. Bárbara has the swimming pool emptied with the excuse of having seen a rat (Jéssica) in order to curtail the young woman's brazen occupation of what she sees as her space. At the end of the film, when Jéssica has already left, Val having decided to quit her job finally enters the water. In this scene her figure occupies the central position of a long shot. Lights in the background surround her as if she were a star in a theater show, a visual trope that signifies her upward mobility.[40] Her daughter's force of character to challenge old class divisions has motivated her to at least aspire to climb the social ladder.

A similar significance attached to the swimming pool in *Que horas ela volta?* is highlighted in Lucrecia Martel's *La ciénaga* (2001). The opening scene of this Argentine film depicting the malaise of a middle-class family also takes place at a swimming pool. In her analysis of *La ciénaga*, Amanda Holmes has argued that Martel "draws attention to spatial order and categorization,"[41] and that "the construction of spatial representation reflects questions about the formation of social and personal order in the complexity of contemporary Argentine society."[42] In other words, the swimming pool in *La ciénaga* takes part in social categorization and class division. The same applies to space in *Que horas ela volta?* with regard to contemporary Brazilian society, but while the swimming pool in *La ciénaga* evokes the "passivity, almost despondency"[43] of the Argentine middle classes, in *Que horas ela volta?* it symbolizes both the upward social mobility of the lower classes and the fear of traditional middle classes for the *new* middle class that emerged in the twenty-first century as a result of the policies that the governments of the Brazilian Workers' Party put into place: Lula da Silva and Dilma Rousseff.[44] Hence, the pool is fraught with social conflict.

Jéssica is depicted as an ambitious character who uses space to push class boundaries. From the moment this student from the Northeast, who is aspiring to study at the university, enters Bárbara's home, her movements and her body language display an irreverent attitude toward established house rules and more general social conventions. When Bárbara's husband shows her the guest room, she sits on the spacious bed and jokingly suggests that she occupy this comfortable bedroom instead of sharing the cleaner's confined room. Carlos, who likes Jéssica from the beginning, asks Bárbara whether Jéssica can be accommodated in the guest room. Bárbara feels forced to agree, but this moment is visually conveyed as the realization of a class conflict. A close-up of Bárbara looking at Jéssica is followed by an eyeline match of Jéssica looking at her, with Carlos in the middle. Carlos will gradually fall in love with Jéssica, later asking her to marry him.

The cinematography in *Que horas ela volta?* emphasizes social conflict within neoliberal parameters, according to which Jéssica and Val should only interact with Bárbara's family, members of the middle class, insofar as they provide a service to them. Unable to stand a dangerous situation in which Jéssica clearly takes advantage of every opportunity to live comfortably in Bárbara's home, Bárbara requests first that Jéssica vacate the guest room and later that she remain within the limits of the helper's room. Jéssica's entrance into the domestic helper's area is visually rendered as Jéssica's occupation of an animal's space. A bird's-eye view of the space in this scene allows the audience to perceive Jéssica's confinement to the lowest floor of the house and her gaze at the sky, a visual metaphor of her current social position and her aspirations alike. The staircase inside the home next to the guest room is another space symbolizing social mobility. There are several eye-level shots of the empty staircase, the camera zooming in to invite the viewer to contemplate this possibility.

Spatial arrangements in the house also underscore the social segregation that neoliberalism promotes. The kitchen doorframe is unquestionably the most important space in the film as it represents the boundaries between classes. The original title of the film was, in fact, *The Kitchen Door*, a door that, in this film, serves as a threshold between the worlds of employer and employee. Many scenes are filmed from Val's point of view from the kitchen sink, from where she sees the dining room through the doorframe (Figure 2.2). The kitchen is not only Val's workplace but also the family's breakfast room. In her first morning in São Paulo, Jéssica wakes up before her mother and finds Bárbara in the kitchen making juice for breakfast. In this scene, Bárbara stands next to the sink usually occupied by Val while Jéssica sits at the table. In just one night, Jéssica has shaken up the social order of the household. Jéssica is now symbolically occupying Bárbara's space in the house, something that Bárbara quickly realizes and resents. In another scene, Carlos invites Jéssica to eat with him in the dining room. Whereas Val's view of and access to the dining room has always been limited, Jéssica's is now unrestricted.

Anna Muylaert's depictions of the protagonists Val and Jéssica in connection to Bárbara's home and the relationship between Bárbara and Val as employer and employee are part of a *cine clasemediero*. Another example that allows us to classify this film as *cine clasemediero* is the reluctance to represent a favela in the film. *Que horas ela volta?* revisits the common favela/sertão theme only toward the end of the film. Jéssica and her mother are originally from Pernambuco, the Northeast, and the land of the sertão. When Val visits her daughter right before resigning and moving in with her, we see them arguing in the small apartment rented by Jéssica. The favela of Embu-Guaçú appears in the background, seen through the apartment door (Figure 2.3). Parallel to the framing of the family dining room in Bárbara's middle-class kitchen from Val's perspective, the framing of the favela from Jéssica's new apartment suggests that Val and Jéssica do not belong to this space either.

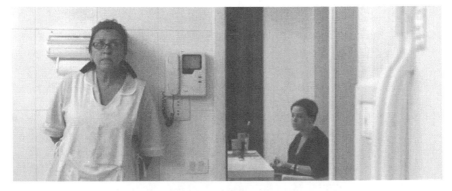

Figure 2.2   Val's Point of View from the Kitchen Sink. *Source: Que horas ela volta?*

Figure 2.3 The Favela in the Background. *Source: Que horas ela volta?*

The favela has enjoyed a long tradition of cinematic representation. Igor Krstić has identified a general transition from a referential to a symbolic representation of the favela on the Brazilian screen since the first films set in the favelas in the 1930s to contemporary cinema.[45] Throughout the decades, the favela has been approached as a romanticizing setting, a location for stories about struggling characters, a politicized space, and, in more contemporary films, a place associated with extreme violence—Ivana Bentes' "cosmetics of violence"—such as in *Cidade de Deus* and *Tropa de elite* (*Elite Squad*, José Padilha, 2007), and a space for creativity, such as in *Orfeu* (Carlos Diegues, 1999).[46] Despite this long history of the favela on screen, Director Anna Muylaert keeps the favela "outside." Just as Val was incapable of crossing the boundaries to the dining-room table, so is Director Anna Muylaert reluctant to enter the favela, a territory that she, as a member of the Brazilian middle class, does not seem to know well. For this reason, she remains in the safety of the interior of Jéssica's home and frames/contains the favela as a lit picture in the distance.

CONCLUDING REMARKS

Post Tenebras Lux and *Que horas ela volta?* exhibit a similar emerging awareness of the filmmaker's social position and the ensuing *limitations* in trying to depict the lives of the members of the lower classes. The films' strategies of containment are made evident through several means. At a narrative level, members of lower classes are presented as service providers for the middle classes.[47] Cinematography and the depiction of space demonstrate Reygadas' and Muylaert's strategies of containment. Lastly, both films exhibit a fear of the lower classes. The "fear of violence and anxiety about security"[48] is palpable in *Post Tenebras Lux*. In the case of *Que horas ela volta?*, there is the traditional middle class fear of downward social mobility combined with their fear of the rise of the lower classes. The most interesting aspect of both films is the combination of an awareness of the limitations concerning knowledge about "the other" and a critical view toward the middle class that might be construed as a creative liberation.

Spatial representation in these two films is tied to the effects of neoliberalism in Mexican and Brazilian societies. In *Post Tenebras Lux*, the innovative connotation of the rural space as a setting for class segregation and class conflict leaves behind earlier associations of the countryside with innocence and virtue,[49] backwardness, and even spirituality.[50] Anna Muylaert's *Que horas ela volta?* is a more positive spin for social mobility, which might be attributed to the effects of socio-political policies aimed at reducing inequality in Brazil between 2003 and 2016, when the Workers' Party (PT) was in power. In any case, the camera has turned its attention from underprivileged to middle-class characters, and sees working-class people as their employees.

A relational approach to space allows us to identify the social position assumed by filmmakers and cinematographers. In *Post Tenebras Lux* and *Que horas ela volta?*, the camera films from a middle-class "position" even in shots that are from the point of view of working-class characters. The construction of middle-class spaces in contrast to the spaces traditionally associated with the lower classes clearly indicates that the fear of invasion in *Post Tenebras Lux* and the anxiety toward the new middle-class upward social mobility in *Que horas ela volta?* are central to the understanding of these films as political.

Moving from the home and the close neighborhood to larger communities brings us necessarily to the State and how institutions configure our perception of and interaction with large underprivileged groups. The progressive period of the Turn-to-the-Left enabled the emergence of counter-narratives and politics challenging the power that the State has to perpetuate social discrimination. The following two chapters discuss the ways in which entrenched class ideologies are reinforced or brought into question through films produced in two of the most important Turn-to-the-Left representatives: Brazil and Venezuela.

NOTES

1. See Francisco H. G. Ferreira et al., *Economic Mobility and the Rise of the Latin American Middle Class* (Washington, DC: World Bank, 2013); Jorge Castañeda, *Mañana Forever?: Mexico and the Mexicans* (New York: Vintage, 2011). There is a consensus about the rise of a new class that most scholars identify as a middle class,

although Brazilian sociologist Jessé Souza prefers to call it *os batalhadores* (the fighters): Uirá Machado, "É um erro falar que existe nova classe média, diz sociólogo," *Folha de São Paulo*, February 13, 2011, http://www1.folha.uol.com.br/poder/2011/02/874777-e-um-erro-falar-que-existe-nova-classe-media-diz-sociologo.shtml. These references illustrate differing views about the causes for this rise.

2. Calle, Luis de la, and Luis Rubio. "Clasemedieros." *Nexos* (May 2010). http://www.nexos.com.mx/?p=13742.

3. Kathleen Newman, "A Different Mexican Postcard: Fernando Eimbcke's *Lake Tahoe* (2008)." *Studies in Spanish & Latin American Cinemas* 12, no. 2 (2015): 159.

4. Leslie L. Marsh, "Reordering (Social) Sensibilities: Balancing Realisms in *Neighbouring Sounds*," *Studies in Spanish & Latin American Cinemas* 12, no. 2 (2015): 155. Newman's and Marsh's studies refer specifically to the Mexican film *Lake Tahoe* (Fernando Eimbcke, 2008) and the Brazilian film *O som ao redor* (Kleber Mendonça Filho, 2012), not necessarily to a group of films.

5. Misha MacLaird, *Aesthetics and Politics in the Mexican Film Industry.* New York: Palgrave Macmillan. 2013; Ignacio M. Sánchez Prado, *Screening Neoliberalism: Transforming Mexican Cinema 1988–2012* (Nashville: Vanderbilt University Press, 2014); see also the statements of one of the most prominent Brazilian filmmakers, Lucia Murat, in Alain Arias Barreto, "Lucía Murat y el cine," *La Jiribilla. Revista de cultura cubana* 397 (December 13–19, 2008).

6. Cacilda Rêgo and Carolina Rocha, eds., *New Trends in Argentine and Brazilian Cinema* (Bristol: Intellect, 2011), 9.

7. Vinicius Navarro, "Local Filmmaking in Brazil: Place, Politics, and Pernambuco's New Cinema," *Studies in Spanish and Latin American Cinemas* 14, no. 1 (2017); Leslie L. Marsh, "Reordering (Social) Sensibilities."

8. Fredric Jameson, *The Political Unconscious: Narrative as a Socially Symbolic Act* (London: Routledge, 2002), 37.

9. The renowned Argentine director Lucrecia Martel declared in a recent interview that cinema's weakness worldwide is that it is only in the hands of the upper-middle class (Iván Pinto Veas, "Lucrecia Martel," *La fuga* 17 [2015], http://2016.lafuga.cl/lucrecia-martel/735); film scholar Lúcia Nagib noted earlier that, "There is still an economic cleavage which reserves cinematographic activity for the middle and upper classes" (*O cinema da retomada. Depoimentos de 90 cineastas dos anos 90* [São Paulo: Editora 34, 2002], 15).

10. Jorge Luis Borges, "Juan Muraña," *Doctor Brodie's Report*, trans. Norman Thomas di Giovanni (New York: E. P. Dutton & Co., 1972), 82.

11. Paul Dallas, "Culture Wars: Talking Brazilian Cinema and Its Discontents with Director Kleber Mendonça Filho," *Filmmaker*, January 28, 2013, http://filmmakermagazine.com.

12. Michael Janoschka and Axel Borsdorf, "Condominios Fechados and Barrios Privados: The Rise of Private Residential Neighbourhoods in Latin America," in *Private Cities: Global and Local Perspectives*, eds. Georg Glasze, Chris Webster, and Klaus Frantz (London: Routledge, 2006), 105. Néstor García Canclini has aptly observed, "Latin American elites . . . live in gated communities and consume in the segregated shopping centers of their cities," *Imagined Globalization* (Durham and London: Duke University Press, 2014), 73.

13. Michael Janoschka, Jorge Sequera, and Luis Salinas, "Gentrification in Spain and Latin America: A Critical Dialogue," *International Journal of Urban and Regional Research* 38, no. 4 (July 2014): 1244, 1245, 1247, 1248; Ermínia Maricato, "The Statute of the Peripheral City," in *The City Statute of Brazil: A Commentary*, eds. Celso Santos Carvalho and Anaclaudia Rossbach (São Paulo: Cities Alliance and Ministry of Cities, 2010), 31–32; Teresa P. R. Caldeira, *City of Walls: Crime, Segregation and Citizenship in São Paulo* (Berkeley: University of California Press, 2000), 251.

14. Mexican filmmaker Iria Gómez Concheiro had a project titled *Los inquilinos* about this forced gentrification at the time of writing, but attention to this urban and social phenomenon is not yet common.

15. Fredric Jameson, "The Aesthetics of Singularity," *NLR* 92 (2015): 130.

16. Jameson, "The Aesthetics of Singularity," 130–31.

17. Doreen Massey, "Politics and Space/Time," *NLR* 1 no. 196 (November–December 1992.): 66–67.

18. Massey, "Politics and Space/Time," 79.

19. Massey, "Politics and Space/Time," 84.

20. Miriam Haddu, *Contemporary Mexican Cinema 1989–1999: History, Space and Identity* (New York: The Edwin Mellen Press, 2007), 9.

21. Navarro, "Local Filmmaking in Brazil," 70.

22. Ignacio M. Sánchez Prado, *Screening Neoliberalism: Transforming Mexican Cinema 1988–2012* (Nashville: Vanderbilt University Press, 2014), 201.

23. Cynthia Tompkins, *Experimental Latin American Cinema: History and Aesthetics* (Austin: University of Texas Press, 2013), 160.

24. John Hopewell and Emilio Mayorga, "Reygadas Looks to 'Lux,'" *Variety* 418, no. 2 (2010): 8.

25. Tiago de Luca, *Realism of the Senses in World Cinema: The Experience of Physical Reality*, (London: I. B. Tauris, 2014), 90–91. De Luca concentrates on Reygadas' first three features, not on *Post Tenebras Lux*.

26. De Luca, *Realism of the Senses in World Cinema*, 240.

27. In contrast to *Post Tenebras Lux*, in some Mexican and Brazilian crime dramas about the invasion of middle-class homes or neighborhoods, the protection of middle-class residents is foregrounded and "safe" and "dangerous" spaces are often visually rendered as interdependent with each other (*O som ao redor*, Kleber Mendonça Filho, 2012; *La zona*, Rodrigo Plá, 2007; *Redentor*, Cláudio Torres, 2004; *Era uma vez...*, Breno Silveira, 2008; *Amar te duele*, Fernando Sariñana, 2002; *O invasor*, Beto Brant, 2002; *Os inquilinos*, Sergio Bianchi, 2009).

28. Michel Foucault, "Of Other Spaces," *Diacritics* 16, no. 1 (1986): 24.

29. Foucault, "Of Other Spaces," 27.

30. Laura Podalsky, "Landscapes of Subjectivity in Contemporary Mexican Cinema," *New Cinemas: Journal of Contemporary Film* 9, nos. 2 & 3 (2011): 168.

31. José Castillo, "Carlos Reygadas," *Bomb* 111 (2010): 72–73.

32. Marsh, "Reordering (Social) Sensibilities, 151.

33. David Harvey, *A Brief History of Neoliberalism* (New York: Oxford University Press, 2005), 2.

34. Jean-François Lyotard, *The Postmodern Condition: A Report on Knowledge* (Manchester: Manchester University Press, 1984), 7.

35. Fredric Jameson, *Postmodernism or the Cultural Logic of Late Capitalism* (Durham: Duke University Press), 55–57.

36. This is according to data gathered by Thiago Stivaletti shortly after the film's release in 2015 ("*Que horas ela volta?* é vendido para 22 países," *Filme B*, July 17, 2015, http://www.filmeb.com.br), but the popularity of the film continued growing after 2015.

37. For more on Casé's performance as a "Brazilian style" star, see Randal Johnson, "Television and the Transformation of the Star System in Brazil," in *A Companion to Latin American Cinema*, eds. Maria M. Delgado, Stephen M. Hart, and Randal Johnson (Malden: John Wiley & Sons, 2017), 29–31.

38. Lígia Lana,"'Da porta da cozinha pra lá'. gênero e mudança social no filme *Que horas ela volta?*" *Rumores* 19, no. 10 (January–June 2016): 121–37; Rui Fernando Correia Ferreira and Lívia Almada Neves, "O conceito do ócio vicário no filme 'Que horas ela volta?': Revisitando Thorstein Veblen em uma nova perspectiva dos fenômenos socioeconômicos," paper, XL Encontro da ANPAD, September 25–28, 2016.

39. Leslie L. Marsh, "Women's Filmmaking and Comedy in Brazil: Anna Muylaert's *Durval Discos* (2002) and *É Proibido Fumar* (2009)," in *Latin American Women Filmmakers: Production, Politics, Poetics*, eds. Deborah Martin and Deborah Shaw, (London: I. B. Tauris, 2017), 151.

40. Anna Muylaert felt the need to reflect on her own social class when asked in an interview about the swimming pool's symbolism. For her, in addition to being "the place for leisure and for the priviliged," it is also the place for *machismo* (male chauvinism), and in this sense Muylaert would identify with both Jéssica and Val in such a place, even though she "belong[s] to the other social class. "Director Anna Muylaert Interviewed by French Journalist Pierre-Michel Meier," DVD Extra Features, 2016, Oscilloscope Pictures.

41. Amanda Holmes, "Landscape and the Artist's Frame in Lucrecia Martel's *La ciénaga/The Swamp* and *La niña santa/The Holy Girl*," in *New Trends in Argentine and Brazilian Cinema*, eds. Cacilda Rêgo and Carolina Rocha, 131.

42. Holmes, "Landscape and the Artist's Frame," 133.

43. Holmes, "Landscape and the Artist's Frame," 134.

44. As Lima has noted, "Fifteen years ago, a work dealing with the relationship between a wealthy Morumbi family and its maid, played by a well-known and charismatic actress like Regina Casé,would hardly have resonated in the same way as *The Second Mother* does today." Bruna Della Torre De Carvalho Lima, "Criticism and Condescension: The Triumph of the Poor in *The Second Mother*," *Latin American Perspectives* 211, no. 6 (November 2016): 141.

45. Igor Krstić, *Slums on Screen: World Cinema and the Planet of Slums* (Edinburgh: Edinburgh University Press, 2016), 196.

46. Krstić, *Slums on Screen*, 196, 202.

47. There is a significant number of films on domestic and security services in contemporary Latin American cinema, such as *Doméstica* (*Housemaids*, Mascaro, 2012),

Benjamín Naishtat's *Historia del miedo* (*History of Fear*, 2014), Rodrigo Moreno's *El custodio* (*The Bodyguard*, 2006) and *Réimon* (2014), and Jorge Gaggero's *Cama adentro* (*Live-in Maid*, 2004), but the Chilean-Mexican coproduction *La nana* (*The Maid*, Sebastián Silva, 2009) is probably the best known internationally. The growing number of films about domestic helpers has lead film scholar Deborah Shaw to classify them as a genre (Deborah Shaw, "Intimacy and Distance-Domestic Servants in Latin American Women's Cinema: *La mujer sin cabeza* and *El niño pez*/*The Fish Child*," in *Latin American Women Filmmakers: Production, Politics, Poetics*, eds. Deborah Martin and Deborah Shaw, 124).

48. Teresa P. R. Caldeira, "From Modernism to Neoliberalism in São Paulo: Reconfiguring the City and Its Citizens," in *Other Cities, Other Worlds: Urban Imaginaries in a Globalizing Age*, ed. Andreas Huyssen (Durham: Duke University Press, 2008), 52.

49. Haddu, *Contemporary Mexican Cinema*, 213.

50. Sánchez Prado, *Screening Neoliberalism*, 205.

Chapter 3

Class and the State[*]

State Institutions: Slum Pacification and Prison Riots in Brazil

In the twenty-first century, Brazilian cinema has continued to adopt transnational strategies of production, distribution, and exhibition in line with other Latin American cinemas since the 1990s. This is a practice that makes evident the gradual dissolution of the nation-state as the privileged site of cultural practice which Martín Hopenhayn diagnosed, although some argue otherwise.[1] Between 2008 and 2012, Brazil produced sixty-two official co-productions with countries in Latin America as well as Europe, a huge increase in co-productions compared to previous years.[2] In international relations, Brazil was propelled to an unprecedented level in the global arena as part of the BRICS group of emerging economies, challenging the hegemony of the United States in Latin America (at least up to 2016) much like China does. Up to 2016, Brazil enjoyed a new leading status as the sixth economy of the world by hosting international events such as the 2014 World Cup and the Rio 2016 Summer Olympics, the latter being held during the impeachment of the last of the PT (Workers' Party) Presidents, Dilma Rousseff, and which deeply divided Brazilian society along class lines.

This global rise was concurrent with the heralded growth of the Brazilian middle classes.[3] The diverse groups of a new middle class includes precarious and salaried workers, *nouveaux riches* and provincial middle classes that have become more visible on the screen and in the society at large in the twenty-first century. However, while Brazilian society continues adapting

---

[*] Chapter 3 has been published as "Brazil at a Socio-Cinematic Crossroads: State Intervention on Screen," in *Brazil in Twenty-First Century Popular Media: Culture, Politics, and Nationalism on the World Stage*, edited by Naomi Pueo Wood, 113—138 (Lanham, Md.: Lexington Books, 2014).

to the new status, huge inequalities persist in the country, as can be seen not only in favelas (Brazilian term for "slums") and prisons but also in the *asfalto* (paved streets in well-built middle-class areas) and other spaces typically inhabited by the middle class such as universities.[4]

This chapter examines three co-productions released in the first decade of the twenty-first century, when Brazil was at a crossroads, engaging in the Turn-to-the-Left at continental level while continuing to be affected by the global spread of neoliberalism, two phenomena that deeply influence class mobility. The films selected, *Carandiru* (Héctor Babenco, 2003), *Tropa de elite* (*Elite Squad*, José Padilha, 2007), and *Tropa de elite 2: O inimigo agora é outro* (*Elite Squad 2*, José Padilha, 2010) focus on the relationship between the state and the underprivileged under two presidents, both intent on reducing inequality in Brazil but from different political stances (Fernando Henrique Cardoso—1995–2003—and Luiz Inácio Lula da Silva—2003–2011). The three films under scrutiny were immensely popular on a national and international level, painting an image of the country at a critical period (around the beginning of the two presidential terms of Lula da Silva and near the end of his presidency). In a way, these films contradicted official self-congratulatory messages and served as reminders of the nation's challenges when Brazil's standing in supra-national organizations from the Global South was rising but the political ideology of the films cannot be wholly separated from their insertion in a transnational commercial operation.

Regarding their aesthetics, and bearing in mind Laura Podalsky's skepticism toward a "stagist" model of film history,[5] it must be noted that none of these three Brazilian films follow NLAC theory and revolutionary practice. Their attention to collective social problems also distances them from a prevailing interest in "the micropolitics of emotion" identified as a marker of contemporary Latin American cinema by Paul A. Schroeder Rodríguez, although they are part of a contemporary trend toward genre cinema also pointed out by this scholar.[6] More importantly for our query of the films' critical geography of class is Ismail Xavier's comparison between oppositional documentaries dealing with the same themes as *Carandiru* and the two *Tropa de elite* films. Xavier's perceptive analysis sheds light on the narrow perspective of *Tropa de elite* (limited to that of the "tough-guy cop" unlike the earlier documentary *Notícias de uma guerra particular*—*News from a Personal War*—João Moreira Salles, 1999) and its skewed moral mission to "clean up" the social environment. Likewise, Xavier succinctly describes Babenco's main interest in idiosyncratic confrontations "not clearly linked to the repressive dynamics of the institution."[7] It is against this background that the following analysis is set.

GLOBAL PRODUCTION AND CONSUMPTION

Notwithstanding the limitations of the use of a national framework for the description of cinemas within the postnational audiovisual cultures of the twenty-first century, the success and consumption of these three internationally acclaimed films might be better comprehended within the context of competition and cooperation, or coopetition,[8] between Brazilian cinema and Hollywood in Brazil, and in the case of *Carandiru* in particular, also within the context of global art cinema.

Nagib noted the redundancy of framing the discussion of World Cinema in dichotomies such as Hollywood–World Cinema but in the cases of *Tropa de elite* and *Tropa de elite 2* there is more justification when we consider the overwhelming prevalence of American cinema on Brazilian cinema screens and the Brazilian films' use of a Hollywoodian style. What Paulo Emílio Salles Gomes claimed about the marginalization of Brazilian cinema within its own borders and the occupation of the Brazilian film market by foreign films has remained pertinent.[9] In this regard, it is not by mere chance that the opening scene of *Tropa de elite 2* contains explicit visual and verbal references to American cinematic clichés, as we can observe at the beginning of *Tropa de elite 2* when a car is ridden by bullets.

I will not evaluate whether Brazilian cinema benefits from Hollywood's competition and cooperation or not, but will instead highlight some possible effects of this interconnection with regard to narrative and ideology in the selected case studies. I contend that this competitive market influences the films' narrative design as well as their political agendas. While *Carandiru*'s appeal to the audience relies on a more underprivileged-centered approach to filmmaking than the two *Tropa de elite* films (which align more with Hollywood action films), an analysis of the three texts and their alleged underpinning ideologies of class reveal significant similarities and dominant narratives of the poor that perpetuate class differences.

Concerning production, distribution and exhibition, Brazil not only leads Latin American cinema as a producer of Latin American films (along with Mexico and Argentina), but is also a leading distributor and consumer of Hollywood cinema. According to the study *Global Entertainment & Media Outlook* by the group PricewaterhouseCoopers, the Brazilian film market was expected to grow 6.7 percent annually from 2012 to 2016, by which time Brazil would be responsible for 50 percent of the whole Latin American film market revenue.[10] Brazilian entertainment industries are important for Hollywood's growth in the areas of distribution and exhibition since, as Miriam Gottfried reports, international ticket sales have been the only source of Hollywood's growth in this area. According to this *Wall Street*

Journal reporter, in 2011, 69 percent of Hollywood's total box-office earnings in 2011 was derived internationally, and Cinemark Holdings, a US theater operator with a booming Latin American business, received roughly 30 percent of its revenue from Latin America (60 percent of which came from Brazil).[11]

Brazilian and Hollywood industries are interconnected in Brazil as in many countries in the world. When Brazilian films are released, they have to compete with Hollywood blockbusters in their own country, which may affect not only marketing strategies, but also the design of projects from the pre-production phase. In the particular case of *Tropa de elite 2*, to fully appreciate the significance of its phenomenal box-office success, it is important to keep in mind the much greater popularity of the ever-present Hollywood movies which usually outperform Brazilian and other Latin American films in Brazilian cinema theatres. This film was produced with an estimated budget of US$7.16 million. It is "the most popular film of all time in South America (out-grossing even *Avatar*)"[12] and was one of the main factors for the increase in the market share of Brazilian films exhibited in Brazil in 2010. The film broke box-office records, earned (BRL) R$102 million and was seen by more than 11 million people in Brazil alone. When the film was released in October 2010, it was the only month when the number of viewers of Brazilian films exceeded that of foreign films shown in the country.[13] A comparison of these optimistic-looking figures with those of Hollywood sales in Brazil, however, casts a more sober tone, such as, in week 33 of the year 2012, the American film *The Avengers* (Joss Whedon, 2012), which had been occupying the number one spot in terms of Brazilian ticket sales in 2012 up to August, had already been seen by the same number of Brazilians and had earned more than a (BRL) R$129 million in the country.[14] In 2010, there were only three Brazilian films among the top twenty in terms of ticket sales in Brazil, the others being American films, a trend that continued in 2011.[15]

The previous comparison is not aimed at characterizing Brazilian cinema as a lack, but instead provides an insight into the dynamics of film making, film distribution and exhibition in the region in order to interpret the three films in focus here, and together with the comments by the Brazilian producers of all three films can provide a clearer picture. *Tropa de elite* was produced by the local Zazen Produções, Universal Brazil, the (currently embattled) American Weinstein Company, and the Latin American film producer Eduardo Constantini Jr. Zazen's mission statement combines a preoccupation with producing quality films (the main priority) and recruiting the best talent available with a social commitment.[16] The same applies to films like *Cidade de Deus*, about which Else R. P. Vieira says that "ultimately, the question to be addressed concerns the achievement of the commercial film in advancing a social cause."[17] In addition, *Tropa de elite* was the first film produced by the film fund The Weinstein Co., managed by Eduardo Constantini Jr. and successfully tried a new funding formula for Latin American cinema aiming at providing regional productions with a wider stage.[18] As Constantini Jr. explains: "We want to find films that show the reality of Latin America and can travel beyond the country where they are produced"[19]—this is also what Dylan Leiner, senior vice-president of acquisitions and productions at Sony Pictures Classics, looks for in Latin American films when selecting them for distribution.[20] At continental level, Argentine director Daniel Burman echoes this sentiment when stating, "We have to give people a good reason to watch our films instead of the latest James Bond. We don't have a developed industry to compete hand to hand. We have to compete with stories, emotions."[21] Therefore, *Tropa de elite* forms part of a contemporary strategy of Latin American cinema to gain international prominence and increase its international market share without neglecting cinema's potential for social transformation.

Keeping this global outlook in mind, the film directors' backgrounds also play a part in this business/art/social dynamic. Director José Padilha studied business, politics and economics in Brazil, and English literature and international politics at Oxford.[22] Before producing his first fiction film, *Tropa de elite*, he had built a reputation as one of the most important Brazilian documentarists with *Ônibus 174* (*Bus 174*, 2002). Thanks to the success of *Tropa de elite* and *Tropa de elite 2* and to Padilha's capacity to combine action with social commentary, he later directed the Hollywood reboot *RoboCop* (2014) and the Netflix series *O mecanismo* (*The Mechanism*, 2018), a continuation of his interest in public corruption schemes already present in *Tropa de elite 2*.

Likewise, Argentine-born Héctor Babenco, the director of *Carandiru*, initiated his feature film career with a documentary after showcasing a series of works within the film/theatre industries in different countries. He was an internationally renowned director who, following the success of his fiction feature *Pixote* (1981), worked in Brazil, Hollywood and Argentina. His 1985 film *Kiss of the Spider Woman,* a 1985 Brazil-US co-production, was one of his major successes. *Carandiru*, released in 2003, was the most expensive Brazilian film ever made at the time, with a budget of US$4 million, and it went on to become the most successful film in the box-office that year. Its success was subsequently surpassed by *Tropa de elite* and *Tropa de elite 2*, which were produced with estimated budgets of US$4 million and US$7.16 million respectively.[23]

THE CINEMATIC CONSTRUCTION OF SOCIAL
CLASS AND FIGURATION OF INSTITUTIONS

The previous examination of some aspects of the Brazilian film industry serves as a foundation for the following textual analysis. I first look at ways in which the narrative design and the use of authoritative male narrators are symptomatic of a continuation of dominant modes of socio-cinematic representation in the three films, despite their apparent differences. I then tie together the cinematographic dichotomy between a focus on individuals versus a cinematography that privileges the view of characters as members of a collectivity with Michel Foucault's view on the politics of personal identity. This serves to examine the discursive mechanisms used to construct class identity and establish boundaries between social groups by identifying the *habitus* of main characters (a socially constituted system of dispositions that serves as a class marker in Pierre Bourdieu's terms). I base my critique on the cinematographic representation of state apparatuses such as the university and the police on Foucault's consideration of the educational institutions and the police as two main sites for the propagation of a technology of power aimed at protecting the interests of the middle classes.

CLASSIFYING THROUGH NARRATIVE DESIGN,
CHARACTERIZATION, AND CINEMATOGRAPHY

Tropa de elite and *Tropa de elite 2* are narrative feature films that follow character-driven classic narrative structures with linear sequencing and continuity editing combined with sporadic use of fragmented MTV style editing, in similar fashion to the influential *Cidade de Deus*, which "decidedly . . . [took] the side of narrative cinema against postmodern fragmentation."[24] *Carandiru*, on the other hand, uses a more unconventional auteuristic style, with a narrative structured in three "acts" that, broadly speaking, evolve from a focus on individuals throughout most of the film to a greater attention to the underprivileged collectivity and the effect of institutions on them—what Ismael Xavier calls "true state terrorism"[25]—toward the end of the film.

In *Tropa de elite*, BOPE Captain Nascimento (Wagner Moura) is given orders to "pacify" and "clean" a favela in Rio de Janeiro in preparation for the Pope's visit. The BOPE is the "batalhão de operações policiais especiais" (battalion of special operations). Nascimento's voice-over commentary interspersed throughout the film serves to represent him as an authoritative narrator, an interpretation which illustrates Foster's view that "the film's rhetoric was designed to ensure approval of the activities and the conduct of the elite squad, whose struggle for survival is glorified by the film. The double violence the elite squad must confront, from both the drug dealers and regular police, mutes interest in the ways in which they duplicate the barbarism of their foes."[26]

A good example of the postclassical editing or MTV style characteristic of *Cidade de Deus* can be found in the introductory scene of *Tropa de elite* in which viewers see quick cuts and freeze frames of a party at a favela while listening to the "Rap das Armas" (Rap of Guns) whose lyrics define Brazil as a tropical country full of favelas. The soundtrack is intermittently overlaid with the didactic voice-over narration of Captain Nascimento. Under this ambience, the favela residents resemble a seething horde without individual characteristics. This opening scene, undoubtedly designed within the conventions of mainstream crime fiction, illustrates José Padilha's ability to tune in to the tastes of young audiences, a skill that might have been precisely one of the main reasons for the film's global appeal and box-office success.

The film's main plot revolves around the search for a replacement for Nascimento, as he is having personal problems and wants to quit the BOPE. However, BOPE members are highly specialized, and finding an honest new recruit in the regular police force is not easy, as social stability in the favelas depends on the corrupt engagement between the regular police and the drug lords. André Mathias (played by the Afro-Brazilian actor André Ramiro) and Neto (Caio Junqueira) are finally selected and are made to undergo intensive and humiliating training, but this does not prevent Mathias from pursuing a Law degree at university among white middle-class students. Among these students, there is a group who runs an NGO in the *Prazeres* favela and welcome him, but when they discover that Mathias is a police officer, Maria (Fernanda Machado), a white middle-class student who had become his girlfriend, shuns the young man without hesitation.

Tropa de elite 2 also managed to attract audiences worldwide because of its film language and content.[27] *Tropa de elite 2* begins with the aftermath of a violent shoot-out involving Nascimento that injects in the introduction the initial dynamism that the favela party provided for *Tropa de elite*. The flashback that ensues starts with the crosscutting of two authorities in their respective spaces. On the one hand, we see the scholar-activist Fraga, who is based on a real figure—the professor and National Secretary of Public Security in 2003 Luiz Eduardo Soares, who co-wrote the book *Elite da tropa* (2006) with two ex-police officers. In *Tropa de elite 2*, Fraga, the fictional rendition of Prof. Soares, is giving a lecture at a university in Rio de Janeiro on the negative role of the security forces in Brazil for which the maximum security prison Bangu 1 serves as a case study. On the other hand, we see Nascimento controlling his men during an anti-riot operation at the real Bangu 1. Inside the prison brutal scenes of rival gangs burning detainees alive and shooting each other are unfolding, their names barely mentioned, their faces embodying unscrupulous brutality. When Fraga, who has gained the trust of the inmate population, is called to help at Bangu 1, he meets Colonel Nascimento. Despite the Colonel's instructions to his men not to shoot, Mathias does otherwise and a massacre ensues. Fraga escapes unscathed, though the image of the human rights T-shirt worn by the professor stained in blood makes the headlines. Public sentiment is divided between those who think that violence should be employed to get rid of "the scourge of society" and those who prefer a softer approach to resolving these conflicts.

Politicians exploit this divisiveness in the public sphere to punish Mathias and "promote" Nascimento to the position of Sub-Secretary of Intelligence with the intention of effectively neutralizing him. However, from this position he will be able to supervise wiretapping operations which will be instrumental in unveiling the corrupt operations by the same politicians who had originally tried to neutralize him. Throughout the film, it is made clear that corrupt politicians in collusion with the police and the media are the major enemies of society. I examine the significance of the intertwining of institutions such as the police, the prison, and the university below, but for the time being it is suffice to say that the film's conclusion (a seemingly conventional closed ending but one in which nothing is really resolved) explains the meaning of the full title of the film: "*Elite Squad: The Enemy Within.*" In Portuguese the title is "*O inimigo agora é outro*," literally translated as "Now the enemy is another"—that is, now the enemy is not hiding in the favelas, but in the government, the political establishment, and the media. Nascimento's verbal accusations toward the end of *Tropa de elite 2* are visually conveyed with a scrutinizing aerial shot of emblematic monuments in the capital of the country and the flag representing the nation.[28]

However, this apparent frontal attack against the establishment is undercut by the classic narrative design and the privileging of the voices of the representatives of the upper and middle classes, such as government representatives, the police, the media, and middle-class academics. The establishment's prominence in the narrative at the expense of the voices of the inmates and the favela dwellers undermines the possibility of a radical social commitment.

Released seven years earlier than *Tropa de elite 2*, *Carandiru* is set in the other major Brazilian city, São Paulo. It is an adaptation of a bestselling book written by Héctor Babenco's doctor named Drauzio Varella, who practiced voluntary medicine for fourteen years at the Brazilian detention center called Carandiru to prevent the spread of an AIDS epidemic. He worked there until the massacre of 1992 during Fernando Collor de Mello's presidency, which ended with 111 inmates dead, most of them killed by the police special forces (none of whom died).[29] After the massacre, the inmates were gradually transferred to other centers and Carandiru was finally demolished in 2002, a decade after the event. It is not uncommon for

Brazilian crime films to be based on real events and to capitalize on their popularity, and this has been the case from very early on in the history of Brazilian film. *Os estranguladores*, by Antonio Leal, was the first—or at least one of the first—Brazilian fiction films. Shot in 1908, with a duration of more than half an hour and a plot based on the killing of two brothers who were strangled by a gang of criminals, this film became a total success and encouraged others to produce films based on real violent events for decades.[30]

Carandiru's narrative is structured around a narrator who appears, as in the previous two films, in the form of a voice-over. In this case the narrator is a physician (Luiz Carlos Vasconcelos), a "committed chronicler" in Herlinghaus' words,[31] and the fictional rendition of Dr. Varella. Director Babenco came across the book he adapted for the film *Carandiru* while he was being treated for a serious illness; his personal physician was in fact the original author. Notwithstanding Babenco's life-long commitment to the marginalized and underprivileged, his personal involvement in this project stemmed from his involvement with a narrator and character who, however sympathetic to the predicament of the inmates and their tragedy, lives in another world and returns to his safe middle-class apartment at night. The choice of this narrator instead of, say, an inmate, for instance, predetermines the director's position as a member of the middle class, regardless of his origins or the doctor's as a member of the working class.[32]

To sum up, all three films have male narrators who are also characters in the film and address the audience through a voice-over, narrating the story from their point of view. In principle, it seems evident that the two narrators belong to the middle class or are at the very least in a position of superiority to the inmates or favela residents: the prison doctor in the case of *Carandiru* and the Chief of the BOPE, Captain (later promoted to Colonel) Nascimento, in the other two films. However, in the case of *Tropa de elite* and *Tropa de elite 2* there is an interesting oscillation of social position depending on the particular social field where the characters are situated. This instability is connected to the diverse identification of classes with the police force in Brazil as observed by Teresa P. R. Caldeira.[33] Both the Chief of the BOPE, Nascimento, and the BOPE agent, Mathias, assume identities which neither distance them from the university students nor allow them to identify with the group of *favelados* (favela residents).

Captain Nascimento's explicit references to class differences also point in this direction. In *Tropa de elite*, we hear his inner thoughts that reveal his opposition to Mathias' romantic ambitions with the middle-class girl, indicating that he believes this to be an impossible relationship due to class and race differences. His premonition is later confirmed, as is the impossibility of Mathias' ascent of the social ladder. Toward the end, there is a scene in the film when a group of middle class students and citizens demonstrate against the assassination of two NGO activists killed in the *Prazeres* favela. At this point, the voice-over of Nascimento claims that people do not protest when a police officer (Neto) is killed, only when rich people die. Colonel Nascimento's reflections are accompanied by images of Mathias attacking a university student while he addresses the masses of middle-class demonstrators with class-infected accusations. The cinematography supports Nascimento's Manichaean divisions. This scene has a stark color contrast: all the demonstrators are dressed in white, their white faces and occasional blond hair contrasting markedly with Mathias' black complexion and black T-shirt. Furthermore, the shot's composition emphasizes physical distance, with Mathias appearing larger than the middle-class demonstrators and situated closer to the audience (Figure 3.1).

Nascimento is also highly critical of the middle-class university students who deal in and consume drugs. These moments situate the BOPE members in opposition to the middle class but this is not always the case. This oscillation in social class calls to mind Jean-Claude Bernardet's identification of this oscillation as characteristic of the Brazilian middle class represented in Cinema Nôvo,[34] but in *Tropa de elite*, *Tropa de elite 2* and *Carandiru*, the representation of the middle class is more nuanced than in Cinema Nôvo's works.

Contrary to the unstable social class of the narrators of *Tropa de elite* and *Tropa de elite 2*, the narrator of *Carandiru* is unquestionably a character belonging to the middle class both inside and outside the prison because of the particular cultural and symbolic capital he possesses. Even though the social divisions

Figure 3.1   Mathias Confronting the Middle-class Demonstrators. *Source: Tropa de elite.*

effective inside the prison do not correspond necessarily to those of the outside world (for instance, the prisoner head chef is the real head of the prison, not the warden) the power the physician possesses to help inmates prevent or treat AIDS endows him with authority. The way the film is narrated also invites us to imagine that the doctor is in fact the alter ego of the director and therefore there are no signs of problematization of the doctor's views as they are taken for testimony. In the film itself, there is an explicit reference to the doctor's scopic drive when he associates in his thoughts the prison and the films that he used to watch at the cinema when he was a child. At one point, the doctor says that his feelings when crossing the detention center's door are similar to the ones he felt when going to the cinema. And we actually see him peeping through the cells' holes in the first part of the film.

This feeling is transmitted to the audience, who can also peep through the hole, as it were, of the cinema screen in a sort of mise-en-abîme operation and assume the doctor's position. And like the doctor, Lucía Herrera Montero argues, the audience remains unperturbed and comfortably seated while watching the film,[35] and despite the doctor's presence in most scenes, he is not the main character. According to Robert Stam, Varela "is less a character than a function."[36] We learn nothing about his life other than his experiences at the prison. Unlike Nascimento in *Tropa de elite* and *Tropa de elite 2*, the doctor is important only insofar as he opens the door that allows us access to the prisoners' voices and their hearts' yearnings. The doctor's reflections near the end of the film as well as the extract from the prologue of Drauzio Varella's book selected by the director Héctor Babenco for the coda justify this interpretation. Here, Varella affirms that only God, the police and the inmates really know what happened in Carandiru and only they are able to tell the full story. He only heard the prisoners, meaning that in a way he is only important to the extent that he serves to make the prisoners' testimonies public.

In addition to these observations on the narrative design and the use and position of narrators, other narrative differences between *Tropa de elite* and *Tropa de elite 2* and *Carandiru* are worth highlighting—in particular, the view of the underprivileged as individuals with a history or as a mass without history, and the technology of power executed in their social fields. It is here that we find a major difference between the *Tropa de elite* films and *Carandiru*. Similar to *Elite Squad 2*, *Carandiru* begins with a fight between inmates, but at the beginning of *Carandiru* the special police forces are not called in to intervene and the audience only see them when they enter the prison to initiate the massacre at the end of the film. This film makes ample use of flashbacks, a device employed to afford the audience a deeper insight into the lives of the prisoners, particularly into their past. During his regular visits to the center, the physician conducts medical check-ups and talks to the prisoners. At the beginning, these scenes follow in quick succession to provide a general framework and atmosphere and produce a strong initial impression that inmates have different personalities, pasts, and problems. As the film progresses, the narrative will focus on a small number of them and we will come to know more about their lives outside of the prison through conventional flashbacks. The figure of the doctor serves to establish a mechanism whereby we can hear the inmates relate their past and express their inner feelings in the first person.

Moreover, the inmates are generally portrayed in unconventional forms. For instance, the day the new doctor begins work at the center, he encounters a situation where one young prisoner—Lula, played by Dionísio Neto— wants to kill another called Peixeira (Milhem Cortaz). The warden, Mr. Pires, appears to prevent a fight between the two convicts, but the doctor sees that it is the Head Chef—Negro Preto, played by Ivan de Almeida—who intervenes and manages to placate the two. This scene demonstrates that, despite the fact he is just a prisoner, Preto is in fact the one who has power over the inmates, not the official representative of the Brazilian government.[37]

Carandiru's approach differs from the one taken in the *Tropa de elite* series, where the silence and insignificance of favela dwellers and inmates renders them invisible subaltern objects. The power of the favela's drug lord Baiano in *Tropa de elite* is not foregrounded and is minimized by the power of the BOPE, a representation that does not give justice to the power generally attributed to drug lords in journalistic accounts, for instance.

Carandiru's individualized and historical approach is consistent in subsequent sequences; however, as Herlinghaus has observed, *Carandiru* offers an interesting shift from Babenco's initial individualized perspective of the inmates to a more distant gaze toward the end, in accordance with a generic change from melodrama to tragedy.[38] Figures 3.2 and 3.3 illustrate this shift. In the first one, we see two of the inmates when they were children. One of them had been abandoned by his parents and later became a drug-dealer, a consumer, and eventually the assassin of his own step-brother, who ends up in prison for killing the men who allegedly raped their sister. The second frame shows the inmates lying almost naked on the prison's courtyard, faceless and defenseless against the power of the BOPE. In other words, the focus on the collective predicament of inmates toward the end of the film produces what Herlinghaus has called "images of impersonal state violence."[39]

To provide these two different approaches (individual–collective) with a deeper meaning, it is worth bringing to this analysis Foucault's observation of the consequences of the cult of the individual and individual freedom in liberal politics. Foucault noted that, in the Ancient Regime, the public exposure of an identity was a sign of the royal power, whereas the visibility of the criminal as an individual later became a sign of disempowerment. As Schawn and Shapiro interpreted,

Figure 3.2 A Personalized View. *Source: Carandiru.*

Figure 3.3 Shift to an Anonymous Approach. *Source: Carandiru.*

Foucault radically implies that the politics of personal identity, from the late 1960s onward, was a mistake, given that in the modern system of discipline, we could say that to be marked as having an identity is a feature of disempowerment.[40]

In *Carandiru*, with the combination of an individualized perspective in most of the film and a more distant gaze toward the end, the disempowering attention to individuality coexists unproblematically with an empowering attention to the collectivity of inmates. The film's end retains a certain degree of attention to the exploitation of the disenfranchised in an unfair system sustained by modern institutions of the state within a film that mostly highlights the individuality of the inmates observed from the perspective of a middle-class character. In the following section, I point out diverse ways of "marking" these individuals as members of different classes.

Habitus and Ethnicity

As seen in the previous section, the comments on class differences made by Nascimento and Mathias in *Tropa de elite* are not veiled. I will now turn to less explicit forms of constructing social difference such as the deployment of ethnicity, sexuality, and authentic experience for this aim. Beverley Skeggs, and earlier Bourdieu, have noted the new forms that class struggle is taking in contemporary societies and have demonstrated how the construction of class is always performed from a certain ideological position, not from an inexistent neutral point. And very importantly for our aim of highlighting some aspects of the social classification embedded in these films, Skeggs has also emphasized the importance of the visual in contemporary class construction.[41] A number of scenes are illustrative of these operations.

In regard to ethnicity in *Tropa de elite*, for instance, Mathias is an Afro-Brazilian with a Caucasian girlfriend. Mathias is, in fact, the only African-Brazilian student in his class, a situation that has been changing in recent years thanks to the affirmative action policies gradually implemented by the Brazilian government since 2002—such policies aim at achieving a racial composition in university lecture theatres that is equal to that of Brazilian society at large, where approximately 50 percent of the population are non-white.[42] As *Tropa de elite* and *Tropa de elite 2* both demonstrate, the racial composition of a lecture in a Law degree like the one portrayed in *Tropa de elite* was almost exclusively Caucasian before the implementation of these measures, whereas a History lecture like the one we see in the opening scene of *Tropa de elite 2* tended to traditionally incorporate a larger number of *pardos* (brown-skinned people) and *pretos* (African-Brazilians).[43] Racial inequality in Brazil has been connected to other forms of social, economic, and political inequality long before the 1980s in Brazil.[44]

The racial composition of the lecture theatres of *Tropa de elite* and *Tropa de elite 2* show how the films manage to accurately portray recent changes in the racial composition of university lecture theatres in contemporary Brazil. The relative social positions of students of different ethnic backgrounds (André Mathias and his classmates) are visually rendered by director José Padilha as opposed and irreconcilable (in other words, struggling) in the form of medium shots where Mathias is usually presented in opposition to either his white classmates or a white mass of middle-class demonstrators. Might it be implied from this choice of cinematography that Padilha has little faith in the peaceful resolution of this struggle, even if there exists a romantic relationship? A romantic relationship between two members of different ethnic groups does work in the same film, but only when the lovers belong to the stratum of the underprivileged (drug lord Baiano and his partner).

In *Carandiru*, a variation of the theme of the interracial relationship exists. Sexuality features more prominently in Babenco's film, as unconventional sex is one of the director's authorial signatures. Majestade (Ailton Graça) is an African-Brazilian man with two wives of different ethnic backgrounds, Dalva, played by Maria Luísa Mendonça, and Rosirene (Aida Leiner). Both women love him and have children with him, and he loves them both, but neither woman accepts polygamy. When Majestade meets white Dalva for the first time, in order to convince her to marry him, he argues that the mixture of their skin color will produce a wonderful effect, a remark that is visually illustrated with a beautiful shot of the black man and the white, blond woman, who appear side by side and facing the camera in a rather theatrical position, as if they were ready to take a picture (and, significantly, not in opposition to each other as is often the case between Mathias and Maria in *Tropa de elite*).

The connection between ethnicity and class is performed differently in *Carandiru* and *Tropa de elite*. Babenco's approach apparently offers an optimistic view of the power of love to overcome ethnic obstacles—even obstacles originating from class position, if the film's press kit (including explicit references to class differences in relationship to ethnicity which were not even included in the final cut of the film) is taken into account. In spite of this, Majestade's depiction is not exempt from a stereotypical ascription to the lower classes because of the connection usually established between ethnicity and sexuality.[45] In *Carandiru*, Majestade uses his body and his capacity to have children as a strong argument to convince Dalva to marry him. The scene where he meets Dalva for the first time presents him as the epitome of the macho guy, and sexuality is also important in the portrayal of his relationship with his second wife, Rosirene (Afro-Brazilian), a union between two black persons marked by uncontrollable passion.

In contrast to the aristocracy and the lower classes, the middle class generally observes some degree of sexual restraint. This restraint, however, does not preclude the middle-class fascination with the excesses of the lower classes as a way for the middle-class individuals to define themselves and to establish the constitutive limits of each class. The voyeuristic attitude of the doctor in *Carandiru*, peeping through the windows of the prison cells at night, fits the same pattern. Yet another instance of this disposition (habitus) is his role as a witness (together with another figure of authority, the prison warden) of the confrontation between Majestade and his two wives. Apart from its humor and theatricality, this moment is unequivocal. While Majestade argues with his two spouses, the warden asks the doctor, "Two women, doctor! What do *these crooks* have that *we* haven't?" [emphasis added]. The doctor replies with the question: "Have you kissed your wife today?" (replays the gazing privileged character). In sum, Majestade's characterization based on his sexual life-style, in addition to his dark skin, positions him in a lower class from the doctor's point of view, which is the one the audience is invited to assume. Compared to the implicit lack of desire of the representatives of the middle class, his ability to keep two demanding women sexually satisfied marks him as a member of the lower class. Sex is readily associated with the lower classes.

Another example of how the disposition of a character unmasks a class position via the concept of "authentic experience" can be found in *Tropa de elite*. There is a sequence where Mathias betrays his class position by strongly disagreeing with his classmates' predominant view on the role of police in Brazil. During this sequence, Maria is presenting her group's work on the Brazilian penal system. In a simplifying fashion and drawing from Foucault, the character of Maria argues that Brazil's penal Law articulates a network of repressive public institutions designed to protect the rich and punish almost exclusively the poor. In this classroom discussion held between Law undergraduates, there is neither an explanation of the diffuse character of power nor of the non-repressive character of other forms of power, such as education at a university where students are "disciplined" to accept and propagate a certain view of a "normal society." When the teacher asks students in this class to apply this to a particular institution, Maria chooses the police, a repressive state apparatus. The students, one of whom self-reflectively classifies the students in this classroom as members of the middle and upper classes, debate whether the police beat only the poor or also the rich. There is disagreement over whether the rich are treated as badly as the poor. The son of a judge expresses his father's strong rejection of the use of torture by police in the favelas, which prompts Mathias to intervene and position himself against everyone. They all laugh at his judgment unaware that he is a policeman. In defense of the police force, Mathias states his belief that the police are generally honest and argues for the need of repression to avoid the consequences of drug consumption. These problems, he adds, cannot be perceived by those who live in nice apartments that most of the students occupy in the South of the city (which is recognized by Rio de Janeiro's residents as a predominantly middle-class neighborhood).

At this moment, we can observe how the stance on a social issue necessarily positions individuals in two different classes. Their opinions on the police in effect produce their class. It is not the disagreement over whether the middle classes suffer police abuse as much as the lower classes that divides this group of students into two social classes. A clear dividing line is drawn when Mathias speaks from a position of a person who has authentic experience of the police interventions and the consequences that drug consumption has on poor people. There is a displaced class content in this discussion about the role of the police: those who speak in abstract terms and the student (Mathias) who knows the situation well.

The argument that authentic experience marks its users as belonging to a certain social class (the lower classes, in the case of Mathias) also works for the white students, but this time it operates in their favor. Some middle-class students use evidence gathered during their encounters with the lower classes as members of an NGO to better write essays, that is, through their experiences with the poorest members of the society, they acquire the cultural capital that helps them maintain their social status. In *Tropa de elite*, students use the expertise gained at the NGO established in the favela to support their arguments. The favela dwellers themselves are not able to capitalize upon their own experiences or culture, but these students are able to increase their individual value by writing essays about this experience, which will help them earn a university degree. Education is confirmed as a major means of establishing one's status in the middle class. Incidentally, the NGO serves in *Tropa de elite* to highlight the hypocrisy of the middle class and seems to follow a general line of criticism against the role of NGOs in such places.[46]

THE ROLE OF INSTITUTIONS

Rather than being exclusively limited to Rio de Janeiro or São Paulo, the three films in focus here clearly show a concern for a "national" problem, particularly in regard to governmental institutions. As the lyrics of the "Rap das Armas" used as the introductory soundtrack of *Tropa de elite* go, *"O meu Rio de Janeiro é um cartão postal mas eu vou falar de um problema nacional"* (My Rio de Janeiro is a postcard, but I am going to talk about a national problem). The portrayal of institutions in these features goes against the trend noted by Ivana Bentes according to which "the majority of the films do not relate violence or poverty with the elites."[47] In contrast to *Cidade de Deus*, what we observe timidly in *Tropa de elite* and decisively in *Tropa de elite 2* and *Carandiru* is an equation of elite and criminality. The institutions amply represented in these three films are the police, the prison, and the university.

As I explained earlier, the three films in this chapter deal with the operations of a special police unit, the BOPE, trained to take temporary control of areas that are traditionally under the control of drug traffickers, such as favelas and prisons. In fact, these operations function as central themes in the three films and even serve to anecdotally link them—the title *Carandiru* is based on a historical flawed operation of the BOPE in 1992 at the now demolished Carandiru detention center where 111 inmates were executed, and this operation is even mentioned in *Tropa de elite 2* as a failed operation (and a stain on the BOPE's name), the likes of which should be avoided in the future.

Tropa de elite is based on the historical visit of Pope John Paul II to Brazil in 1997 and his first visit to the city of Rio de Janeiro, the location where both *Tropa de elite* films are set. In *Tropa de elite*, as in real life, Pope John Paul II wants to reside next to a dangerous favela, and the BOPE has been assigned the task of cleaning it up for the Pope's protection. In actuality, the cleanup operation to receive John Paul II cost the lives of thirty people.[48] Since 2008, the BOPE coexists in Rio's favelas with a new type of military police, the *Unidade de Polícia Pacificadora* (UPP) (Pacifying Police Unit). The UPPs do not appear in *Tropa de elite* as they did not exist yet when the film was released in 2007; neither do they feature in *Tropa de elite 2*, released three years later, when the UPPs were already established in some favelas.

This significant absence notwithstanding, it is important to note here with regard to this analysis that, unlike the BOPE, whose extremely violent and sporadic invasions of the favelas or the prisons are amply documented in the three films, the UPPs in real life are conceived of as permanent police units aimed at improving the lives of favela residents and incorporating the favelas into the "divided city." However, a report based on extensive research published in May 2012 concludes that the areas where the UPPs were established were paradoxically not the most in need of these units, but the ones nearest to middle-class areas or locations selected for the celebration of some of the future large-scale events. This seems to suggest that the UPPs have a more classist and temporary role than was originally thought.[49]

There is an interesting correlation between these research findings on the UPP and the representation of the BOPE in *Tropa de elite*. In *Tropa de elite*, the BOPE's image is more ambiguous than in *Tropa de elite 2*, as it corresponds to a film whose social critique is somewhat more reticent than its sequel's. One of the major findings of Colonel Nascimento in *Tropa de elite 2* is precisely the realization that the BOPE operations to clean up the favelas of drug dealers throughout the four years that the narrative evolves (2006 to 2010) were in fact contributing to the corruption of the military police in the favelas and maintaining a corrupt political system in Brazil. This fictional image seems to correlate to the hypothesis outlined above regarding the possible unwanted effects of the UPP's operations in real life. Both this hypothesis and the fully-fledged accusation made in *Tropa de elite 2* (where a Brazilian governmental institution such as the BOPE is accused of effectively supporting the maintenance of a deeply corrupt socio-political system that ensures the dominance of the middle class in a capitalist economy) serve as a real and fictional illustration of Foucault's argument on the function of punishment as a political tactic. One of the four general rules of his *Discipline and Punish* is "Analyse punitive methods not simply as consequences of legislation or as indicators of social structures, but as techniques possessing their own specificity in the more general field of other ways of exercising power. Regard punishment as a political tactic."[50]

Thus, institutions and the state are scaffolds for a certain technology of power. Foucault observed how the substitution of non-corporal punishment for physical punishment in the penal system around the year 1760 did not respond to a disinterested development toward a more humanitarian society, but to the gradual establishment of a different technology of power which involved different interconnected institutions, such as those devoted to surveillance and repression (the police, the prison) and educational institutions. The fictional image of the university in the *Tropa de elite* series, particularly the scene in *Tropa de elite* in which the undercover BOPE agent André Mathias is working with his classmates on the application of Foucault's work to the Brazilian penal system, prompts the reflection on Foucault's contention of a single process of "epistomological-juridical" formation in which the development of penal law and human sciences were intimately interrelated. As I have stated, these two forms of exercising power belong to a single technology of power. Punishment, surveillance and knowledge are not dissociated from each other, an idea not reflected in Maria's presentation (*Tropa de elite*) and Fraga's lecture (*Tropa de elite 2*) which focused only on a repressive state apparatus without mentioning the role of the university. In both films, there is a clear association of "power" to "repression"; however, Foucault noted that "power" is not always associated to repression, but also to the construction of knowledge. In *Tropa de elite,* there is a significant silence about the existing asymmetries of power in the classroom itself. The existing racial inequality characteristic of Brazilian tertiary institutions is highlighted by José Padilha but he stops short of pointing to a structural root-cause of this inequality.

CONCLUSION

In the preceding analysis, I attempted to highlight that the classification made by male authoritative narrators based on differences in life-style practices betrays their own position as middle-class classifying agents. At times, it is evident that the characters adopt different class positions depending on their relation to other characters situated at lower or higher positions. Robert Stam has noted that the use of music in *Carandiru* "reflects the social vantage point from which the prisoners are being pitied but also judged from a kind of ethically panoptical position. In short, it reflects the cultural norms of both author and auteur, the middle class director and the middle class doctor."[51] I have

observed significant differences between these films in the representation of
the underprivileged as unknown others or nameless casualties of the social
violence exerted against them.

Moreover, in filmmaking phases other than production, it has been noted
that the use of crime narratives functions successfully as a national branding
strategy to increase the market share and internationalize Brazilian cinema.
The present study reflects on and raises awareness of some of the implications
that such representations and business strategies might have for the perpetu-
ation of class differences.

The films' potential as classploitation narratives can also be discussed following the analyses and, in the case of these three films, there are arguments
to support different views in this regard. Despite the explicit and perhaps
stereotypical defense of the lower class in opposition to the middle class in
Tropa de elite, the great attention paid in this film to generic conventions tied
to entertainment values and the superficial portrayal of relationships and characters other than that of Nascimento point to the primacy of entertainment
rather than a genuine interest in addressing a social problem. This is further
supported by the use of emotional elements with the aim of manipulating the
audience's emotions.

In *Carandiru*, it is precisely the depth of the depiction of the inmates as
individuals and the avoidance of stereotypes that seems to point in the other
direction. Director Babenco claimed in an interview that he did not use any
emotional manipulation and that it was his intention to make an original film
that was "entertainment with ethics and values of respect and solidarity."[52]
None the less, individualization is fraught with problems. Instead of trying
to differentiate these films sharply, it might be more advantageous to simply
admit that these two seemingly different directions (entertainment-social
commitment) are important components of the three films in different ways.

Identifying the class dynamics inherent in these texts can raise our awareness of the symbolic constructions that we are creating or reinforcing, which
in turn may affect the capacity of someone living in the favelas or in detention
centers to improve his/her job prospects or to be perceived as a non-dangerous
individual. Ultimately, class analysis of these texts and their industries might
help to avoid complaisant attitudes and to keep in mind that class struggle is
still very important, although it "is not the only struggle."[53]

More importantly, these three films form part of the twenty-first-century
Brazilian cinematic response to the challenges posed by global and national
film industries and the globalization of Brazilian society and economy as a
whole. The aesthetics of the 1970s Cinema Nôvo that moved the Argentine
Héctor Babenco to Brazil are no longer effective or attractive to modern
audiences, critics, and scholars alike, but this does not necessarily imply that
the concept of class struggle has been rendered ineffectual, as Arnaldo Jabor

maintains.[54] Cinema Nôvo's characteristic politics and social commitment have also been transformed in twenty-first-century Brazilian cinema in order to adjust to the spirit of the new century. Both *Tropa de elite* films (particularly *Tropa de elite 2*) and *Carandiru* have managed successfully to portray the profound discontent of contemporary Brazilian society with the inability of the state to tackle persistent social problems, in particular extreme poverty and the "medieval"[55] conditions in which many Brazilians subsist despite the country's success at the macroeconomic level. These films anticipated the mass protests in Brazil in the summer of 2013, when tens of thousands of middle-class and poor Brazilians took to the streets to protest against poor social services and corruption,[56] two of the main issues in these films, amid official celebrations of a prelude to the 2014 World Cup, the Confederations Cup. The contemporary class struggle of Brazilian society is embedded in their narratives at the same time that they have successfully appropriated socio-economic problems to their advantage in order to create engaging narratives that enabled them to successfully compete with the much more powerful American industry in Brazil and attract the attention of audiences worldwide.

The rigid conceptions of the nation as well as the stagnant class divisions constructed within it as seen in these Brazilian blockbusters contrast with the notion of the nation in the films examined in the following chapter 4, where this concept does not necessarily reside in established institutions.

NOTES

1. Martín Hopenhayn, "¿Integrarse o subordinarse? Nuevos cruces entre política y cultura," in *Cultura, Política y Sociedad. Perspectivas latinoamericanas*, ed. Daniel Mato (Buenos Aires: CLACSO, 2005), 20. This diagnosis has been challenged in the field of Latin American cinema in Joanna Page's *Crisis and Capitalism in Contemporary Argentine Cinema* (Durham: Duke University Press, 2009).

2. John Hopewell, "Venice Film Festival: Brazil Sees Co-Prod Surge Via Festivals," *Variety*, August 30, 2013.

3. Ferreira et al., *Economic Mobility and the Rise of the Latin American Middle Class* (Washington, DC: World Bank, 2013).

4. The ratio of lower-class and dark-skinned students in universities has been steadily increasing since 2002, when the Government of the then President Fernando Henrique Cardoso passed the Law 10.558 whereby the Programa de Diversidade na Universidade was created with the aim of addressing the huge differences between racial and class composition in universities and the Brazilian society at large.

5. Laura Podalsky, "Unpacking Periodization," in *The Routledge Companion to Latin American Cinema*, eds. Marvin D'Lugo, Ana M. López, and Laura Podalsky (Oxon: Routledge, 2018), 63.

6. Paul A. Schroeder Rodríguez, "After New Latin American Cinema," *Cinema Journal* 51, no. 2 (2012): 108.

7. Ismail Xavier, "Ways of Listening in a Visual Medium: The Documentary Movement in Brazil," *NLR* 73 (January–February 2012): 116.

8. Term used by Alejandro Pardo to describe European cinema vis-à-vis Hollywood. For different opinions on the effects of Hollywood on other "minor" cinemas, read also Octavio Getino, *Cine iberoamericano. Los desafíos del nuevo siglo* (Buenos Aires: CICCUS, 2007) and Andrew Higson, "The Limiting Imagination of National Cinema," in *Cinema & Nation*, eds. Mette Hjort and Scott MacKenzie (London: Routledge, 2000).

9. Paulo Emílio Salles Gomes, *Cinema: Trajeto ria no subdesenvolvimento* (São Paulo: Paz e Terra, 1996), 97.

10. PricewaterhouseCoopers, (PwC), *Global Entertainment & Media Outlook 2010–2014* (New York: PricewaterhouseCoopers, 2010).

11. Miriam Gottfried, "Theater Firm Cinemark Has Riveting Global Story," *Wall Street Journal*, July 30, 2012: 30.

12. "*Elite Squad 2*: Press Kit," Variance Films, 2011, 2.

13. Brazil, ANCINE, *Informe 2010*.

14. PricewaterhouseCoopers, *Global Entertainment & Media Outlook*.

15. Brazil, ANCINE, *Informe 2010; Informe 2011*.

16. "Zazen Produções," Zazen Produções, http://www.zazen.com.br/.

17. Else R. P. Vieira, *City of God in Several Voices*, ix.

18. John Hopewell, "New Type of Patron Boosts Latin Biz," *Variety*, June 12–18, 2006: 55.

19. Charles Newbery, "Local Biz Needs New Models and Aud-Friendly Films to Compete with Hollywood," *Variety*, February 5–11, 2006: C8.

20. Tamara Falicov, "Hollywood's Presence in Latin America: Production Participation to Distribution Dominance," in *The International Encyclopedia of Media Studies*, gen. ed. Angharad N. Valdivia, Vol. 2: *Media Production*, ed. Vicki Mayer (Chichester: Wiley-Blackwell, 2013), 14.

21. Charles Newbery, "Local Biz Needs New Models," C8.

22. "José Padilha," *IMDb Database*.

23. "Elite Squad: The Enemy Within." *IMDb Database*; Guss De Lucca, "'Tropa de Elite 2' é o melhor investimento do ano," *Último segundo*, November 23, 2010.

24. Lúcia Nagib, *Brazil on Screen. Cinema Novo, New Cinema, Utopia* (London: I.B. Tauris, 2007), xxii.

25. Else R. P. Vieira, *City of God in Several Voices*, 104.

26. David William Foster, "Films by Day and Films by Night in São Paulo," in *Latin American Cinemas: Local Views and Transnational Connections*, ed. Nayibe Bermúdez Barrios (Calgary: University of Calgary Press, 2011), 110.

27. I witnessed the enormous enthusiasm that this film generated among young audiences of very different cultural backgrounds in 2011 when I attended screenings in locations as distant as Havana (Festival Internacional del Nuevo Cine Latinoamericano) and Hong Kong (HKIFF).

28. Thanks to Tatu Laukkanen for this interpretation.

29. Years later, on the 13th of July, 2013, amid nationwide mass protests to press the Brazilian government for improvements in education and health, Varella is still urging the government to conduct infrastructural improvements, not just add more medical practitioners to areas lacking good health services: http://www1.folha.uo l.com.br/fsp/ilustrada/118585-mais-medicos.shtml.

30. Paulo Emílio Salles Gomes, *Cinema: Trajeto ria no subdesenvolvimento*, 28.

31. Hermann Herlinghaus, "Affectivity Beyond 'Bare Life': On the Non-Tragic Return of Violence in Latin American Film," in *A Companion to Latin American Literature and Culture*, ed. Sara Castro-Klaren (Malden M.A.: Blackwell, 2008), 599.

32. "*Carandiru*: Press Kit," Sony Pictures Classics, 2003, 17.

33. Teresa P.R. Caldeira, *City of Walls*.

34. Jean-Claude Bernardet, "Trajectory of an Oscillation," in *Brazilian Cinema*, Expanded ed., eds. Randal Johnson and Robert Stam (New York: Columbia University Press, 1995), 281–89. Bernardet later retracted from his previous analysis.

35. Lucía Herrera Montero, "Memorias, cuerpos y narraciones en el espacio de la prisión. *Carandirú* de Héctor Babenco," *Miradas al margen: Cine y subalternidad en América Latina y el Caribe*, ed. Luis Duno-Gottberg (Caracas: Fundación Cinemateca Nacional, 2008), 186.

36. Randal Johnson and Robert Stam, eds., *Brazilian Cinema*, Expanded ed. (New York: Columbia University Press, 1995), 114.

37. This is explained by director Héctor Babenco in the DVD extras of the film.

38. Herlinghaus, "Affectivity Beyond 'Bare Life,'" 599.

39. Herlinghaus, "Affectivity Beyond 'Bare Life,'" 600.

40. Anne Schwan and Stephen Shapiro, *How to Read Foucault's Discipline and Punish* (London: Pluto Press, 2011), 127.

41. Beverley Skeggs, *Class, Self, Culture* (London: Routledge, 2004), 106.

42. André Cicalo, "Nerds and Barbarians: Race and Class Encounters through Affirmative Action in a Brazilian University," *Journal of Latin American Studies* 44, no. 2 (2012): 239.

43. According to André Cicalo, before the recent implementation of quotas reserved for lower-class and non-white students, the Law degree was one of the more notable university degrees to have a fewer number of these students. The results of an ethnographic study that he conducted at a public university in Rio de Janeiro between 2007 and 2008 show that the divisions between middle-class white students on the one hand and non-white and lower-class students on the other persisted in the classroom and were even spatially demarcated in those years. Cicalo, "Nerds and Barbarians."

44. George Reid Andrews, "Racial Inequality in Brazil and the United States, 1990–2010," *Journal of Social History* 47, no. 4 (2014): 829–54; Cicalo, "Nerds and Barbarians;" Marcelo Neri, *A nova classe média. O lado brilhante da base da pirâmide* (São Paulo: Saraiva, 2011).

45. George W. Stocking, for instance, has analyzed how race has been negatively associated to lower moral standards (*Victorian Anthropology*, New York: Free Press, 1987); more famously, Foucault showed how sexuality could be a means of expressing class (*The History of Sexuality* [New York: Pantheon Books, 1978]).

46. Mike Davis' *Planet of Slums* (London: Verso, 2006) contains ample evidence of this fact.

47. Bentes is referring here to works made between 2003 and 2005. Ivana Bentes, "The Aesthetics of Violence in Brazilian Film," 86.

48. Mauricio Becerra Rebolledo, "Latinoamérica maquilla su pobreza: El cambio de rostro de Río de Janeiro," *Panoramas News*, October 25, 2011.

49. Cano, Ignacio, et al., *"Os donos do morro": Uma avaliação exploratória do impacto das unidades de polícia pacificadora (UPPS) no Rio de Janeiro*. Fórum Brasileiro de Segurança Pública and Laboratório de Análise da Violência (LAV–UERJ), 2012.

50. Michel Foucault, *Discipline and Punish: The Birth of the Prison* (New York: Vintage, 1995), 23.

51. Robert Stam, "The Carandiru Massacre: Across the Mediatic Spectrum," in *New Argentine and Brazilian Cinema: Reality Effects*, eds. Jens Andermann and Álvaro Fernández Bravo (New York: Palgrave Macmillan, 2013), 146.

52. *"Carandiru*: Press Kit," 12.

53. Enrique Dussel, "Philosophy of Liberation, the Postmodern Debate, and Latin American Studies," in *Coloniality at Large: Latin America and the Postcolonial Debate*, eds. Mabel Moraña, Enrique Dussel, and Carlos A. Jáuregui (Durham: Duke University Press, 2008), 343.

54. Arnaldo Jabor, "Preface," in *City of God in Several Voices: Brazilian Social Cinema as Action*, ed. Else R. P. Vieira (Nottingham: CCCP, 2005), iii–iv.

55. Term used by Babenco to describe Carandiru in the DVD extras.

56. John Hopewell, "Brazil: A Case Study in Anger, Sound and Fury," *Variety* July 17, 2013.

Chapter 4

The Return of the People

Wrestling with the State:
"Up with Populism!" in Venezuela

The political Turn-to-the-Left in the twenty-first century had cultural ramifications that were not always obvious to researchers.[1] In cinema, this short wave brought with it new production, distribution and exhibition strategies, and new infrastructures that attempted to challenge or expand existing public and private practices and institutions. Compared to the effects of globalization, neoliberalism, and the competition from Hollywood on production and distribution in the subcontinent, these new Turn-to-the-Left initiatives had a minimal impact on Latin American cinemas. However, if we aim to foster and respect audiovisual diversity and sovereignty, it is of paramount importance that we recognize the value of these types of projects. This chapter contributes to the in-depth study and visibility of one of them.

As can be expected, the most idiosyncratic films released in the period of the Turn-to-the-Left were Venezuelan. In no other Latin American country where the Turn-to-the-Left took root were efforts toward audiovisual independence from Hollywood and against the *dictadura mediática* (mainstream media dictatorship)[2] more concerted than in this country. In the first chapter, I focused on one paradigmatic example (*La clase*) that revisited the trope of social ascension through romantic relationships. In the present chapter, my interest lies in the formation of collective identities alongside and in relationship to the state. To the extent that these films and their narratives propose a viable political alternative to corrupt and bureaucratic political systems through a new cinematic practice, they contrast sharply with the ideologically conservative and Hollywood-imitative films from Brazil studied in chapter 3.

At this point, it is necessary to distinguish two types of films that constitute a unique contribution to twenty-first-century Latin American cinema: *Libertador Morales, el Justiciero* (*Libertador Morales, the Justice Maker*, Efterpi Charalambidis, 2009) is a "committed comedy" and a melodramatic farce, an attempt at creating a light genre that combines local comedy with an explicit social message of the type that is constantly heard on Venezuelan radio stations. Its genre and approach to history are unique when compared to a number (perhaps a "series") of FVC films created to reevaluate historical figures like Simón Bolívar as well as when contrasted with ealier socially engaged cinema in other Latin American countries across the subcontinent.

The second film in focus in this chapter is a choral political drama, *Macuro, la fuerza de un pueblo* (*Macuro, the Strength of the People*, Hernán Jabes, 2008). It is the first feature by Hernán Jabes, a director familiar with the language of musical videos and commercials. *Macuro* is a film rich in intertextual postmodernist references and well suited to demonstrate that the apparent simplicity of films produced at FVC can hide revealing complexities. A noteworthy characteristic of these features is that both are directed by first-time directors and script-writers that do not belong to the established Venezuelan film elite (still strong after nearly two decades of Bolivarian cultural policies). Moreover, Charalambidis is a female director in a country where the filmmaking sector is overwhelmingly male. These facts, among others, illustrate FVC's efforts toward the democratization of film production, although these can be regarded more as timid attempts at diversification than systematic efforts to diversify the medium, which could have been implemented more effectively by training and supporting native Venezuelan filmmakers and other minorities. This has yet to happen in a coordinated and systematic manner, in spite of all the Venezuelan state's rhetoric about a new humanity.

Considered for their capacity to foster the constitution of collective identities, many of the filmic effects of the Turn-to-the-Left (both FVC and non-FVC productions) can be called "populist" in Ernesto Laclau's terms. Laclau arrived at his influential and non-stereotypical conception of populism thanks to his interest in the formation of collective identities. *Libertador Morales, el Justiciero* and *Macuro, la fuerza de un pueblo* are primarily concerned with this process of forming a collective identity.

In contrast to the immense popularity of the term populism in fields such as political theory and history, populism is a neglected concept in film studies that has experienced a relatively timid resurgence in recent years, particularly in discussions around cinema and *el pueblo* (the people).[3] During the explosion of the Cinema Nôvo, Glauber Rocha wrote the well-known manifesto *Down with Populism!* which is still useful for tracing the uncharted history of populism in Latin American film and questioning contemporary practices. Two other useful theoretical tools for examining these films are Fredric Jameson's conception of "aesthetic populism"[4] and Luis Britto García's use of the term. Britto's role as an artist and intellectual involved in the Bolivarian revolution provides a counterpoint to foreign views on these cultural dynamics.

The concept of "populism" is "extremely elastic."[5] In a colloquial sense of the word, it usually refers to particular right-wing or left-wing political practices invariably led by charismatic leaders who establish a direct link with "the people," and is often negatively connoted in discourses produced by middle-class intellectuals and artists. Venezuelan artist and intellectual Luis Britto, for instance, uses it in such a pejorative light to criticize governments prior to the establishment of the Bolivarian revolution. Britto holds the view that consumer subcultures like pop must be comprehended within the panorama of populist movements, which are not exclusively political but also cultural and ideological. In this sense, populism, for Britto, aims at "explicitly or implicitly overcoming or ignoring class struggle in the name of some national or traditional ideology."[6] According to Britto, class struggle is substituted by the constitution of small communities following a cultural populism of late capitalism according to which cultural production is more centered around aesthetics than "acciones concretas" (concrete action).[7] Britto's claim is related to Raymond William's observations of the treatment of aesthetics into an "isolable extra-social phenomenon" discussed earlier,[8] which is pertinent for evaluating the critical praise by the intelligentsia (particularly that of universities and film festivals) of some Latin American filmmakers who employ auterist aesthetics. Although this latter aspect of Britto is useful for this volume as a whole, Britto's rather defensive conception of populism[9] seems less applicable than Ernesto Laclau's to the films that concern us in this section.

Contrary to most conceptions of populism, in his *On Populist Reason*, Laclau defines populism as a logic inherent in the actual working of any communitarian space, or "a way of constructing the political" and not a social content perceived as marginal.[10] Populism is not "the ideology or the type of mobilization of an *already* constituted group" but is "one way of constituting the very unity of the group."[11] The group does not exist before the functioning of a populist articulatory practice (social classes for Laclau do not exist prior to their articulation). The smallest unit found in this practice is the "social demand," whose functioning Laclau explains in the following terms:

Let me give an example of how isolated demands emerge, and how they start their process of articulation. This example, although it is imaginary, corresponds pretty well to a situation widely experienced in Third World countries. Think of a large mass of agrarian migrants who settle in the shantytowns on the outskirts of a developing industrial city. Problems of housing arise, and the group of people affected by them request some kind of solution from the local authorities. Here we have a *demand* which initially is perhaps only a *request*. If the demand is satisfied, that is the end of the matter; but if it is not, people can start to perceive that their neighbours have other, equally unsatisfied demands—problems with water, health, schooling, and so on. If the situation remains unchanged for some time, there is an accumulation of unfulfilled demands and an increasing inability of the institutional system to absorb them in a *differential* way (each in isolation from the others), and an *equivalential* relation is established between them. The result could easily be, if it is not circumvented by external factors, a widening chasm separating the institutional system from the people.[12]

Laclau's theorization of populism has found its cinematic expression in the Venezuelan state-producer FVC *Libertador Morales* and *Macuro*. Three different aspects of cinematic populism are considered here: (1) realist portrayal of populist dynamics; (2) aesthetic populism; and (3) populist action through exhibition and community engagement.

LIBERTADOR MORALES AND *MACURO*: CONSTRUCTING POPULIST FICTION AND REALITY

Both films in focus in this chapter (*Libertador Morales* and *Macuro*) are firmly rooted in contemporary events. The correspondence between numerous fictional and factual events is blatantly obvious. In *Libertador Morales*, the protagonist (Libertador, played by Rafael Gil) is a young man who works as a *mototaxista* (a motorcycle taxi driver) in the congested roads of Caracas. Mototaxistas are everywhere in this city and often criminalized, although they are prone to robberies and fatal attacks. As Luis Duno-Gottberg points out, they form part of the group of *motorizados* (a mixed group of messengers, mototaxistas, and criminals) which prompted "phobic reactions" from some well-to-do Venezuelans as they emerged "as new political subjects" in recent decades.[13] The mototaxistas' defense of the population that descended from the slums in the popular mobilizations of the Caracazo on February 27, 1989 (which, as discussed in chapter 1, was a crucial event in Venezuelan history still influencing contemporary politics) and the demonstrations that led to the reversal of the coup against Chávez on April 11, 2002 continued in 2014 with the mototaxistas' support for President Nicolás Maduro during the protests against him led by opposition leaders. At the time, extensive roadblocks called *guarimbas* were set up by the opposition, sometimes with cables across each side of a road, which caused a number of fatalities. The precarious livelihood of the motorizados is not reflected in *Libertador Morales*, but all these events in the country's upheavals explain why a mototaxista was chosen as the protagonist for a film funded by a governmental institution.

A touch of humorous dogmatic *chavismo* (support for Hugo Chávez's socio-political program) is on show with the mototaxista Libertador displaying tattoos of the independence leader Simón Bolívar on his body, living in a home decorated with pictures of his idol, and riding a motorbike adorned with stickers of images and quotes by the leader. Simón Bolívar (1783–1830) is known as *el Libertador* (the Liberator) because he liberated five Latin American nations from Spanish colonial rule. Libertador, the fictional character, was given this name by his mother in honor of the historical figure, and he, in turn, gave the name of Simón to his son for the same reason. Moreover, his middle name is Morales, referring to Simón Bolívar's motto "moral y luces" (morality and enlightenment) based on the principles of the French Enlightenment that inspired independence revolutions in Latin America. Steve Ellner translates this term as "morality and illumination" and points out that the major thrust of the Chávez government from 2006 was to promote "education with socialist values" in educational as well as non-educational contexts.[14] The respect for independence leaders has always been present in Venezuela as elsewhere in Latin America, but the constant reference to Simón Bolívar, Miranda, and other national icons in officially dominated media has become constant and repetitive. The persistent exhibition of Bolivarian enlightenment of the fictional character represents well the bombarding of messages in Venezuelan media as well as codes such as the need to publicly exhibit allegiance to the government by the wearing of red T-shirts.

Libertador Morales' plot is a melodramatic one that is easy to follow. Libertador falls in love with Daisy (Alba Valvé), a receptionist who soon becomes his girlfriend and the fictional version of the historical figure of Manuelita, "la libertadora del Libertador"–the female liberator of the Liberator–as she was called. At the same time, there is a criminal gang operating in the area led by Chaparro (Yugui López). In the film, Libertador realizes that the police Chief is in collusion with the gang instead of working to protect the neighborhood and embarks on a mission to fight crime by assuming the role of "mototaxista superhero." Donning a mask and assisted by a beggar (his "squire" Paloadeagua–Alberto González), he thwarts most of the gang's criminal activities thus propelling him to the spotlight as his fame grows and the people start to talk about the mysterious hero protecting them, whom they nickname "El Justiciero" or "The Justice Maker." As mentioned above, motorizados are generally considered supporters of the government but their relationship with the state is "complex" and "can be better assessed in light of Ernesto Laclau's recent discussion on the political logic of 'populist identification' and popular agency," a point in which Duno-Gottberg's analysis coincides with my own.[15]

This crime fighter is basically a Bolivarian version of "El Zorro" and other similar action heroes, as explicitly stated at the end of the film. At his home, Libertador discovers that his son (José Manuel Suárez) is involved in Chaparro's dealings. The father and son have a strained relationship in which the son blames the father for the death of his mother. After a series of incidents that bring Libertador and his son to jail for different reasons, the collusion between the police inspector and the gang is finally brought to light and Libertador is set free thanks to the strong support shown by his followers (mirroring President Hugo Chávez's liberation from coup leaders in 2002). His son, who had committed a crime with the gang, is also set free and Libertador is reunited with his girlfriend. Every detail is explained to the audience in a way that Glauber Rocha would critique as "speak simply so that the people understand."[16]

Macuro's film language also "speaks simply" and is set in rural Venezuela, in an actual small village called Macuro. At the beginning of the film, Macuro appears to be an idyllic, albeit undeveloped coastal village where the locals lead a traditional way of life either working in the local cement factory or as fishermen. The village festivals are attended by the village folk: pretty young girls and their boyfriends, the local band, and the village priest.[17] On one such evening, the people have gathered to attend a much-anticipated band concert when there is a power outage and all celebrations have to be suspended. When it is discovered that the small power generator that serves the village has broken down, three village representatives volunteer to ask for help at the cement factory (a privately owned company), where there is an unused power generator that could solve the problem temporarily until the authorities supply the necessary parts to make the repairs. The meeting between the villagers and the factory manager does not go well and the film unravels the conflict between the villagers and the manager. Even though the villagers are granted permission to use the spare generator by the factory owners in Caracas, the manager refuses entry to the factory, and this erupts into a violent confrontation between the villagers and the police. When a policeman defending the interests of the factory manager kills one of the protesting villagers, a mentally challenged boy called Aeroplano, the emotionally charged atmosphere is such that the remaining villagers enter the factory unobstructed and take the spare generator.

Real-life Macuro differs little from its fictional rendition, except for the absence of smuggling activities in the film for which the remote area, well connected with other Caribbean countries, is known. Historically, it is the only continental area of Latin America that Christopher Columbus set foot on, in the mistaken belief that it was an island. The film is based on a real event in 1989 and is inspired by continuing underdevelopment and other similar incidents. Eight years prior to the film's release, this area had its first road connecting it to Güiria, where the municipal government resides. As in the film, the municipal government of Güiria in real life has not supported the artisanal fishermen of Macuro in their conflicts with the owners of the cement factory and of a port, which the fishermen wanted to use for the development of the fishing industry. Initially, the fishermen who fought for the nationalization of the port encountered the opposition of the local government and the police force, but the strong popular movement pushing for its nationalization finally succeeded in leaving the "International Harbour of Güiria" in the hands of the local population.

The two narratives portraying corrupt and inefficient authorities and justice prevailing through the collective efforts of the community fall under a populist rationality. As in reality, the people in the films express their demands and resort to taking justice into their own hands when they realize that the authorities (the municipal police in *Libertador Morales* and the municipal government in *Macuro*) are not serving the interests of the general population. Libertador acts as a vigilante. In an episode reminiscent to the liberation of Chávez by his supporters in 2002, when Libertador is in trouble with the Court, the people manage to have him reinstated as a policeman. In other words, both *Macuro* and *Libertador Morales* take a view that the "will of the people" finds a way to impose itself.[18]

The events that trigger the creation of an "antagonistic divide" (in Laclau's terms) are the breakdown of the power generator in *Macuro* and the lack of security in *Libertador Morales*, neither of which are resolved by the public institutions in charge of solving these problems. In *Macuro*, the community seek help from a private company, but the refusal of the cement factory manager to help with the spare generator creates a series of subdemands derived from the first one: the fish caught by the fishermen rot, the convenience store has no fresh produce because the refrigerators are inoperative, the hawker cannot sell the usual food, and so on. As neighbors gather at the convenience store, ideas about mobilization and organization form in the community and they start seeing themselves as "the people."

This divide between the people and the rest is not just characteristic of this Latin American country where extreme inequalities and polarization have been exacerbated in the last few years. Bill Fletcher observes that in the United States, for example, "The right-wing populists postulate 'the people' vs. the rich; 'the people' vs. the 'vampire state.' But the 'people' are, in reality for the right-wing populists, only a segment of those who are actually the people."[19] This is what Laclau denominates the change of the "*plebs*" into "*populus*," the former being a part of the latter that becomes the totality when an antagonistic frontier is created. I will approach the term "the people" from a formal perspective in the next section.

As some communities in Venezuela, the characters in these films are building a "social-based" and radical democracy, in Steve Ellner's terms, where the disenfranchised masses of the population have been invited to bypass the bureaucratic institutions to communicate directly with the leadership and also to participate directly in decision-making processes.[20] In the film *Macuro*, one of the main characters is an Afro-descendant, played by the Venezuelan actress Malena Alvarado. The "social extension" of the film[21] is coherent with the policies introduced in some Latin American countries in the last twenty years to grant more visibility to multiple ethnicities (recognized in recently modified constitutions).[22]

However, the films' alignment with the Bolivarian cultural vision and mission does not necessarily imply that the directors support the Bolivarian government. Contrary to what could be expected from *Macuro*, Hernán Jabes is a vocal opponent of the Venezuelan government of the *V República* (the Fifth Republic) and has moved to Mexico. In his reading of *Libertador Morales*, the prominent critic Alfonso Molina, praises Director Charalambidis for intelligently avoiding to take sides in the narrow-minded political polarization that affects the country.[23] Efterpi Charalambidis is currently filming her second feature in Venezuela with the support of the two Venezuelan film institutions Centro Nacional Autónomo de Cinematografía (CNAC) and FVC, on the life of a middle-aged woman[24]. The processes that the narratives elicit in viewers exist independently of the directors' affiliations. The confluence of different interests involved in the production and distribution of these projects results in the texts' complex readings. *Libertador Morales* and *Macuro* contributed to the promotion of new social dynamics in line with other political, economic, and social endeavors of the Bolivarian revolutionary government. This cinema plays a crucial role in the socialist fight for "una nueva humanidad" (a new humanity) and "la revolución de las conciencias" (the revolution of the conscience)—two phrases commonly used by the ideologues of twenty-first-century socialism.

AESTHETIC POPULISM

FVC productions tend more toward classical narratives than modernist art. The importance attached to the script by Venezuelan filmmakers like Charalambidis and Jabes contrasts with the loose scripts of many contemporary auteur Argentine films that are successful at prestigious film festivals. This aesthetic choice begs questions about the intended audience and the legacy of NLAC in contemporary Venezuela.

Although some NLAC directors are more didactic than others (Solanas clearly more so than Gutiérrez Alea), they all famously rejected populism on cinema. Among these rejections, the clear stance against populist film practices by Glauber Rocha stands out. In his 1969 manifesto "Down with Populism!," Glauber Rocha described populist cinema in these terms: "Like the *caudillo* [the military strongman], the artist considers himself the father of the people: the motto is 'speak simply so that the people understand.'"[25] Clearly, this notion of populism corresponds to "populism as content," populism understood as the clientelist practice of presidents like Fujimori, not to

Laclau's notion of populism. NLAC works are proof of this rejection of "populism as content" in practice, and it is precisely NLAC's complexity at multiple levels that helped the movement gain international recognition and an important place in the history of cinema.

Two examples of NLAC's formal complexity, one from Brazil (Glauber Rocha himself) and another from Cuba (Sara Gómez), serve to illustrate this point. With regard to Rocha's *Deus e o diabo na terra do sol* (*God and the Devil in the Land of the Sun*,[26] 1964), Lúcia Nagib observes that "The exclusion of oppositional binaries, as much as the concepts of 'otherness' and 'difference,' makes Rocha's project incompatible with any preestablished political agenda, and in this sense *God and the Devil* has very little in common with what is normally understood under the rubric of political cinema."[27] Likewise, Sara Gómez's *De cierta manera* fulfills the principle of imperfect cinema by "[offering] no single internally consistent discourse" and by, in García Espinosa's words, "[showing] the process which generates the problems . . . [submitting] it to judgment without pronouncing the verdict."[28] In other words, these films are not didactic in a straightforward sense of the term.

Contrasting this, the dismissal of FVC productions as "heavy-handed and didactic,"[29] is common. The little critical attention devoted to FVC in the US media and the international scholarly community predominantly highlights the "propagandistic" use of FVC productions. They are also readily linked to populist demagogy.[30] Film scholar Libia Villazana warned that "un proyecto como el de la Villa, que es histórico para el desarrollo del cine venezolano, debería optar por el pluralismo y no por el propagandismo" (it should be advised that a project like Villa, a historical development in Venezuelan cinema, opt for pluralism and not for propaganda).[31] Although it is understandable that the first impression of many FVC's productions fits our common sense understanding of propaganda, a deeper analysis of particular film texts and their context of production complicates the films' multilayered meanings considerably. A paper presented by Gonzalo Chacón Mora in 2014, an otherwise interesting study of the evolution of the figure of the malandro in Venezuelan cinema referred to in chapter 1, ends on a similar note to Villazana's. Chacón Mora's diachronic approach leads his study to FVC productions, which he calls propagandistic even before studying them.[32] Granted, many of FVC productions are contemporary agitprop promoting participatory political action and historical revision but this statement does not exhaust the multi-layered richness of the texts.

Libia Villazana states that some Venezuelan cultural projects "[evoke] the initial rationale of the New Latin American Cinema," meaning that such projects aim "to create a new cinematic language that would reflect Latin American's own images and voices" and "to unite the continent culturally and politically in order to confront imperialism."[33] Old and new texts dealing with "class differences" and "social problems" are listed in Villazana's study, and data on specific agreements are duly recorded, but the question of the specific form that differences between NLAC narratives, Hollywood cinema (also mentioned in her chapter as a counterpoint to FVC creations) and contemporary films might adopt remains unanswered.[34]

Equally useful for the purpose of distinguishing FVC's unique contribution from NLAC is Noah Zweig's view of FVC productions like *Libertador Morales* as sites where global dynamics like Hollywood's global presence and Venezuela's reliance on oil revenue are played out against anti-neoliberal policies. The incorporation of the Hollywood superhero narrative in *Libertador Morales* would be a sign of the neoliberal features of the film whereas the call for "individual and collective forms of action when public institutions do not work" would be characteristic of the anti-neoliberal features.[35] Zweig concludes his analysis remarking that FVC "deploys a populist strategy"[36] and that the major difference between NLAC and these FVC productions is that the Venezuelan state plays a role as a counter-hegemonic force in the contemporary cultural conjuncture of Venezuela (hegemonic forces include the private media, the Church, etc.), whereas the Cuban State and the ICAIC in Cuba in the 1960s–1970s (NLAC) were the hegemonic forces.

Reception is key for a deeper understanding of the Venezuelans films studied here, and this necessarily brings this discussion to the forgotten and recently reignited question of "the people." Gilles Deleuze describes the trajectory of "the people" from classical to modern political cinema as a transformation that goes from "the presence of the people" (in Soviet Cinema, for instance) to "the people are missing." For Deleuze, Rocha's films "invent" the people and in them "the missing people are becoming"—not in the sense of transforming the Old into the New through a revolution (as in the famous Soviet Cinema's film *The General Line*), but by the "juxtaposition or compenetration of the old and the new 'which makes up an absurdity,' which assumes 'the form of aberration.'"[37] In Deleuze's view, in modern political cinema, "there will no longer be conquest of power by a proletariat, or by a united or unified people." More specifically, Deleuze claims that Rocha's films result in "the invention of a people" through an operation on the myth whereby the "[intolerable] lived present beneath the myth" is isolated and reworked as "a speech-act" which becomes "collective utterances capable of raising misery to a strange positivity."[38]

For Gonzalo Aguilar, the people of NLAC, *el pueblo*, have been transformed into *la gente* or a "postmodern mass" in New Argentine Cinema of the 1990s and 2000s because the people to whom Fernando Solanas and Octavio Getino directed their *La hora de los hornos* in 1968 no longer exist.[39] In contrast to New Argentine Cinema, the return of the people in Solanas' more recent *Memoria del saqueo* (2004) is "odd" and masks the wide support for neoliberalism from *la gente* (not the class-inflected term *el pueblo*) before the Argentine crisis of 2001–2002.

The people represented and addressed in *Macuro* and *Libertador Morales* are neither the 1960s people of Solanas nor la gente of New Argentine Cinema. Aguilar's assertion that the socio-political environment has changed dramatically is correct, but this change has not been homogeneous in Latin America, even in Argentina, where the people in Laclau's terms has resurfaced. FVC productions thus create a third stage in Deleuze's trajectory of the people consisting in a partial return to the first stage adjusted to the transformations of the people in the contemporary ideological and socio-economic conjunctures of Venezuela. Mabel Moraña contends that the term "social inequality" is replacing the liberal conception of "multicultural difference," signaling an attention to social justice that is not generally phrased as "class struggle." For Moraña, the left in Latin America is no longer the traditional left, although there is a "return" to the left in response to the feared threats posed by globalization.[40]

The people in FVC films are no longer missing. Both *Libertador Morales* and *Macuro* are explicit in introducing the notion that the pillar of social revolution is the union of the people—"United we are strong," reads the coda of *Libertador Morales*. This is reminiscent the cry "¡Suframos juntos! ¡Estemos siempre juntos!" (Let us suffer together! Let us be together!) uttered by the social leader Miro in the 1936 Mexican oppositional film *Redes* (Emilio Gómez Muriel and Fred Zinnemann), which demonstrates that, it might be more productive to consider the existence of similar intended audiences across times and socio-political conjunctures rather than looking at phenomena as a succession of historical stages. *Redes* is a film produced during the socially progressive Lázaro Cárdenas' administration in Mexico. Despite its temporal and spatial distance from *Macuro* (*Redes* was released in 1936 in Mexico and *Macuro* in 2008 in Venezuela), the comparison between them is apt for *Redes* can be also "understood both as art and as a tool for awakening the consciousness of the workers."[41]

The features share important aesthetic traits that might be interpreted as intertextual references or the common use of generic conventions (natural, since both are political dramas). Firstly, the films make use of frontal medium-close-ups and close-ups of the leaders of social revolt at turning points of the narrative. Secondly, in both cases, the determination to fight is conveyed by the kinetic energy produced by the fast movement of boats and accompanying music—in the final scene of *Redes*, the increasing pace of the rhythm of the violins is punctuated by the growing sound of trumpets as fishermen in their boats unite in their determination to rebel against the oppressor, and in *Macuro*, the clarinet and the guitar introduce a passionate dialogue to convey a sense of struggle and pathos as the fishermen become determined to prevent the corporate ship from berthing in the cement factory. Finally, both films make use of frontal shots of the people as a collectivity positioned in different layers at the climax of the conflict between the owners of the means of production and the people.

Two important innovations of *Macuro* stand out: *Macuro*'s conflict, in contrast to that portrayed in *Redes*, is not circumscribed to the national framework, as the cement factory in the film belongs to a global corporation. This is metaphorically staged by framing the ship and the fisherman in a low-angle shot that makes the fisherman appear defenseless against the mighty corporation. Furthermore, the ethnicity and gender identities of the participants in the struggle in *Macuro* are more varied than in *Redes*, which demonstrates the conscious efforts toward social extension in the newer phase of socially-committed filmmaking that FVC represents (see Figures 4.1, 4.2, 4.3.).

New Genres

As mentioned previously, both *Libertador Morales* and *Macuro* adopt conventional modes of narration, most notably character-driven linear narratives with an Aristotelian tripartite narrative structure (exposition-conflict-denouement). In addition to the similarities and differences with NLAC noted above, their apparent formal simplicity sets them clearly apart from the left-leaning NLAC cinematic practices. From the perspective of a middle-class viewer that appreciates NLAC or the elliptical narratives of much of modern cinema endorsed at international film festivals (e.g., Lucrecia Martel's or Carlos

Figure 4.1 The Unity of the People in the Local Struggle. *Source: Redes.*

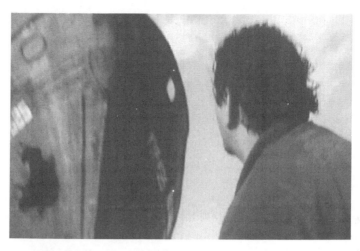

Figure 4.2 Locals Against Large Corporations. *Source: Macuro.*

Figure 4.3 Social Extension Visible on the Screen. *Source: Macuro.*

Reygadas' films), the scripts of *Libertador Morales* and *Macuro* might seem too dialogic and out of pace with developments in World Cinema. In these FVC films, everything is fully explained and nothing left to the viewers' imagination.

However, the apparent clear differentiation in *Libertador Morales* between good and evil typical of melodrama (at least of melodramas like *Nosotros, los pobres*, though perhaps not Chalbaud's melodramas) becomes more complex on closer examination. *Libertador Morales* hybridizes three genres (melodrama, farce and action hero film) in which the ethical axis of "good versus evil" is essential. The revalorization of melodrama (one of the major Latin American film genres) as a genre, a cinematic style and a sensibility in film scholarship in recent decades[42] opens up the possibility of seeing the motto "speak simply so that the people understand" in a more positive light than its presentation in Rocha's manifesto might lead us to think. Some examples of generic traits in the films will be presented before discussing the possible implications of this choice of form.

Two subplots led by the main character can be distinguished in *Libertador Morales*, as in the classical narrative cinema of Hollywood: the first plot concerns the social theme of public criminality whereas the second deals with the romantic relationship between Libertador and Daisy, who in turn also have to cope with bereavement and chronic illness in their families respectively. They are intertwined so that "the private affair merges with the social—or political—immediate."[43] By reinforcing meaning, the music clearly differentiates the subplots and guides the viewer through them. Generally, the music in the subplot relating to family relationships corresponds to its typical use in melodrama, that is, the music is there to provoke or intensify emotions, an effect reinforced by the mise en scène. One of the scenes that best exemplifies this is when Libertador captures a criminal who turns out to be his son. Referring to his mother's death, the son calls Libertador a coward, but Libertador sends him to jail for the crime regardless. At this point, the strains of violins burst into song to express the father's feelings of impotence and his sense of failure; Libertador drops down to the ground in a world-weary posture (Figure 4.4). At other times the music switches to a farcical mode to reflect a change in mood, for instance in the scene when the Police Chief is going to meet a buxom newsstand owner and also when three members of Chaparro's gang members break into a watch shop. At this moment, we can see the crude characterization of the three thieves, who are reduced to puppet shadows (Figure 4.5).

The people in *Libertador Morales* "return" to film in a formulaic form that is essentially tied to generic conventions. Characterization in this comedy in general follows Eisensteinian typage, as evidenced in a scene of a community meeting, where in attendance are the comical types of the two thieves, the Police Chief, Libertador, "the good pregnant wife," "the outspoken Bolivarian," and "the honest and hard-working couple" of Portuguese origin.[44] All of these characters are shown in medium and close-up shots which amplify the crooked gestures of "the bad ones," the false look of the Police Chief, and the honest and innocent looks of the residents, all of which produces either a comical or exaggerated impression. The use of shot-reverse shot technique expresses the antagonism between "good" and "evil" in a conventional form.

Figure 4.4 Melodramatic Mode. *Source: Libertador Morales, el Justiciero.*

Figure 4.5 Crime as Farce. *Source: Libertador Morales, el Justiciero.*

The hybridity of genres in the film is also evident in the use of colors, costumes, and lighting. The predominant use of high-key lighting and bright colors is contrasted with low-key lighting indoors at certain moments that take on a darker tone (the collusion between Police Chief Linares and the thieves is emphasized by the use of low-key lighting and ochre, for example), but generally the use of color and outdoor spaces produce an optimistic outlook throughout the film.

Concerning location and art direction, most of the film scenes are shot on location, but there is a mixture of real elements and murals and props arranged by the art director. Some of the murals and graffiti produce a sense of orderliness and perfection (a few were made specifically for the film), which contrast with the untidiness of some of the real graffiti also captured on screen like the ones seen when Libertador is chasing his son.[45] In sum, this is a feel-good movie that makes no use of social drama or social realism to present social problems and, in this sense, runs counter to the long (and excellent) Venezuelan tradition of "películas de barrio."

In trying to historicize literary genres (instead of simply explaining their meaning or describing them), Jameson has observed how the ethical axis of good and evil is an "ideologeme that articulates a social and historical contradiction."[46] An ideologeme is "a historically determinate conceptual or semic complex which can project itself variously in the form of a 'value system' or a 'philosophical concept,' or in the form of a protonarrative, a private or collective narrative fantasy."[47] The mixed genre chosen by Charalambidis projects on film the disjunctures and conflicts of contemporary Venezuelan ideological and socio-historical conjunctures at the levels of content and form.

Furthermore, both *Macuro* and *Libertador Morales* articulate a preoccupation with constructing a new humanity that is prevalent in Venezuelan society among supporters and detractors of the twenty-first socialist system implemented in the country since 1999. To be productive, the question of "propaganda" raised in some of the reviews of FVC seen above must be tackled from the perspective of its formal configuration. Jabes' *Macuro* is more appropriate than *Libertador Morales* for this discussion because of its political nature. Siegfried Kracauer differentiates the Nazi propaganda from the propaganda of democracies in that the aim of the former is to "suppress the faculty of understanding" whereas the latter's aim is to "appeal to the understanding of its audiences"; undemocratic propaganda films function "to impress people rather than instruct them."[48] *Macuro*'s plot is a fictionalization of an event and presents this event in a non-emotionally manipulative fashion. The focus of the narrative lies on the process by which we "become aware" of the characters: decisions are constantly discussed, the characters have doubts, different views are respected (except for the antagonist of the people, the manager, moved by irrationality), and not every aspect of the film is as straightforward as it might be implied in the term "propaganda." At the formal level, there is an interesting contradiction that will be revealed as follows.

The subtitle of the film—*The Strength of a People*—is reminiscent of intertitles in the political documentary *La batalla de Chile* (*The Battle of* Chile,

Patricio Guzmán, 1975–1979) like "Popular Power" or "The Fight of an Unarmed People"; however, as seen above, FVC fiction features and NLAC features (to which Guzmán's film belongs) are formally distant. *Macuro* is more reminiscent of Sergei Eisenstein's political cinema. Direct references to *Battleship Potemkin* (1925), for instance, are the images of the members of a repressive state apparatus lined up against the people, and the attack of the police against the weakest demonstrator (the mentally challenged Aeroplano) remind us of the attacks against a child and his mother in both *Battleship Potemkin* and *Strike* (1924). The fragmentation of demonstrators' and policemen's bodies and the dialectical montage of medium shots and medium close-up shots with a tempo in crescendo which Eisenstein had devised are employed by Jabes to visually convey the conflict and the high emotional tone of the scene. *Macuro*'s cinematography contains Eisensteinian dialectical techniques as well which contrapose camera angles and movements along the vertical, diagonal, and horizontal axes.

However, *Macuro*'s cinematographic techniques are not exhausted with these Eisensteinian devices. Visually, images of Christopher Columbus and the sea are imbued with a different dynamic than the one suggested by the dialectical montage techniques observed above. The motif of Christopher Columbus' statue occupies a prominent position in the film, appearing near the beginning of the film and reappearing toward the end as the conflict between the villagers and the factory manager is about to start. The explicative intertitles, which appear at the beginning of the film and limit our capacity to play an active role in the viewing experience, proclaim that Columbus first set foot on that land more than 500 years ago. The version of the statue (of which there are many throughout Spain and Latin America) is the one pointing to the "New World," that is, Macuro itself. The second time we see the statue, the background is sombre in tone, as the conflict between the factory and village representatives has come to a climax.

Other motifs that help realize Jabes' vision are the long shots of the pontoon and of floating fishing boats that function more as perception-images (Deleuze) than conventional establishing shots. The initial and final images of the film are almost identical (long shots of the pontoon), except for the fact that at the beginning, our impression of the scenery is a placid one and the non-diegetic music in the background reinforces this effect. The diegetic sound of the breeze mixed in with the music is placid too. At the end, however, when the image of the pontoon reappears, there is no music; we can only hear the breeze, which intensifies, and with it the sound of thunder. At the end, the mad youngster Aeroplano who had appeared at the beginning of the film basking in the sun while wishing that he could fly can no longer contemplate the tranquil scenery because he has fallen victim to the violence generated during the confrontation between the villagers and the police.

Images of fishing boats are strategically positioned to allow for a reflection of the flow of events. The camera panning over the vessels seems to be questioning the possibility of a self-sufficient world where there is no need to venture overseas. The perception-images of the pontoon, the floating boats, and the empty streets contrast markedly with the action-images of the violent confrontation. Extrapolating the possible audience responses motivated by these motifs to the national context, these images might elicit questions about various official initiatives in the field of international relations, including the Venezuelan initiative to construct Pan-American organizations outside the influence of the United States and Canada such as CELAC, ALBA, and UNASUR, the diplomatic tensions between the United States and Venezuela, and the strengthening of relations between Venezuela and China.

In sum, the aesthetics of *Libertador Morales* and *Macuro* are not as simple as they seem at first sight. More importantly, these films signify an attempt at creating a new visual language for a twenty-first socialist cinema. *Macuro*'s innovation toward this aim mainly resides in the combination of two seemingly contradictory functions: a combative camera and an observational camera. *Libertador Morales*' hybrid genre ("farcical action melodrama") constitutes an ideologeme apt for the convulsive situation of one of the most socially polarized countries in Latin America. Thus, the message that seemed so transparent at the narrative level becomes problematized at a visual level, although this formal complexity is far from that of the most radical NLAC experiments and would probably fit into what Rocha regarded as a populist "disrespect for the audience" (feeding the public with simple and obvious narratives as if the uneducated masses were incapable of understanding formally complex works).[49] Although distant from NLAC radical innovations, these films follow in the footsteps of NLAC in their principles and strategies for distribution and exhibition, which will be described in the next section.

COMMUNITY ENGAGEMENT: CIRCULATION OF STATE-FUNDED VENEZUELAN FILMS AND AUDIOVISUAL EDUCATION

FVC films have become closer to NLAC in modes of circulation. The former productions are not mainly conceived as entertainment of the masses (First Cinema in Third Cinema theory) or art for art's sake typical of urban middle-class viewers (Second Cinema). *Macuro* addresses the underprivileged sectors of Venezuela—rural and urban—while *Libertador Morales* focuses on the urban working class and the lower-middle-class community, including the migrants of European descent that the director is very familiar with (her Greek parents emigrated to Venezuela in the 1950s and ran a hardware store in the Caracas central area of El Silencio) (*La clase*, in chapter 1, aimed mainly at an underprivileged audience from the urban barrios).[50]

NLAC aspired to engage the audience in social transformation by transforming dominant exhibition and distribution patterns. The Cuban strategy described in the documentary *Por primera vez* (*For the First Time*, Octavio Cortázar, Cuba, 1967) is an optimal example of this line of action. The Cuban documentary describes a successful initiative to bring cinema to communities in Cuba where the population had never seen a film projection. Thanks to a sustained systematic effort to provide audiovisual education to the general population, Cuban audiences are sophisticated viewers and they are still enthusiastic about cinema. During film festivals in Cuba, long queues line up to watch films of all kinds, from auteur cinema to commercial features, and due to Cuba's socio-economic situation, audiences are not segregated according to class.

Similarly, *Libertador Morales* and *Macuro* were exhibited in four kinds of venues: commercial cinemas, the network of cinemas of Cinemateca Nacional 'the National Film Archive,' community centers, and (national) film festivals like the *Festival de Cine Latinoamericano y Caribeño de Margarita* (Margarita's Festival of Latin American and Caribbean Cinema). When I visited Margarita in 2009, temporary canopies were set up as exhibition venues in addition to the main theatre. What caught my attention the most was the wide variety of audiences that were drawn to the festival: among the public, composed mainly of the middle-class audience, there were also rambunctious, underprivileged kids from the barrios. For these youths, this was probably the first time that they had gone to a film festival, let alone watched films whose ethics and aesthetics differed immensely from those of *Secuestro express* and *Cidade de Deus*.

In fact, such a dynamic is often observed in Venezuelan cultural and official events where members from underprivileged groups are in general welcome. During the Margarita Festival, organizers of community cinema participating in the festival regaled me with anecdotes about their Sunday community screenings for children, one of which I found to be illustrative of the spirit of these events and its people. Usually, the cinema theatre in a community in Margarita (Porlamar) is reserved for the children on the last day of the week, but one Sunday the cinema had been reserved for other purposes. The children were very disappointed and made enquiries about the decision, which they said deprived them of their "rights." This is the kind of spirit that *Macuro* and *Libertador Morales* embody: empower and inform the people.

The Bolivarian Government of Venezuela embraces cultural and audiovisual policies as a major component of twenty-first-century socialism. This is hardly surprising since socialism traditionally regards culture as essentially steeped in politics, as was the case in the Soviet Union and is still the case in

Cuba since the revolution of 1959, albeit in radically different incarnations. Among the measures that demonstrate the commitment of the Venezuelan Government to build a counter-hegemonic mediascape is the creation of the public TV station TeleSUR on January 24, 2005 (conceived as the new television of Latin America that runs counter to media conglomerates such as CNN, Univisión, BBC, TVE, and Deutsche Welle).[51] The suffix "SUR" in TeleSUR is used as "a geopolitical concept which promotes people's struggle for peace, self-determination, respect for human rights and social justice."[52]

Critics of the socialist government's audiovisual policies claim that freedom of speech has been gradually curtailed since 1999. One such case that generated public outrage was the rejection of RCTV's application for renewal of access to the public airwaves in 2007. RCTV is one of the channels that supported the *coup d'état* and went off the cable networks in 2010 for not complying with the Resorte Law. The contrast between TeleSUR and RCTV serves to hint at the type of alternative culture that the socialist Venezuelan government has been promoting since its inception. The success of RCTV's *telenovelas* (soap operas that have a wide viewership in Latin America) and the channel's emotional public appeal when it was taken down from the public airwaves in 2007 contrast with the number of TeleSUR programs dealing with political debate and education.[53]

To regulate the audiovisual sector, the Bolivarian Government of Venezuela unified under the Ministry of Popular Power for Culture the institutions devoted to audiovisual production and distribution in a platform called the *Plataforma del Cine y Medios Audiovisuales* (Cinema and Audiovisual Platform). This platform is made up of *Centro Nacional Autónomo de Cinematografía, Fundación Cinemateca Nacional, Fundación Villa del Cine, Distribuidora Nacional Amazonia Films*, and *Centro Nacional del Disco*. The first four are dedicated to film and audiovisual production. The *CNAC* (Autonomous National Centre of Cinematography) was created in 1994 and is the main institution of the platform. According to the Cinema Law of 2005 (Ley de la Cinematografía Nacional), the CNAC is in charge of designing film policies, keeping a registry of all film activities and products and administering FRONPROCINE, a fund to promote Venezuelan filmmaking.

FVC is the cultural flagship of the Bolivarian revolutionary project, as described in chapter 1. Its function is the integration of cinema and community interests. During its twelve years of existence, it has promoted community filmmaking and has enabled a number of first-time directors to produce their first features (such directors include Hernán Jabes, Efterpi Charalambidis, Charles Martínez, Andrés Eduardo Rodríguez, Luis Alejandro Rodríguez, and José Antonio Varela, among others). At the same time, veteran filmmakers like Román Chalbaud, César Bolívar, Luis Alberto Lamata, Fina Torres, and Carlos Azpúrua have benefited from FVC. In its first three years of existence (up to June 2009), this institution alone had produced more than twenty-three feature films and documentaries, and according to Pedro Calzadilla (the minister of Popular Power for Culture) the number of films produced per year is fourteen or fifteen.[54] This is no small figure given that between 1973 and 1993 an average of 8.3 films per year were released in Venezuela.[55]

Moreover, until 2016, it was usual for the release of a film produced by FVC to be postponed in order to ensure that there were few Venezuelan films competing at the national box-office. With some exceptions, there is general agreement about the unquestionable improvement in the Venezuelan film scene in terms of number of films produced since 2006, although this is not generally attributed to FVC. The institution's efforts to create a national film culture, to rescue the historical memory of the country and to produce quality films while promoting moral education through better technology, appropriate infrastructure and the nurturing of talent to carry out innovative national projects (as pledged on FVC's webpage[56]) are hardly acknowledged.

The mention of technological independence is not a minor matter since dependence on vital film technology from the West has proved highly damaging for some industries at times when it was deliberately denied by the United States for ideological reasons. The state distributor, Distribuidora Amazonia Films, was created with the aim of diversifying distribution (according to filmmaker Luis Alberto Lamata, distribution and exhibition in Venezuela are in the same hands). Distribution is one of the major challenges for Venezuelan (and Latin American) cinema. José Antonio Varela, the director of FVC between 2010 and 2014, remarked in an interview at the 8th edition of the Festival of Poor Cinema in Havana in 2010 that "the weakest element of our cinema, not only in Venezuela but in the whole region and even in the whole South of the world is the distribution."[57] To transform this hegemonic system, the Law of 2005, building upon the Law of 1993—a historical law pushed by filmmakers that was passed despite American interference[58]—made compulsory the promotion and exhibition of Venezuelan cinema[59] and also set screen quotas for distributors.[60] This law ensures relative independence of non-FVC productions since the projects are selected by representatives from all sectors of the filmmaking community.

Policies for Audiovisual Circulation and Education

As in other matters, opinions on strategies for the circulation of films and the promotion of audiovisual education are divided in contemporary Venezuela. Opposing strategies for the development of the sector could be summarized in protection of individual private initiatives versus cooperatives. The founder of the private school ESCINETV (Escuela de Cine y Televisión) María

Cristina Capriles would be a defender of the former model whereas the director of the school COTRAIN (Comunidad de Trabajo e Investigación, founded the same year as ESCINETV and also still active as far as the crisis allows it), Liliane Blaser, would defend the latter.[61]

In terms of circulation, Venezuelan audiovisual representatives regularly promote Venezuelan films in national and international film festivals and nominate films for the Oscars, and CNAC-funded features have gained impressive international critical acclaim in recent years. This success contrasts with the lack of attention that Venezuelan cinema has received in scholarly publications and professional magazines. The size and stage of development of Venezuelan cinema is not comparable to that of the three major industries in Latin America, but this might not be the only reason for this neglect. What I call "Venezuelan populist cinema" (of which *Macuro* and *Libertador Morales* are two examples) does not fit the politics and aesthetic preferences of most international film festivals—"never forget that film festivals have equally, over the years, been political sites[,] [b]oth expressions of the political and battlegrounds of ideology."[62] Due to this inadequacy, the diversified exhibition strategies employed in the cases of *Macuro* and *Libertador Morales* seem to be the best option for the dissemination of films that constitute a viable alternative to dominant modes of filmmaking.

Libertador Morales is clearly part of an effort of the Venezuelan government to empower the excluded and semi-excluded masses of the population by increasing their literacy, cultural, and ethical levels and to ultimately change the society. The Gramscian notion of the need for ideology in the struggle to create a new socialist society underpins these efforts. Films like *La clase*, *Macuro*, and *Libertador Morales* obviously aim at promoting ethical values amongst the population. As to whether they have succeeded, "there is little evidence of a fundamental change in ethical values" in the Venezuelan society,[63] but as this chapter has shown, some elements of community may have left their mark on cinema audiences, however minor this might be.

CONCLUSION

From the analysis of both *Macuro* and *Libertador*, it is clear then that both directors have made aesthetic choices where explanation is preferred to intuition and classical narratives to counter-cinema. These aesthetic choices respond to the need to produce popular films that appeal to a broad spectrum of the population and recuperate the age-old pedagogic and didactic function of art repudiated in bourgeois aesthetics.[64] And the recuperation of the function of art to raise awareness among the exploited classes is related to broader socio-political changes in Venezuela, Brazil, and Argentina, as anthropologists Mario Sanoja Obediente and Iraida Vargas-Arenas have noted:

> It is not accidental that the main national objective of Presidents Chávez, Lula and Kirchner, as well as the Bolivian people exploited and despised by their oligarchs, is the battle against poverty and exclusion . . . . Neither is it accidental that, due to the inertia generated during the puntofijista political system, cultural policies are still designed to benefit a few, preventing the excluded sectors (the majority of the Venezuelan population) from becoming aware via culture-action of the class interests that unite them politically and recognize their common interests as exploited classes.[65]

The debate of the appropriate aesthetics for a culture-action that raises awareness of exploitation has a long tradition in Venezuela. Contemporary Venezuela is at a crossroads, and FVC has been adopting a new form of popular cinema in response to the new situation. In his *The Viewer's Dialectic,* Tomás Gutiérrez Alea, who believed that theoretical reflection was necessary for the advancement of filmmaking, distinguished two possible meanings of "popular" cinema. The first is based on a quantitative criterion: popular cinema would be the cinema that is accepted, enjoyed, and viewed by many people; the second would reflect the cinema which "expresses the people's most profound and authentic interests and responds to those interests" and aims at "transforming reality and bettering humankind,"[66] an option that challenges (and respects, in Rocha's terms) the viewer, as we have seen. The films by Charalambidis and Jabes examined here represent a populist materialization of popular cinema which rejects radical formal innovations while retaining the aim to critically engage with the audience. Regarding the representation of social classes, in both cases the upper and upper-middle classes are either absent or evil, but the representation of the lower-middle class, the working class and the underprivileged is nuanced, and the latter classes are portrayed as agents of social transformation.

NOTES

1. Two attempts to describe the cultural turn associated to the Turn-to-the-Left show that this subfield of study is in need of more investigation. See Marc Zimmerman and Luis Ochoa Bilbao, eds., *Giros culturales en la marea rosa de América Latina* (Puebla: LACASA, 2012); Mabel Moraña, ed., *Cultura y cambio social en América Latina* (Madrid: Iberoamericana; Vervuert, 2008).

2. This term is often applied by intellectuals justifying the need to create new audiovisual imaginaries and media outlets suitable for new socialist programs. Two of the most prominent intellectuals associated to it are Ignacio Ramonet and Luis

Britto. See Luis Britto García, *Dictadura mediática en Venezuela. Investigación de unos medios por encima de toda sospecha* (Caracas: Ediciones Correo del Orinoco, 2012).

3. The Introduction to this volume discusses this question in detail. Gonzalo Aguilar claims that Argentine cinema (the country where the landmark *La hora de los hornos* was directed by Solanas and Getino in 1968) has reached a point "más allá del pueblo," (beyond 'the people'), but this stage is obviously not over in other Latin American cinemas. Gonzalo Aguilar, *Más allá del pueblo. Imágenes, indicios y políticas del cine* (Buenos Aires: Fondo de Cultura Económica, 2015).

4. Fredric Jameson, *Postmodernism or the Cultural Logic of Late Capitalism* (Durham: Duke University Press, 1991), 54–55.

5. See, for instance, Silvio Waisbord, "Media Populism: Neo-Populism in Latin America," in *The Media and Neo-Populism. A Contemporary Comparative Analysis*, eds. Gianpietro Mazzoleni, Bruce Horsfield, and Julianne Stewart (Westport: Praeger, 2003), 197–216; Ryan Brading, *Populism in Venezuela* (London: Routledge, 2013), 8; Luis Britto García, *El imperio contracultural: del rock a la postmodernidad* (La Habana: Editorial Arte y Cultura, 2005), 54.

6. García, *El imperio contracultural*, 54–55.

7. García, *El imperio contracultural*, 55.

8. Williams, *Marxism and Literature*, 153.

9. Britto supports the Bolivarian government and probably rejects the endless qualification of 'populist' to Bolivarian governments.

10. Ernesto Laclau, *On Populist Reason* (London: Verso, 2005), 11.

11. Laclau, *On Populist Reason*, 72–73.

12. Laclau, *On Populist Reason*, 73–74.

13. Luis Duno-Gottberg, "Social Images of Anti-Apocalypse: Bikers and the Representation of Popular Politics in Venezuela," *A contra corriente* 6, no. 2 (2009): 147.

14. Steve Ellner, "Venezuela's Social-Based Democratic Model: Innovations and Limitations," *Journal of Latin American Studies* 43 (2011): 428.

15. Duno-Gottberg, "Social Images of Anti-Apocalypse," 163.

16. Michael Chanan, ed., *Twenty-Five Years of the New Latin American Cinema* (London: BFI, 1983), 15.

17. The priest José María Korta could have inspired this fictional character. In life, Korta welcomed the improvement of the legal framework to enable indigenous people to become a juridical body but criticized the Bolivarian government for its contradictions in the implementation of measures aimed at the improvement in the status of the indigenous. José María Korta, "Pronunciamiento del Padre Korta sobre los recientes asesinatos de los yupka," *Aporrea*, June 28, 2012; Jorge Arreaza, "Carta pública ante la desaparición física de el Hermano José María Korta Lasarte," *Aporrea*, July 12, 2013.

18. Slavoj Žižek, *In Defense of Lost Causes* (London: Verso, 2008), 64.

19. Bill Fletcher Jr., "Right-Wing Populism: The Herpes in the System of Racial Capitalism," How Class Works Conference. Address (SUNY-Stonybrook, June 4, 2010).

20. Ellner, "Venezuela's Social-Based Democratic Model," 421–49.

21. Raymond Williams, "A Lecture on Realism," *Screen* 18, no. 1 (1977): 61–74.

22. Juan Luis Mejía Arango, "Apuntes sobre las políticas culturales en América Latina, 1987–2009," *Pensamiento Iberoamericano* 4, 2ª etapa, no. 1 (2009): 105–30.

23. Alfonso Molina, "Un héroe de la justicia popular," *Ideas de Babel*, August 7, 2009.

24. The title of the feature produced in 2018, *Qué buena broma, Bromelia*, points to a continuation of the generic choice made in her previous feature.

25. Chanan ed., *Twenty-Five Years of the New Latin American Cinema*, 15.

26. Robert Stam and Lúcia Nagib use this translation for the film *Deus e o diabo na terra do sol* instead of the usual *Black God, White Devil*. For the justification of this translation, see Robert Stam and Louise Spence, "Colonialism, Racism and Representation. An Introduction," *Screen* 24, no. 2 (1983): 2–20.

27. Lúcia Nagib, *World Cinema and the Ethics of Realism* (New York: Continuum, 2011), 58.

28. Chanan, *Cuban Cinema*, 13.

29. Noah Zweig, "Villa Del Cine (Cinema City): Constructing Bolivarian Citizens for the Twenty-First Century," *Situations* 4, no. 1 (2011): 146.

30. Juan Forero, "Venezuelan Film Studio Tries to Counter Hollywood: Populist Government Dives Headfirst into Movie Business," *The Washington Post*, October 7, 2007.

31. Libia Villazana, "De una política cultural a una cultura politizada: La República Bolivariana de Venezuela y su revolución cultural en el sector audiovisual," in *E Pluribus Unum? National and Transnational Identities in the Americas = Identidades nacionales y transnacionales en las Américas*, edited by Josef Raab and Sebastian Thies (Münster: LIT; Tempe, 2008), 167.

32. Gonzalo Chacón Mora, "Imagining the Malandro: Anti-Politics and the Representation of the Malandro in Venezuelan Cinema," Proc. of the Conference on The Aesthetics of Politics and the Politics of Aesthetics in Contemporary Venezuela, Centre of Latin American Studies, Venezuela Research Network, University of Cambridge, September 19–20, 2014.

33. This particular part of her chapter refers to ALBA-TCP's cultural project, but FVC is presented in this text as "founded with similar ideological tenets." Libia Villazana, "The Politics of the Audiovisual Cultural Revolution in Latin America and the Caribbean," in *Counter-Globalization and Socialism in the 21st Century: The Bolivarian Alliance for the Peoples of Our America*, ed. Thomas Mur (New York: Routledge, 2013), 190–91.

34. In any case, this is not the main purpose of Villazana's study and other aspects of her article are nevertheless very useful for the study of this cinema.

35. Zweig, "Villa Del Cine (Cinema City)," 147.

36. Zweig, "Villa Del Cine (Cinema City)," 142.

37. Gilles Deleuze, *Cinema 2: The Time-Image* (London: Continuum, 2005), 210. Here, Deleuze quotes Roberto Schwarz's definition of "tropicalism."

38. Deleuze, *Cinema 2*, 211, 214.

39. Gonzalo Aguilar, *New Argentine Film: Other Worlds* (New York: Palgrave Macmillan, 2008), 125–26.

40. Mabel Moraña, ed. *Cultura y cambio social en América Latina* (Madrid: Iberoamericana; Vervuert, 2008).

41. Roberto Kolb-Neuhaus, "Silvestre Revueltas's *Redes*: Composing for Film or Filming for Music?," *The Journal of Film Music* 2, nos. 2–4 (2009): 127.

42. John Mercer and Martin Shingler, *Melodrama: Genre, Style, Sensibility* (London: Wallflower, 2004).

43. Deleuze, *Cinema 2*, 210.

44. This fictional meeting reflects the creation of government-financed community councils in April 2006 that were enabled by the Law of Community Councils, a law aimed at promoting the participation of community councils in decision-making processes. The idea was intended as a practical measure to promote participatory democracy, but the lack of control in the use of public finances and poor organizational skills of its members led to a high failure rate. See Ellner, "Venezuela's Social-Based Democratic Model."

45. Sujatha Fernandes offers an analysis of the use of graffiti in the last decade in Venezuela: *Who Can Stop the Drums? Urban Social Movements in Chávez's Venezuela* (Durham: Duke University Press, 2010).

46. Jameson, *The Political Unconscious*, 96.

47. Jameson, *The Political Unconscious*, 102. For instance, the ideologemes of History and Nature appear in *La casa de auga* (Jacobo Penzo, Venezuela, 1983) in the narrative forms of political persecution and leprosy. For more on this example, read Fredric Jameson's "On Magic Realism in Film." *Critical Inquiry* 12, no. 2 (1986): 301–25.

48. Siegfried Kracauer, *From Caligari to Hitler: A Psychological History of the German Film* (Princeton: Princeton University Press, 2004), 278.

49. Glauber Rocha, "Down with Populism!," in *Twenty-five Years of The New Latin American Cinema*, ed. Michael Chanan (London: BFI and Channel Four, 1983).

50. The diversity of the target audiences of these three films fully funded by the current Venezuelan government lends support to the claim that Chavistas are not only "young, poor, politically unsophisticated, antidemocratic masses that prefer political violence to democratic and constitutional processes," which is how they are usually "mischaracterized by the media, the opposition, and some academic analysts." Cristóbal Valencia Ramírez, "Venezuela's Bolivarian Revolution: Who Are the Chavistas?," *Latin American Perspectives* 32, no. 3 (2005): 80–81.

51. "TeleSUR." *EcuRed*. N.d.

52. TeleSUR, "Acerca: SUR," http://www.telesurtv.net/pages/sobrenosotros.html.

53. On November 21, 2007, RCTV posted a video on their webpage where some broadcasters sang the melodramatic song "Un corazón que grita" "A heart that screams" as a farewell and appeal to their followers. The emotional tone of the farewell message is symptomatic of the vision of the company with regard to their audience, which contrasts markedly with the aim of raising the critical thinking skills of its audience. http://www.rctv.net/.

54. Statistics provided in CNAC bulletin n. 71, October 2011.

55. José Miguel Acosta, et al., *Panorama histórico del cine en Venezuela* (Caracas: Fundación Cinemateca Nacional, 1997), 52.

56. "Villa del Cine: Quiénes somos." Villa del Cine. N.d. http://www.villadelcine. gob.ve/index.php/quienes-somos/sobre-la-villa.

57. "José Antonio Varela. Presidente de la Fundación Villa del Cine (Venezuela). Parte 1." Interview. *Cubainformación TV*, April 2010. Video.

58. Getino, Octavio Getino, *Cine iberoamericano. Los desafíos del nuevo siglo* (Buenos Aires: CICCUS, 2007), 32.

59. Article 27. "Exhibitors must screen in all their cinema theatres non-propagandistic or non-commercial shorts recently premiered in Venezuela. The trailers of national and international films and audiovisual productions which are about to be released must also be advertised. Similarly, they must show national newsreels programmes." Article 30. "All Venezuelan films will be guaranteed their release. In order to give preference to Venezuelan films, a minimum screening quota will be established, which will vary annually. This applies to Venezuelan films prepared to be released."

60. Article 31. "Individuals or companies dedicated to film distribution in the national territory, must distribute a minimum of 20% of Venezuelan films, of the total number of films to be distributed in each fiscal year."

61. See María Cristina Capriles, "La investigación y la formación cinematográfica en Venezuela insertas en el sistema educativo venezolano," II Simposio de Investigación y Formación Cinematográfica, CNAC, Centro Nacional Autónomo de Cinematografía (Caracas. July 27–29, 2012) for more on Capriles' approach; and Liliane Blaser, "Instituto de formación cinematográfica Cotrain: Diez años aprendiendo a enseñar" *Objeto Visual* 4 (1997); 9–15, for more on Blaser's film activism.

62. Ruby B. Rich, "Why Do Film Festivals Matter? (2003–2004)," *The Film Festival Reader*, ed. Dina Iordanova (St Andrews: St Andrews Film Studies, 2013), 158.

63. Ellner, "Venezuela's Social-Based Democratic Model," 433.

64. Fredric Jameson, "Postmodernism, or the Cultural Logic of Late Capitalism," *NLR* 146 (1984): 89.

65. Mario Sanoja Obediente and Iraida Vargas-Arenas, *La revolución bolivariana. Historia, cultura y socialism* (Caracas: Monte Ávila Editores Latinoamericana C.A., 2008), 160.

66. Tomás Gutiérrez Alea, *The Viewer's Dialectic*. Part 1, trans. Julia Lesage, *Jump Cut* 29 (1984): 18–21.

Chapter 5

The Globalization of Class on Screen

Amat Escalante's "Engaged Visuality"

This chapter delves into cinematic figurations of a transnational or borderless class system[1] typical of neoliberal societies affected (or enriched) by migration. The largest groups of films on migration in the Americas belong to the Hispanic and Mexican cinemas. The second feature by the celebrated Mexican and global auteur Amat Escalante (*Los bastardos, The Bastards,* 2008) constitutes a unique contribution of the twenty first century to the branch of migration-themed films in Mexican cinema and can enlighten us in the way the tradition of representing migration and, with it, transformations in class figurations, has evolved in accordance to global filmmaking trends.

The migrants in this film belong to a group that Guy Standing has termed "the precariat." Standing presents this group as a "new" and "distinctive socioeconomic group" resulting from "a . . . fragmented global class structure," consisting of "[m]illions of people, in affluent and emerging market economies" who work in insecure conditions that do not correspond to those typical of the working class or "proletariat" ("workers in long-term, stable, fixed-hour jobs with established routes of advancement, subject to unionisation and collective agreements, with job titles their fathers and mothers would have understood, facing local employers whose names and features they were familiar with"). In contrast to these, "many entering the precariat would not know their employer or how many fellow employees they had or were likely to have in the future."[2] The term has been questioned by "old-time Marxists" (in Standing's terminology), to which he responds that the precariat is not a class ("Precariousness . . . is more than a 'social condition.' A social condition cannot act. Only a social group with common or compatible aims can do that. . . .").[3]

Although the term "precariat" is felicitous (and for this reason I use it here to designate the class of proletarians that have seen their labor rights considerably curtailed in the last few decades), its definition is not, as it seems that Standing is trying to re-invent the Marxist wheel while contradictorily attempting to distance himself entirely from an "old-time" Marxism. The discussion of this new term falls out of the scope of this book, but I must note that this confusion about class and its concomitant rejection of Marxism resonates with other attitudes described in parts of this volume.

Nobel Prize winner in economics Joseph Stiglitz highlights transportation and communication and the flows that they facilitate as defining character-istics of globalization;[4] this is in the same vein as professor in media and culture Arjun Appadurai, who defines globalization as "a cover term for a world of disjunctive flows." According to Appadurai, these flows are disjunc-tive because they follow different speeds and directions, and the relations between "objects in motion" such as migrants, hackers, street gangs, and commodities are problematic and frictional.[5] Both Stiglitz and Appadurai are concerned with the destructive power of globalization if it only ends up serving the powerful rather than producing a more equitable world, and both scholars consider their academic and non-academic works as interventions toward harnessing the possible beneficial forces of globalization (Appadurai, for instance, speaks of a "globalization from below," a mode of globalization which empowers the disenfranchised).

The filmmaker in focus in this section also intervenes in this global discus-sion through visual means and forms part of the relation between economics and culture that Appadurai contemplates in discussions on globalization. Appadurai's approach falls within a broader interest in the figurations of cur-rent socio-economic changes embedded in cultural objects in the sense that, for the scholar, it is via a perspective "from below" that culture becomes not the typical counterpoint of economics, but the site of imagination where the poor can develop "the capacity to aspire." In answer to the question of "why culture matters for development and for the reduction of poverty," Appadurai states: "[I]t is in culture that ideas of the future, as much as those about the past, are embedded and nurtured."[6]

GLOBALIZATION AND TRANSNATIONALISM

Globalization is not simply a thematic concern of the films studied in this and the following chapter but is embedded in the films' mode of production. Both the terms "transnationalism" and "globalization" have been critiqued. The term "globalization" is applied to the study of social processes such as migra-tion and cinema, and scholars in various fields have observed limitations in its usage. Some social science scholars have critiqued common celebratory narratives of globalization and free trade agreements by noting the marked contrast between the easy flow of markets on the one hand, and the erection or reinforcement of walls and other types of barriers to prevent people from migrating freely across the world on the other.[7] In film studies, another type of criticism has been leveled against the term globalization, namely concerning its unproductive generalization, which is seen as a reason to prefer the concept "transnationalism" over "globalization" in film studies.[8]

Transnationalism in film studies has gained increasing currency in the last decade, as evidenced by the launching of a new journal devoted to transnationalism (*Transnational Cinemas*) by two Latin American film scholars in 2010, and more recently by the prominence given to a metacritical approach to transnationalism by Latin American film scholars in the 2014 Fall issue of *Cinema Journal*, a sign of both the maturity of the approach and its continued currency.[9] Four years earlier, Will Higbee and Song Hwee Lim had already shown dissatisfaction with the most common uses of the term "transnationalism" up to 2010 because of what they interpreted as either an inability of the term to account for power imbalances in transnational connections (typical of celebratory transnationalism narratives), or its inapplicability to cinemas other than diasporic or postcolonial cinemas developed in the interstices of the nation. To address these shortcomings, Higbee and Lim proposed the term "critical transnationalism," a practice that serves not only to highlight the effects that transnational connections produce, but also to describe them, retain the relevance of the national within a transnational approach,[10] and address a group of films which, according to these scholars, has hitherto been neglected within the transnational research framework: art-house films. One of the three major theorizations of transnationalism that these two scholars attempt to improve with their proposal of critical transnationalism (namely Sheldon Lu's theory of "transnational Chinese cinemas") does, however, address film art.

By funding their production through transnational capital and distributing the films within the international film market, all the films studied in this chapter and the following one fit Lu's definition of transnational cinemas.[11] Nevertheless, as migration and trade are often studied in tandem with globalization, and because the thematic concern with global processes affecting class figurations stands in the foreground of the methodology employed here, I retain globalization as the main perspective while bearing in mind that the conditions of these films' production modes are embedded in their narratives.[12]

GLOBALIZATION AND NEOLIBERALISM

Neoliberalism is "in the first instance a theory of political economic practices that proposes that human well-being can best be advanced by liberating individual entrepreneurial freedoms and skills within an institutional framework characterized by strong private property rights, free markets, and free trade,"[13] or, in a more critical tone, "a vision of society in which competition for wealth is the only recognized value and virtually all decisions are left to unregulated markets."[14] In contrast, globalization has a broader application in fields other than political economy such as migration, social networks, culture, and so on. Jyostna Kapur and Keith Wagner embrace neoliberalism instead of globalization for their study because "the former term identifies a history, structure, and a set of relations—that is, free market capitalism" that can be studied within Marxist theory, whereas "globalism" mystifies this structure and the root causes of the predominant forms of social relations in our age as well as their cultural expressions.[15] In this chapter, the neoliberal agreement North American Free Trade Agreement (NAFTA)[16] plays a central role, but since my overarching study covers five national cinemas connecting two cultures and spaces in the world as distant as Asia and Latin America, the term "global," which contains a spatial connotation lacking in the term neoliberalism, gains prominence in this section, and for this reason I have chosen to look at class struggle "through the prism of globalization."

CLASS STRUGGLE REVISITED THROUGH THE PRISM OF GLOBALIZATION: AMAT ESCALANTE'S "ENGAGED VISUALITY"

The Mexican director, producer, and screenwriter Amat Escalante has reached the status of world auteur and, as such, his works are often showcased at international film festivals familiar with the work of filmmakers like Carlos Reygadas (México), Pablo Trapero, Lucrecia Martel and Lisandro Alonso (Argentina), Walter Salles and Fernando Meirelles (Brazil), Jia Zhangke (People's Republic of China, PRC), and Nuri Bilge Ceylan (Turkey), directors whose films prominently feature class conflicts. Escalante's films invariably stage the tension between the local and the global in distinctly Mexican situations and are firmly located in Guanajuato, a focus that links him to Jia Zhangke but distinguishes him from Carlos Reygadas, the associate producer of all his feature films. Although Escalante has also worked on Reygadas' films as an assistant director, Reygadas' films often contain narratives that would not typically be associated with a Mexican imaginary to the same extent that Escalante's are (see Reygadas' 2007 *Stellet Licht*, for instance). *Los bastardos* is part of a film trilogy: *Sangre* (*Blood*, 2005)-*Los bastardos* (2008)-*Heli* (2013). Though Escalante did not originally conceive them as such, he concedes that all three features share a common concern with the consequences of globalization. *Los bastardos* is an indictment of the effects of economic neoliberalization on Mexicans and, specifically, on the effects of the NAFTA, which since its inception in January 1994 has resulted in increasing numbers of undocumented (and thus unprotected) laborers, deteriorating working conditions for the Mexican population, and a subsequent disruption of the well-being of some middle-class communities in the United States.

Los bastardos revolves around two undocumented Mexicans (Jesús and Fausto, played by Jesús Moisés Rodríguez and Rubén Sosa) who find casual work as construction workers, contract killers, and farm hands in Los Angeles. The man who hires them to murder his middle-aged wife never appears on screen, but his wife is one of the main characters. Karen (Nina Zavarin) is separated from her husband and alienated from her uncommunicative teenage son, and uses drugs to relieve her feelings of frustration and solitude. Before being shot, Karen surprisingly shares some intimate moments at home with the migrants, particularly with Jesús (they watch TV, have bizarre sex, and take drugs together), until the youngest (Fausto), fearing that Jesús will be unable to kill the woman, decides that the moment has come to kill her himself. When Karen's son returns home and finds the Mexicans there, he kills Jesús. Fausto manages to escape and later continues to work in the United States as a day laborer on a farm.

All of Escalante's films are inscribed within a Mexican cinematic history of representation of violence, although they are also imbued with a large dose of humour that is perhaps foreign to an international audience. In *Los bastardos*, different types of violence pervade US society. The structural violence of the class struggle between the precariat and the middle classes is foregrounded in different forms and contexts, more prominently the exploitation of migrants by middle-class employers, the clash between migrants and the use of migrants to indirectly perform gender-based violence. I will explore them in this order in the following analysis.

COLLECTIVITY VERSUS MULTIPLICITY

The middle classes in the United States are relentlessly portrayed as exploitative in this film. The employers that these undocumented migrants encounter are exploitative: they offer the migrants miniscule wages, target Latin Americans for sex, bargain ruthlessly and try to trick them whenever possible, or even hire them to kill people. In contrast to the American classic film on Mexican migration to the US *El Norte* (Gregory Nava, 1983), where the American employers of both main characters were appreciative of the migrants' skills and were willing to compensate them with promotions and good working conditions according to their merits, Escalante points an accusatory finger at the American middle class.

The first scene where this is made obvious occurs when potential employers visit undocumented day laborers waiting to be hired at an industrial area. To kill time, the laborers amuse themselves with stories of past work experiences, like being unknowingly hired to work as sex workers. A middle-aged man then appears and offers them US $8 an hour for construction work, but the migrants demand a minimum of US $10. They agree on US $10 and a ride back to the place where they were picked up. While on their way, the employer tries to establish a friendly conversation with the migrants, but the latter do not respond openly or simply choose to ignore him in a gesture that suggests that, even though the American employer and the Mexican workers are physically close, a Durkheimian social harmony is impossible. In contrast to Marx and Weber, who were "conflict theorists," "Durkheim believed that harmony, rather than conflict, defined society."[17] The construction of successive conflicts in different scenarios situates the film in a conflict-based view of society. When the group of migrants in *Los bastardos* finish their work, the employer returns to pay them and initially refuses to take them back to where he had picked them up—however, the migrants outnumber him and their body language silently expresses a resolute determination of a possible revolt. The tension of the situation forces the American employer to agree to bring them back. It is worth noting that the migrants are always framed nearest to the fourth wall when they talk to the employer (Figure 5.1), an aesthetic choice that tends to put the audience on the side of the migrants and their plight, although different audiences might react differently, as Lapsley and Westlake point out.[18] Likewise, when the employer appears and starts bargaining with the migrants to reduce their wages, he is shown right in front of the spectator at eye level, which also invites the audience to adopt the point of view of the migrants.

Figure 5.1   The Migrant Workers Positioned on the Viewer's Side. *Source: Los bastardos.*

The scene where the laborers demand that the American employer honor their agreement is worth comparing to another scene in a classic film about Mexican laborers demanding an improvement in their labor conditions titled *Salt of the Earth* (Herbert J. Biberman, US, 1954). The film is based on a real strike by mostly Mexican-American miners at the Empire Zinc mine in New Mexico in 1950. The miners and their families, particularly their wives, went on a strike for fifteen months and endured various attacks from their employers aimed at forcing them to return to work. In one of the scenes of the film, some policemen, enacting an eviction order, take possession of the personal belongings and the furniture of the two main characters, a miner and his wife Esperanza (a name which means "hope" in Spanish). As the policemen are about to confiscate the worker's personal property, mining families whose facial expressions indicate a determination to prevent the eviction from happening peacefully surround them. This scene is similar to the one in *Los bastardos* where the employer is deterred from abandoning the workers in a barren land by the demeanor of the workers described above, but the socio-historical context of the 2000s is starkly different from that of the 1950s.

Labor unions were strong back in the 1950s on both sides of the US-Mexican border. In fact, they were already active at the beginning of the twentieth century. Norman Caulfield describes how Mexican workers who opposed the Porfirio dictatorship and supported the Mexican Revolution of 1911 had by then "developed a myriad of ideologies, such as reform socialism, anarchism and syndicalism."[19] As early as 1906, during the Porfirian dictatorship, there was a strike at the Cananea mine in Mexico to demand equal pay for Mexicans and "Anglos" as well as better working conditions, similar demands to the ones presented in the 1950 strike of the Empire Zinc mine depicted in *Salt of the Earth*. It was a time when discrimination against Hispanics was rife. In 1917, the union leader José Rodríguez "rallied that American corporations and the United States government had made Mexican workers 'slaves.'"[20] In those times, there was a large group of literate workers who exhibited a high degree of worker consciousness. Unions on the side of the United States and Mexico also held an international outlook, but unions across the borders gradually started to adopt a more nationally oriented character.

During World War II and in the economic boom that followed the war in the United States, American unions allied with the US government to silence the most radical factions of the labor movement, a move that was replicated in Mexico. Caulfield explains that American unions, in a bid to exterminate radicalism, also collaborated with the US government to make the anarcho-syndicalist unions and leaders in Mexico gradually disappear throughout the first half of the twentieth century. One of this project's most infamous tactics was the implementation of the *charro* system in Mexican unions, consisting in the designation of a union leader who served the interests of the company rather than the workers. This process constitutes a case of US intervention in Mexico within the realm of the unions that fits in with the United States' use of Cold War tactics and their fight against communism in Latin America. The incredible efforts of the US government to ban *Salt of the Earth* in the United States are part of the same anti-Communist campaign at home. Despite the initial popularity of the film among groups from diverse spheres of the political spectrum when it was released in 1954, the US government successfully suppressed it and used it as a warning sign to any future creative endeavors following similar lines.[21]

In the 1970s, when the American economy was threatened by the rise of Japan and Europe as world economic powers, American businesses and the government pressed for free trade as a way to develop their economy. American unions accepted the free trade agenda dictated by the American government because it initially meant that Americans would have to produce more products to export, but now in the twenty-first-century companies are not always constrained by the nation-state and many industries in the United States have been dismantled. Companies are constantly in search of markets and cheap labor all around the globe, and the flow of capital invested in these companies, usually in the form of shares, force companies to constantly increase profits in order to keep attracting investors.

The NAFTA, signed in 1994, was a trial test of the global market, and the effects of the deregulation of markets and the weakening of unions within the framework of this neoliberal agreement have already had a profound effect in the United States and Mexico over the twenty years of its existence. Contemporary unions serve more the function of pressuring workers to accept the employers' terms so that companies do not relocate elsewhere rather than demanding better conditions for the workers and mediating with the employers to accept those conditions. Even worse, whether we accept the new terminology of "precariat" or maintain the term "working class," in the case of undocumented workers like Jesús and Fausto, these negotiations with the union are inapplicable.

Turning back to the scenes that stage conflict between employers and employees in *Los bastardos* and *Salt of the Earth*. In *Salt of the Earth*, after the workers form a united front to deter the police from taking away Esperanza's property, the camera pans over the "collective" surrounding her house and at the same time we hear Esperanza's inner thoughts about the success of the workers' struggle. The camera movement intensifies the sense of joy and success felt by the workers and visually conveys the message that it was not just the determination of a simple group of workers to fight the eviction that prevented the police from carrying out the orders, but the backing of the union and the fact that they all acted as a collectivity. Moreover, the fight would not have been won were it not for the support of the miners' wives.

Esperanza's last thoughts are dedicated to the future of the children, who, as the salt of the earth, must carry the responsibility of constructing a better future. This collectivity thus includes the workers as well as their relatives and friends (see Figure 5.2 & Figure 5.3).

Figure 5.2   The Camera Panning over the Collectivity. *Source*: *Salt of the Earth*.

Figure 5.3   Miners and their Relatives after Emerging Victorious from the Confrontation. *Source*: *Salt of the Earth*.

Unlike this community, the workers in *Los bastardos* are separated from their families, display no signs of knowing each other, and work in different places with different colleagues. The possibility of being replaced by others who are more in need is ever present. The unemployed form part of the capitalist system and are not outside it because they constitute the reserve army that capitalists can use to pressure the slave wage earners into accepting dire working conditions. The effects of the continuation of the implementation of neoliberal policies in Mexico through the NAFTA agreement have resulted in "economic failure by almost any economic or social indicator. This is true whether we compare Mexico to its developmentalist past, or even if the comparison is to the rest of Latin America since NAFTA."[22] The negative consequences of neoliberalism, which Caulfield, Stiglitz, Weisbrot, and Bacon[23] each individually show to be a direct effect of the NAFTA agreement, are palpable in *Los bastardos*. At the end of the film, after surviving the nightmarish experience at Karen's home, Fausto arrives at a large strawberry farm with other laborers, who are briefed on their working conditions and wages right before they start to work in the field. The image of the workers while they are being briefed represents not a collectivity but what Fredric Jameson calls a "multiplicity": "Only capitalism constitutes a social formation—that is an organized multiplicity of people—united by the absence of community, by separation and by individuality"[24] (see Figure 5.4). *Los bastardos'* pessimistic ending differs from *Salt of the Earth'*s optimistic final message. Though the film engages the audience with the precariat's plight through a mode that I will call "engaged visuality" later on, no alternatives or avenues for the development of a class consciousness that will lead to class struggle are offered at the film's narrative level.

CLASS AND GENDER

The most multilayered relationship in *Los bastardos* is none the less the one between Karen and Jesús. If the clash with the white employer described above specifically commented on class, then the encounter with Karen is a commentary on gender alongside class. Karen lives in a large house with a swimming pool located in a beautiful middle-class neighborhood, as perceived by Fausto when he and Jesús enter it at night. When Fausto and Jesús break into her house through a rear window, the woman's son has already left for a date with friends, leaving her to smoke crack on her sofa. When she discovers Jesús and Fausto in her living room, her initial reaction is fear, but then she gradually starts to accept the situation and even seems to revel in the company of the intruders. The men first demand food, then tell her to enter the swimming pool with them. Given Jesús' movements and gestures

Figure 5.4　A Multiplicity of Individuals Separated from their Relatives. *Source: Los bastardos.*

in the pool—he flaunts his penis behind her before entering the pool naked—the impression that is given is that he is about to rape her. At the beginning, Jesús takes pleasure in encircling Karen, an image that is contradictorily suggestive of a shark encircling its prey (suggestive of violent death and separation) and of a male animal following a courtship ritual (suggestive of love and union).

After a while, the three of them return to the living room where, instead of raping her, Jesús gives her pleasure by caressing her gently and using his tongue to stimulate her orally. This is one of the most subversive portrayals of intrusion of middle-class homes by lower-class characters. Fausto kneels down close to observe, his eyes fixated on Karen, but does not interfere in the act. At a moment tinged with intimacy and humour, Karen acknowledges Fausto's presence by offering him crack while Jesús has his face in her groin, but Fausto rejects the drug. In other parts of the film she mentions that her husband treats her like a slave, which implies that this experience was probably the first time that a partner derived more pleasure in making her happy than in using her to his advantage.

While Jesús is stimulating her, the camera slowly zooms in on Karen's face. The spectators can hear her breathe deeply and see her silently shedding tears, ambiguous gestures that make us have doubts about whether she is enjoying an orgasm and the effects of the crack she has been smoking or is just enduring the experience. At this intense moment when death is imminent, she is surrounded by Jesús and Fausto, undoubtedly names of religious and metaphysical significance. Even though Jesús (Jesus Christ, the leader, the son of God) was the one meant to kill her, it will be Fausto (Faust, "the one who summons the Devil" in a long literary and visual tradition) who finally performs the criminal act, and Jesús will die at the hands of Karen's son.

The allegory of a religious communion with Jesus Christ through sexual intercourse in the symbolic realm is likewise justified at the visual level. The minimalist style of Escalante is far from the magnificent and exuberant baroque style of Gian Lorenzo Bernini, but Karen's intense experience at this moment of truth in her life makes her adopt a position that resembles the famous 1645–52 depiction of the union of Spanish mystic and writer Saint Teresa of Avila (more commonly known in Spanish as Santa Teresa de Jesús) with God in Bernini's sculpture at Santa Maria della Vittoria, Rome. The perspective is similar in the film and the sculpture as well, and Karen's "ecstasy" is imbued with as much ambiguity as Saint Teresa's during her union with God. It is well known that Spanish mystics such as Saint Teresa of Avila and Saint John of the Cross used the trope of the union between two lovers to represent the communion of humans with God in a way that the climax of spiritual reunion, the ecstasy, is identified with the climax of physical union.

For Escalante, religion in Mexico is pervasive and inescapable, especially in peripheric states like Guanajuato, where the character Jesús comes from. The director has publicly blamed religious indoctrination as one of the reasons for the prevalent problem of teenage pregnancy in the region. These associations in Mexican and pan-Hispanic cultures warrant the plausibility of the interpretation that reconciliation through sexual union is intended in *Los bastardos*. The possibility of redemption resulting from this union is, however, abruptly foreclosed with Karen's interruption to go to the bathroom. This sudden shift from the divine to the mundane prompts Fausto to ask, "¿ya no quiso?" ("Doesn't she want any more?"). Fausto's scopic drive prompts a series of gazes and reflections that Lacanian psychoanalysis permits us to interpret in order to make sense of this scene.

When Karen is urinating in the bathroom, the spectator is voyeuristically positioned to assume what feminist scholar Laura Mulvey would describe as the male (dominant) gaze. Upon finishing, the spectator learns that the position the camera (and the spectator) was occupying was Jesús' subjective view. He, like us, had followed her to the bathroom. In the bathroom, Jesús and Karen exchange a few words while their images are reflected in the mirrors. This becomes significant when we take into account the fact that Lacan placed enormous importance in mirrors in the development of children's self-recognition and sexual difference. We can find further significance in these scenes as a whole in light of Mulvey's famous use of Lacanian psychoanalytic theory to unveil how cinema had developed so as to reproduce the male scopophilic gaze that situated women (female characters) in a passive position (to be looked at) and men (male characters) in the powerful position of active agents of the narrative.[25]

In this scene, the moment when Karen goes to the bathroom is a typical moment of interruption of the narrative, the moment of the spectacle when the female is on display. While she was subjected to Fausto's gaze in the sofa earlier in the scene, she was superficially and falsely positioned as the recipient of pleasure. When Jesús follows her to the bathroom, displaying the gun across his chest as a sign of his power over her, this illusion is broken. The imminence of death prompts her to think about the moment when she was born in that very same house (incidentally, this is again a baroque association of birth and death).

In this scene, sexual difference is thus intertwined with class conflict; in other words, the tension between male and female reproduces class struggle. The multiplicity of images produced by the mirror reflection visually renders the complexity of a relationship marked by mixed and intense feelings of attraction and fear between a woman who is a member of the middle-class and a man who is a laborer. The self-reflection of Karen and Jesús in the mirror interpellates them as social subjects, in Althusser's terms. Althusser explains that the reproduction of capitalist relations of production is ensured by ideological means. For Althusser, "ideology is a 'representation' of the imaginary relationship of individuals to their real conditions of existence."[26] Through their actions, Karen and Jesús stage the rituals of their respective classes.

This is further confirmed with the continuation of the scene. In contrast to Karen's materially comfortable lifestyle, Jesús' fascination with the food and gadgets that he finds around the house points to the conclusion that he is not accustomed to such creature comforts and comes, in fact, from a world of deprivation. Fausto reminds him on several occasions that they should finish the job quickly and leave, but Jesús enjoys reveling in a middle-class household. Given the persistence of these inequalities, the gun (conspicuously displayed on the table or in the hands of Jesús, Fausto, and even Karen) symbolizes the impossibility of overcoming class struggle.

As mentioned earlier, Fausto will eventually carry out the violent act that manifests this conflict, and he will do so with the help of American TV. While Jesús is playing and eating around the house, Fausto is left alone with Karen in the living room, where they are both watching TV. Escalante's use of soundtrack is often an important part of the narrative. In his first feature, *Sangre*, the most common activity shared by the two main characters is watching reality TV shows. In one of these moments, one of the characters selects the classic NLAC documentary *La batalla de Chile* by filmmaker Patricio Guzmán instead of American-inspired TV programs. As in *Sangre*, the television programs watched by Karen and Fausto in *Los bastardos* are off-screen, but their soundtracks invade the scene (and are particularly invasive given that characters hardly speak). At one point, Karen, perhaps in an attempt to build a rapport with Fausto, asks him, in English, "Have you ever been in hell?" to which, after a prolonged silence, he replies, in Spanish, "sí" ("yes"). The talk about violence on the TV intensifies as the volume increases and scenes showing American police violence appear on screen intermittently. Fausto tries to use the remote control to stop the noise coming out of the TV set that accompanies violent images of a suspect caught by three policemen (the type that usually makes the headlines in international news and social media), but his inability to make the TV remote control work pushes him to kick the TV set until he breaks it. Immediately afterward, Fausto has gathered the strength to kill Karen.

As the violence on American screens (and society at large) is unequivocally transferred to the Mexican migrant, the dream of class reconciliation vanishes. Furthermore, since these migrants cannot develop collective class consciousness due to their precarious situation, the necessary conditions for emancipatory class struggle as a collectivity are not met either. The class struggle seen in *Los bastardos* differs from that represented in the NLAC of the 1960s and 1970s precisely in this point.

Moreover, *Los bastardos* not only depicts class struggle idiosyncratically, it also documents the decline of the middle class. The attachment of this class to home ownership, a college education and health care as "expectations associated with a middle class identity . . . even though the historical context that once made those markers realistically attainable for many has long since disappeared"[27] is shown in *Los bastardos* through the absence of markers of prosperity. The worn-out furniture and old wall paint as well as the hobbies of both Karen (watching TV and taking drugs alone) and her son (deejaying, videogaming) instead present a somewhat bleak picture of the middle class.

Finally, this feature is radical in the way it presents an interconnectedness between diverse characters and the cultural traits of United States and Mexican migrant violence, which correlates with the connection between interventions of the government of the United States in Mexico, such as the war on drugs and the increase of violence in Mexico. In contrast to those who have criticized the film for its depiction of migrants as criminals, I view their violent acts as clearly motivated by violence originating in the United States and a precarious existence under neoliberal conditions.[28]

LOS BASTARDOS' "ENGAGED VISUALITY"

As noted previously, *Los bastardos* figures a different kind of class conflict than the one typically represented in classic NLAC documentaries and fiction features of the 1960s and 1970s. In what follows, I unravel how Amat Escalante navigates through contemporary global trends to create a unique approach that successfully balances the efforts to generate a global appeal with a filmmaking tradition of social engagement.

Non-Aestheticized Violence

The differences with NLAC came about not only because the pro-filmic socio-political reality had changed, but also because the politics and aesthetics of filmmakers and producers shifted from "plac[ing] cinema at the service of class struggle and decolonization"[29] to—in Walter Salles' broad terms—"creating new ways of representing the social problems occurring throughout the region, so as to bring this crisis to the attention of the audiences throughout the world." According to Salles, diverse paradigmatic examples of this successful and innovative visual style that "us[es] certain techniques of documentary filmmaking to show the conditions of poverty and underdevelopment in Latin America in a more vérité light" include Salles' own work, *Amores perros* and *Cidade de Deus*.[30]

Leaving aside Salles' filmography, which differs significantly from *Amores perros* and *Cidade de Deus*, and focusing on the comparison with the latter two canonical films, it must first be noted that the new visual techniques in these works of "aestheticized violence" include, according to MacLaird, a "tendency toward a shorter duration of shot," camera movements and editing that disorient the audience at climactic moments of the narrative, and a heavier emphasis on photographic effects than dialogues.[31] Our discussion of *Secuestro express* in chapter 1 already revealed the serious limitations of this postmodern, MTV-like realist mode that Escalante does not follow for the articulation of a progressive figuration of class relations.

None of Escalante's feature films and shorts fits the first two criteria (short-length shots and disorienting camera movements). In fact, MacLaird clarifies with regard to Escalante (and Reygadas) that their works constitute a "countertrend to the boom in aestheticized violence." Instead, they use "slow-paced realism," "long takes with minimal dramatic action," and create scenes in which "violence builds as potential rather than kinetic energy."[32]

Despite not using these techniques, Amat Escalante's name stands out in references to violent Mexican cinema in search engines and social media, even when compared to well-known titles containing extremely violent scenes such as *El violín* (*The Violin*, 2005), *Miss Bala* (2011), *El infierno* (*El Narco/Hell*, 2010), or even *Amores perros*. Due to Escalante's capacity to effectively concentrate moments of extreme violence in the midst of unimportant, quotidian events, *Los bastardos* has often been likened to Michael Haneke's *Funny Games* (2007), but Escalante insists that his is not a conceptual film about violence.

Instead of NLAC directors or González Iñárritu and Meirelles, he cites as his filmic references Robert Bresson, Stanley Kubrick, Buñuel, and Reygadas, among others. A comparison of film covers and posters serves to identify the gap between classic NLAC and Cinema Nôvo works at one corner and

Los bastardos at the other. On the DVD cover of *Los bastardos*, the image of Jesús stained in blood and holding a gun behind a bloody title belongs more to the imagery and style of a Quentin Tarantino film than to the class-inflected imagery of NLAC or Cinema Nôvo.

Moreover, the use of blood and extremely bloody scenes finds an acknowledged visual reference in gory horror movies as well. The effectist technique used to blow off Karen's head and the fixation of the camera on the beheaded body in *Los bastardos* points to an intended youth audience. Lastly, to fit the aesthetic expectations of young and art-house audiences, Jesús' appearance also underwent a transformation from the physique of a wage laborer from Guanajuato to that of a stylized "Mexican Johnny Depp," as mentioned in the film's DVD extras, which show part of the process of this transformation as performed by the hair stylist and Escalante himself.

This aesthetic affiliation with American and global crime thrillers partly originates from the need to resort to transnational film funding and recognition. Alberto Elena has observed the harmful effects of neoliberalism in the Mexican film industry—for instance, the industry suffered the drastic withdrawal of state funding as a result of the application of the neoliberal policies of Salinas de Gortari (1988–1994) after three successive governments that had provided direct subsidies to filmmakers (the Luis Echeverría government of 1970–1976, the government of José López Portillo between 1976 and 1982 and the six-year term of Miguel de la Madrid between 1982 and 1988). From producing more than a hundred films yearly in its Golden Age of the 1950s, there were periods in the 1990s when not even ten films were made.[33]

This process is certainly not exclusive to Mexican cinema, and Mexican filmmakers hold differing views on the need for state funding of filmmaking. For instance, one of Mexico's most successful and well-known filmmakers, Alejandro González Iñárritu, finds state-run film production crippling[34] and claims to "loathe the government-financed movie-making that seems to operate by the maxim: 'If nobody understands and nobody goes to see a movie, that must mean it's a masterpiece.'"[35] In contrast, director Carlos Carrera (*El crimen del padre Amaro–The Crime of Father Amaro*, 2002) and actor-producer Diego Luna have expressed their support, shared by many in the industry, of state protection, particularly in 2004 when President Vicente Fox intended to dismantle the IMCINE (Instituto Mexicano de Cinematografía, Mexican Film Institute, created in 1983), Churubusco Azteca Studios and the CCC (Centro de Capacitación Cinematográfica, one of the major film schools in Mexico), an initiative that was withdrawn thanks to strong public opposition.

In the twenty-first century, the number of films has been steadily growing as Mexican producers, exhibitors, distributors, and filmmakers like Escalante adapt to the new situation and the development of an independent filmmaking sector. Alberto Elena understands "independent filmmaking" within this Mexican context as privately financed by the directors and/or international investors, and presents the case of Carlos Reygadas as a good example of this practice.[36] Reygadas, who has produced some of Escalante's films and owns the production and distribution companies Mantarraya and ND, has also inspired Escalante to seek support from prestigious film festivals. Although Escalante has received public funding, he distributes his own films in Mexico through Mantarraya.

This strategy has proved successful. *Los bastardos* claimed the Best Director award at the Bratislava International Film Festival, and *Heli* was very successful with both international festivals and the Mexican audience. Escalante also won the award for Best Director for this film at the Cannes Film Festival (among many other awards) and, in the week of this film's release, it sold more tickets than any foreign film in Mexico, a market dominated by Hollywood.

However, there is no doubt that these international sources of funding and the international recognition of these films act to condition both Escalante's choice of themes and, to a certain extent, the Mexican audience's reception of them.

MAGIC REALISM IN *LOS BASTARDOS*

Despite its aesthetic affiliation to global crime thrillers, *Los bastardos* is not bound to the ethos linking American crime thrillers. Instead, Escalante's films constitute a twenty-first-century version of the social commitment of NLAC and Buñuelian traditions through magic realism. From his first short, *Amarrados* (*Tied Up*, 2002)—a film about a small, homeless child addicted to sniffing glue who is sexually abused by an old middle-class woman—to his last feature (*La region salvaje–The Untamed*, 2016), Escalante denounces injustices and situations that he knows well. However, unlike *Los olvidados*, Escalante's films are not "thesis films."[37]

Los bastardos signifies the director's shift from a preoccupation with violence in Mexico within the private realm (as seen his first film) to a focus on the violence lived by Mexican migrants across the border in the United States. A critic called *Los bastardos* "a nihilistic high-art film" with "banal minimalist dialogue" and "ultra-violence,"[38] but the film's violence is far from nihilistic or banal.

Amat Escalante has made repeated remarks about how Mexicans have become accustomed to extreme violence through direct experience or media such as the *nota roja* magazine *Alarma!* (a magazine that specializes in the publication of gruesome events), and has informally commented about a possible historical explanation for the phenomenon. When interviewed about a torture scene in his third film, set in twenty-first-century Mexico, the director overheard one of the non-professional actors remarking that the scene was reminiscent of the violence during the conquest of Mexico by the Spaniards, thus prompting Escalante to reflect on the virulence of violence in the following way:

> Escalante: Many things actually are a bit improvised because the actors had never acted before. . . . The guy said that—this is an Inquisition—and it sounded intellectual or something, it sounded interesting, and I left it there like that, and there is also another part that someone also improvised something about the conquest, from Spain, one guy says, "Now you are going to learn what it is like to be an Indian in the land of God," something like that, which to me sounded like something that a Spanish person would say when they came to Mexico 500 years ago, and these are lines that I heard there and were recorded and I put them in the film by the sound only, but those are things that sounded interesting to me.

> Interviewer: To give a historical echo or something like that . . .

> Escalante: No, not so much, but it somehow made sense in a way to me because, at the end of the day, 500 years are not so much time if you see the history of the world and what has been happening here from 500 years till now, still if you see here is very obvious. You see that the indigenous people are the servants of the Spanish white skin people in Mexico still, and for me that's very impressive still. It brings up many contrary emotions, to see how slowly things change. It sounds a bit ridiculous because the conquest happened a long time ago when the Spanish came, but if anybody comes to Mexico you can clearly see that the conquest is still very much here.[39]

Resonances of these traumatic historical experiences in contemporary Mexico are the Tlatelolco student massacre of 1968 and, more recently, the massacre of forty-three students of a teacher college in Ayotzinapa at the hands of the local government of Iguala, the police and the drug cartel Guerreros Unidos (United Warriors) in September 2014. The Iguala student massacre exposes the decomposition of the Mexican state, which has yet to explain more than 26,000 disappearances[40] and supposedly more than 80,000 deaths under the watch of the Mexican security forces and the drug cartels between December 2006 and February 2013, losses caused by the "war on drugs" launched by President Felipe Calderón (2006–2012) with the support of the United States of America. Intellectuals and leaders from the civil society, including filmmakers, are vociferously demanding that the tragedy of 2014 be a turning point in Mexican history.[41]

In contrast to the *nota roja* magazines, the violence in Escalante's *Los bastardos* appears "uncanny." Jameson uses his notion of magic realism to explain the effect of the reduction of the film's narrative dynamic to the attention to violence (and sexuality, to a certain extent) in combination with a use of color that differs from the postmodern use of glossy colors—in Escalante's film, colors regain their singularity and produce an intense visual pleasure and a de-narrativizing effect, displaying at the same time "a strange and poetic visual reality."[42] Jameson applies Freud's notion of the uncanny in his interpretation of the use of color and violence in magic realist films based on the following process:

> A represented event becomes intrinsically marked as the repetition of an older and archaic fantasy of which no independent traces remain in the text. This "return of the repressed" makes itself felt by the garish and technicolor representation of what is given as an essentially black-and-white reality, figures as daubed and rouged as in photorealist painting, objects derealized by the very plenitude of their sensory being, by which the merely perceptual is unmasked as obsession.[43]

Despite the Mexicans' familiarity with extreme violence, in the penultimate scene of the film, the red blood splattered all around the rooms and the static camera on Karen's beheaded body produce a defamiliarizing effect. It seems as though this scene tries to counteract the nonchalance of murder in contemporary Mexico, establishing a connection with the viewer that goes well beyond the consumption of violence for entertainment purposes. In connection to this, when Buñuel arrived in Mexico, he was struck by the "nonchalance of murder" there. An article about a twelve-year-old boy found in a garbage pit is credited as an inspiration for *Los olvidados*, a film that Escalante regards as one of the films that influenced him the most. Escalante shares with Buñuel a "dispassionate eye" for violence, that is, the non-judgmental portrayal of violence.

Certainly, despite the use of a magic realist strain in *Los bastardos*, the film on a whole cannot be considered a magic realist film, although there are two important characteristics of magic realism present. First, disjunction is structurally present. The present historical conjuncture is clearly perceived by many as a moment of disjuncture and crisis due to its unprecedented levels of violence, its "decomposition," and the negative effects of neoliberalism in its society. Second, *Los bastardos* belongs to the tradition of magic realism in its need to convey the excesses of reality (an aspect fully explained in Gabriel García Márquez's acceptance speech of the 1982 Nobel Peace Prize for Literature).

When understood in this way, magic realism poses a deep relationship between art and the socio-political conjunctures from where it emanates, not just as an inspiration, but also as an intervention (in opposition to the

separation of the artistic and the political realms favored by Vargas Llosa[44]).
From this point of view, magic realist literature and film are profoundly
political.

In relation to this, *Los bastardos* allows for an enquiry into the significance
of "political causality" in contemporary Mexican cinema.[45] The discussion on
the new forms of the political in contemporary cinema is by no means exclusive to Mexican cinema, as discussed in different parts of this book. I will
just recall a few examples to highlight *Los bastardos'* position. In Argentine
cinema, Silvana Díaz interprets the shift in forms of social engagement from
the Argentine cinema of the 1960s to that of the 1990s as a transition from
cinema being "a tool for social transformation" to "chronicling the political
and social changes."[46] Likewise, film scholar Joanna Page views some contemporary texts as seemingly depoliticized but still finding a way of being
political and commenting on neoliberalism, as discussed in the introduction.[47]

In view of the film's analysis, *Los bastardos* shares a preoccupation with
class-inflected violence with *Amores perros* and *Cidade de Deus*, but differs
in its ethical stance. While *Amores perros* and *Cidade de Deus* glamourize
poverty to a great extent (what has been called "neotremendismo chafa"[48] in
the former case, and "the cosmetics of hunger"[49] in the latter), *Los bastardos*
manages to balance social commitment more skillfully with visual innovation, an update of visual "class struggle" that I will refer to as "engaged visuality," a form of "politicized" cinema that, unlike populist cinema, has been
sanctioned at international film festivals.

Regardless of whether or not we agree that Third Cinema has a strong
tradition in Mexico,[50] *Los bastardos* updates the meaning of cinematic class
struggle in line with David Harvey's statement:

> Class struggle is, admittedly, a blanket term that conceals myriad variations. To
> simply parrot the phrase without doing the requisite analysis as to exactly what
> it means in different places and times is to disrespect the analytic tradition of
> historical materialism that Marx and Engels bequeathed us.[51]

The film is also new in its lack of didacticism, which according to David R.
Maciel is one of the general characteristics of border or migrant Mexican cinema.[52] Furthermore, there is originality in this film's full embrace of a combination of entertainment values (visual pleasure and engagement with global
cinematic developments) and Marxist class struggle, the latter of which is
demonstrated in the sense that exploitation is undoubtedly a major defining
term for this narrative. The conflict between classes in the film is complex, as
complex as neo-Marxists would admit, but it is tied to the modes of production. This is not a neo-Weberian view where life chances are determined by
a series of factors, just one of which is class.

The first decade of the 2000s saw an interest in the changing conditions of the Mexican middle class captured by the most influential Mexican film of the decade, *Amores perros*. This is a film where this disruption of the middle-class lifestyle is allegorically depicted in the form of a car crash between members of the lower and middle classes that arguably serves to erase differences between them in order to emphasize "the universality of the human condition."[53] Like *Amores perros*, *Los bastardos* "engages with the complexities of neoliberalism in Mexico"[54] but there are qualitative innovations in the way it goes about this task which I hope to have demonstrated. By negotiating a commitment to social reality and aesthetic conventions in line with global aesthetic developments associated with independent sources of funding, Escalante introduces a new form of socially-committed cinema. *Los bastardos* does not correspond to the use of *nota roja* as a producer of class anxieties nor does it closely follow in the footsteps of the NLAC. It is a new form of social commitment anchored in Mexico's and the US' social and historical traditions combining entertainment, art, and a transnational mode of production. Rather than being banal, *Los bastardos* exposes the deep roots of violence, indirectly pointing a finger at particular causes and posing questions about possible solutions for the social problems depicted in his films.

And, despite relying on institutions that primarily support "second cinema" (art for art's sake, in Third Cinema theory), Escalante does not shy away from pressing social problems. The worsening of the situation of the working class as a result of the effects of neoliberal policies is made obvious. Rather than pitting the working class or the proletariat against the middle class, as would be typical of earlier cinema, precariousness has resulted in a fight of all against all: victims turn into victimizers as even the lower classes fight against each other while the middle classes live in a constant culture of fear of the lower classes. Cinema is capturing this heightened lack of control by the state and the ensuing social decomposition.

Now we turn our attention to the use of consumption as a major sign of the current era of globalization as seen on screen.

NOTES

1. For a definition and discussion of this term, see David Harvey, "Introduction," in *The Communist Manifesto*, Karl Marx and Friedrich Engels (London: Pluto Press, 2008), 1–30; Geoffrey P. Faux, *The Global Class War: How America's Bipartisan Elite Lost Our Future—and What It Will Take to Win It Back* (Hoboken, NJ: Wiley, 2006); Steve Derné, *Globalization on the Ground: Media and the Transformation of Culture, Class, and Gender in India* (Los Angeles: Sage, 2008).

2. Guy Standing, *The Precariat: The New Dangerous Class* (London: Bloomsbury Academic, 2011), 6.

3. Guy Standing, *A Precariat Charter: From Denizens to Citizens* (London: Bloomsbury, 2014), 11.

4. Joseph E. Stiglitz, *Globalization and Its Discontents* (New York: Norton, 2003), 9.

5. Arjun Appadurai, *Globalization* (Durham: Duke University Press, 2001), 6.

6. Arjun Appadurai, *The Future as Cultural Fact: Essays on the Global Condition* (London: Verso, 2013), 181.

7. The idyllic narrative concerning globalization was already critiqued in 1996 by Ulf Hannerz, followed in 1999 by Néstor García Canclini, who refers to this phenomenon as "imagined globalization" because he claims that the benefits of globalization and the erasure of barriers across the globe is in fact more imagined than actual. Ulf Hannerz, *Transnational Connections: Culture, People, Places* (London: Routledge, 1996); García Canclini, *La globalización imaginada* (Buenos Aires: Paidós, 1999).

8. Will Higbee and Song Hwee Lim, "Concepts of Transnational Cinema: Towards a Critical Transnationalism in Film Studies," *Transnational Cinemas* 1, no. 1 (2010): 12.

9. Ana M. López and Dolores Tierney," In Focus: Latin American Film Research in the Twenty-First Century. Introduction," *Cinema Journal* 54, no. 1 (2014): 112–14.

10. Higbee and Lim ("Concepts of Transnational Cinema") fall into the paradox observed by Ulf Hannerz as early as 1996, according to which the term transnationalism tends "to draw attention to what it negates—that is, to the continued significance of the national." Ulf Hannerz, *Transnational Connections*, 6.

11. Sheldon Hsiao-peng Lu, ed., *Transnational Chinese Cinemas: Identity, Nationhood, Gender* (Honolulu: University of Hawai'i Press, 1997), 109.

12. Victoria Ruétalo similarly observes this connection between production modes and narratives in the films *Foreign Land* and *Deep Crimson*. Incidentally, her analysis illustrates the unproblematic use of the term "globalization" in film studies which I attempt to avoid here. Victoria Ruétalo, "Border-Crossings and Textual Gaps: A 'Globalized' Mode of Production in *Profundo Carmesí* and *Terra Estrangeira*," *Studies in Hispanic Cinemas* 5, nos. 1&2 (2008): 57–71.

13. David Harvey, *A Brief History of Neoliberalism* (New York: Oxford University Press, 2005), 2.

14. Faux, *The Global Class War*, 5.

15. Jyostna Kapur and Keith B. Wagner, eds., *Neoliberalism and Global Cinema: Capital, Culture, and Marxist Critique*, (New York: Routledge, 2011), 4.

16. Jeff Faux quotes Renato Ruggiero claiming that NAFTA is "the 'constitution' of the global economy," and adds that, "like all constitutions, NAFTA reflects an underlying political philosophy—in this case, what is known throughout most of the world as neoliberalism." Faux, *The Global Class War*, 4–5.

17. Timothy Shortell, "Durkheim's Theory of Social Class," Course materials. Department of Sociology, Brooklyn College, CUNY, n.d.

18. Robert Lapsley and Michael Westlake, *Film Theory: An Introduction* (Manchester: Manchester UP, 2006), xiii.

19. Norman Caulfield, *Nafta and Labor in North America* (Urbana: University of Illinois Press, 2010), 11.

20. Caulfield, *Nafta and Labor in North America*, 35.

21. Robert C. Hodges, "The Making and Unmaking of *Salt of the Earth*: A Cautionary Tale," PhD Thesis (University of Kentucky, 1997).

22. Mark Weisbrot, Stephan Lefebvre, and Joseph Sammut, *Did Nafta Help Mexico? An Assessment after 20 Years*, PDF file (Washington, DC: Centre for Economic and Policy Research [CEPR], 2014), 18.

23. David Bacon, "Globalization and Nafta Caused Migration from Mexico," *The Public Eye*, Political Research Associates, October 11, 2014.

24. Fredric Jameson, *Representing Capital: A Commentary on Volume One* (London: Verso, 2011), 16.

25. Laura Mulvey, "Visual Pleasure and Narrative Cinema," *Screen* 16, no. 3 (1975): 6–18.

26. Louis Althusser, *On the Reproduction of Capitalism: Ideology and Ideological State Apparatuses* (London: Verso, 2014), 256.

27. Thomas Geoghegan, *Only One Thing Can Save Us: Why America Needs a New Kind of Labor Movement* (New York: New Press, 2014).

28. This relative originality of *Los bastardos* is obvious when the film is compared to other recent fiction films and documentaries dealing with the migratory experiences of Latin Americans to the United States, such as the award-winning *La jaula de oro* (*The Golden Dream*, Diego Quemada-Díez, 2013) and the documentary *De nadie* (*No One*, Tin Dirdamal, 2005) where "poverty" in general (not the reason for poverty) is seen as the cause for migration.

29. Zuzana Pick, *The New Latin American Cinema: A Continental Project* (Austin: University of Texas Press, 1993), 101.

30. Misha MacLaird, *Aesthetics and Politics in the Mexican Film Industry* (New York: Palgrave Macmillan, 2013), 116.

31. MacLaird, *Aesthetics and Politics in the Mexican Film Industry*, 117.

32. MacLaird, *Aesthetics and Politics in the Mexican Film Industry*, 195.

33. Alberto Elena, "La nueva era del cine mexicano: Virtudes y paradojas," *Afuera. Estudios de crítica cultural* 5 (2008): n.p.

34. Celestino Deleyto and María del Mar Azcona, *Alejandro González Iñárritu* (Urbana: University of Illinois, 2010), 6.

35. Edward Lawrenson and Bernardo Pérez Soler, "Pulp Fiction," *Sight and Sound* 11, no. 5 (2001): 3, 28–30.

36. Elena, "La nueva era del cine mexicano," 5.

37. For the exact application of this term to this film, see Mark Polizzotti, *Los Olvidados* (London: BFI, 2006), 43.

38. Todd McCarthy, "Review: The Bastards," *Variety* May 20, 2008.

39. "Amat Escalante Interview," *3sat*. January 19, 2014. Video. (min. 30:00–32:00). Christina Jacqueline Johns' study of violence in Mexico establishes historical connections. *The Origins of Violence in Mexican Society* (Westport: Praeger, 1995).

40. According to Human Rights Watch.

41. There was a large public outcry because of the disappearance of the forty-three students. Javier Sicilia—the Mexican poet who founded the *Movimiento por la Paz con Justicia y Dignidad* (Movement for Peace with Justice and Dignity) and who is a victim of the violence caused by the war on drugs—used the poem "Mi país oh mi país" by Efraín Huerta to synthesize the link between violence and macroeconomic measures. Similarly, prominent Mexican filmmakers such as Alejandro González Iñárritu and Guillermo del Toro have also expressed their strong views against the action or lack of action of the Mexican political class as well as the silence of the media.

42. Fredric Jameson, "On Magic Realism in Film," *Critical Inquiry* 12, no. 2 (1986): 315, 302.

43. Jameson, "On Magic Realism in Film," 315.

44. Mario Vargas Llosa, *Sueño y realidad de América Latina* (Barcelona: Arcadia, 2010).

45. Sánchez Prado, *Screening Neoliberalism*, 175.

46. Catherine Leen, "City of Fear: Reimagining Buenos Aires in Contemporary Argentine Cinema," *Bulletin of Latin American Research* 27, no. 4 (2008): 477.

47. As mentioned in the Introduction, this question of the depoliticization of contemporary narratives has attracted the attention of Anthropologist Arjun Appadurai (*The Future as Cultural Fact*, 58).

48. Jorge Ayala Blanco, *La fugacidad del cine mexicano* (México, DF: Océano, 2001).

49. Ivana Bentes, "The Aesthetics of Violence in Brazilian Film," in *City of God in Several Voices*, ed. Else R. P Vieira (Nottingham: CCCP, 2005).

50. Paulo Antonio Paranaguá considers the Mexican cinema of the 1960s–1970s to have evolved "out of step with the rest of Latin America" and that, in any case, "efforts to revitalise the cinema in the 60s and 70s were primarily thematic," not aesthetic. *Mexican Cinema* (London: BFI; IMCINE, 1995), 10. And John Mraz presents examples of Mexican films that seem to fit into the NLAC tradition. *Looking for Mexico: Modern Visual Culture and National Identity* (Durham: Duke University Press, 2009); Sánchez Prado, in his 2014 *Screening Neoliberalism*, questions—as Paranaguá does—the existence of such a tradition in the Mexican film industry.

51. Harvey, "Introduction," 13.

52. David R. Maciel, "Pochos and Other Extremes in Mexican Cinema; or, El cine mexicano se va de bracero, 1922–1963," in *Chicanos and Film: Representation and Resistance*, ed. Chon A. Noriega (Minneapolis: University of Minnesota Press, 1992), 94.

53. Deborah Shaw, *Contemporary Cinema of Latin America: Ten Key Films* (New York: Continuum, 2003), 36–37.

54. Sánchez Prado, *Screening Neoliberalism*, 172.

Chapter 6

Class and Race

Exploring New Class Figurations in Asian-themed Films Produced in Latin America

There are similar upside-down shots in two otherwise different films, one showing a character's view of Hong Kong from Buenos Aires (*Happy Together*, Wong Kar-Wai, 1997) and the other visually conveying the diametric opposition between Buenos Aires and its antipodes (Fujian, China) (*Un cuento chino, A Chinese Take-Away*, Sebastián Borensztein, 2011). Both scenes combine a sense of emotional distance with a feeling of (global) connection (or perhaps disconnection) that is common in films featuring Asian-themed films set in Latin America.[1] This chapter is concerned with the study of changes in social stratification brought about by Asian immigrants settled in Latin America as seen on the screen. Although in principle we may not think about Asians contributing to the reconfiguration of contemporary Latin American societies in a significant way, attention to this particular aspect of globalization is relevant given the rising volume of Asian migration to Latin America and the strong participation of China in the macroeconomic development of the Latin American subcontinent.[2]

Beginning with the rise in global power of the BRICS (Brazil, Russia, India, China and South Africa) and the strengthening of the investment of China in Latin America in the last two decades, Latin Americans have engaged in complex discourses about the geopolitical and economic nature of contemporary relations between China and Latin American countries. Although opinions on the matter are diverse, the latter relations are distant from earlier Western modes based on colonial exploitation and imperialism as well as from the nineteenth-century coolie trade based on agreements between the Chinese Emperor and Latin American presidents.[3]

One of the first observations to be made is that, in comparison to the enormous volume of trade between the two regions, Asian-Latin American cultural relations and their study are minimal.[4] Regardless of the number of

Latin American films registering the Asian contribution to the reconfiguration of contemporary Latin American societies, their importance is, however, undeniable. For this reason, existing films on and by Asian migrants or Asian descendants in Latin America merit attention. This chapter focuses on two such films made in Argentina and Brazil, one by a first-time Argentine director of Taiwanese origin who attended film school in Argentina (*La salada*, Juan Martín Hsu, 2014), and another by a Hong Kong filmmaker associated to mainland Chinese cinema who secured a co-production deal with the major Brazilian producer Gullane (*Plastic City/Dangkou/*荡寇, Yu Lik-wai, Nelson/余力爲, 2008).

The term Latin American cinema has to be expanded to allow for more hybridity and include these types of productions given the continuing transformation of societies due to migration at a global level—which undermines the still common assumption of ethnically homogenous nations—and the increase in transnationalism in film production, especially BRICS co-productions.[5] By questioning the Asian diaspora, cross-cultural identity, and generation gaps, these films equally belong to Lu's category of "transnational Chinese cinemas." The inquiry into the figurations of the restructuring of social differences brought about by globalization in the films of this chapter brings to mind the question that Lu poses concerning what conditions may be required for a national allegory in the new transnational setting.[6] Differences in the filmmakers' backgrounds and the nature of the projects allow for a rich discussion of hybridity and other aspects mainly in relationship to class and race.

THE ASIANS: OUTSIDER AND INSIDER VIEWS

Presumably because of their insider knowledge of Asian cultures, both *La salada* and *Plastic City* avoid stereotypical portrayals of Asians on the screen. Looking back at characters like the exotic Chinese detective Chan Li-Po (*La serpiente roja*, Ernesto Caparrós, Cuba, 1937) played by an actor who was not even Chinese as was typical of the time,[7] and migrant dramas like Tizuka Yamasaki's *Gaijin: Os caminhos da liberdade* (*Gaijin: A Brazilian Odyssey*, 1980) and the more recent *Corações Sujos* (*Dirty Hearts*, Vicente Amorim, 2011) dealing with Japanese communities living in semi-feudal conditions in Brazil, the contemporaneity of Hsu's and Yu's films come to the fore.

In films closer to *La salada* like *Silvia Prieto* (Martín Rejtman, 1999) and *Los guantes mágicos* (*The Magic Gloves*, 2003) the Asians still appear as outsiders. Lower-middle-class characters in *Silvia Prieto* dine out in cheap Chinese restaurants that have names like "Chinese restaurant Tokyo" (mocking local ignorance of Asia). Resorting to eating in cheap Chinese restaurants seems to be the result of the downward social mobility provoked by the 2001 Argentine crisis known as the *corralito* but what is more interesting in *Silvia Prieto* for our purposes is that the Other, in this case the supposedly Chinese owner or waiter of the business, remains invisible.[8] This obliteration contrasts with the overall presence of Chinese small businesses in Argentine society—as Natalia Milanesio observed, there has in fact been an explosion of seven thousand *autoservicios chinos* (Chinese grocery stores that specialize in cheap food for all classes) across the country.[9]

A higher visibility is attained in *Los guantes mágicos*, which contains abundant references to Asian commodities, such as "the magic gloves" themselves. When a character asks his brother for the origin of the gloves that he is wearing, he replies that they were traded via Canada and made in China. The characters decide to start up a business selling gloves shipped from Hong Kong and, subsequently, there is another direct reference to China in relationship to globalization in the form of a comment made by a character in which he postulates that the United States allowed China to join the WTO in order to let China fall into debt like it did with Argentina.

This focus on trade and consumption continues in *La salada* and *Plastic City*, which partake of a visual mode that Gonzalo Aguilar has called "cinema of consumption" due to the centrality of consumption in structuring subjects and their perceptions.[10] Indicative of this trait is the beginning of *La salada* starts in which a Korean businessman (Mr. Kim, played by Chang Kim Sung) is discussing a business transaction with a friend, who recommends him "to buy." As was mentioned apropos of *Los bastardos*, transport, communication, and the flows that these allow are defining characteristics of globalization,[11] but it must be noted that these are "disjunctive flows," as Appadurai has remarked, because the relations of people and objects in motion are problematic and frictional.[12] Some Asian migrants such as the man who inspired the narrative of *Plastic City* are involved in these types of frictional transactions that are portrayed differently in mainstream media and *Plastic City*. To begin with, the scene in *Plastic City* where the global trade of fake goods is first mentioned happens in an encounter with a corrupt Brazilian politician in collusion with the Asian characters, instead of exclusively criminalizing the migrants.

PLASTIC CITY

Plastic City revolves around a Chinese businessman (Yuda, performed by the Hong Kong star Anthony Wong Chau-sang, 黃秋生) who controls several shopping malls and gangs of street vendors selling pirated goods. His businesses thrive with the corrupt protection of the local Brazilian government, but when this protection is withdrawn due to anti-piracy pressure from the US government, Yuda's empire quickly declines. He has an adopted son, Kirín (played by Japanese actor Jô Odagiri, 小田切 讓) and a sentimental partner, Ocho (played by Huang Yi, 黃奕). The Brazilian authorities who were previously protecting his counterfeit business start to clamp down on him and this, combined with the pressure from a Taiwanese competitor (Mr. Taiwan), complicates matters to such a degree that he ends up losing his pirated goods empire, despite Kirín's desperate efforts to save it by fighting with the rival gang.

Kirín doesn't succeed and Yuda ends up in jail, where he pretends to die in order to be secretly transported to the jungle by helicopter. Believing that Yuda is dead, Kirín sinks into a state of total abandonment, sleeping in the streets until his friend Tetsuo rescues him when he is nearly dead. Tetsuo gives him a pouch that Yuda had left for him which contains some gold nuggets and photos of his real parents, who had been shot dead in Oiapoque when he was a child (at which point he had been rescued by Yuda). Upon seeing the photos, he decides to go in search of his origins and of Yuda. When Kirín and Yuda meet in the jungle, the reappearance of a calm white tiger that had first appeared to Yuda when he had rescued the child Kirín many years ago in the same place signals to Yuda the moment of death. He takes his own life in front of his son and, at that moment, the trees release blood. The film ends with Kirín looking out at the sea from a distance.

The businessman who inspired the character of Yuda in *Plastic City*, Law Kin chong, is a man from Hong Kong who migrated to Brazil when he was three years old. He started selling fake watches in the streets and became the owner of several popular shopping malls in São Paulo (such as 25 de Março, Mundo Oriental and Shopping Pari) and factories in China. Despite the fact that he and his two sons (who studied law) speak Portuguese and hold Brazilian citizenship, the media still refers to them as "the Chinese" in an obvious act of segregation from the imagined mainstream Brazilian population that includes Creoles (descendants of Europeans), Mestizos, Afrobrazilians, and native Brazilians. At the end of the 1990s, Brazil was accused by the Office of the United States Trade Representative (USTR) of allegedly failing to enforce respect for copyright laws and, between 2002 and 2006, Brazil was placed in the USTR "Priority Watch List," which affected Brazilian trade privileges in the United States (at the time, the United States was Brazil's largest trading partner, a position now occupied by China).[13]

Under this climate, Law was sentenced to a brief jail term in 2004 for trying to bribe Deputy Medeiros, the president of the Parliamentary Commission of Inquiry on Piracy. After that, he was arrested again for other charges on several occasions and attracted the attention of the press. In 2005,

Deputy Medeiros published a book with the title *A CPI da pirataria* in which Law "is described as a 'cold little Chinese man' and 'a moral monster' with 'painfully slanted eyes,' but also a 'predictable' man due to his 'millennial obedience.'"[14] Mizukami et al. further observe that Law "has . . . served as a convenient personification of Brazilian anxiety toward Chinese immigration and China's rise as an economic power," an anxiety that sometimes turns into a kind of xenophobia such as that felt by Medeiros above.[15]

The rise of China and the subsequent animadversion against the 150 thousand Chinese living in Brazil is undoubtedly on the minds of those in the Chinese community and also on the mind of director Yu Lik-wai. In 2007, the president of the Chinese Cultural Association complained about pervasive prejudices against his community and the need for the Chinese government to press the Brazilian government to improve its treatment toward them.[16] As for Yu, during the preparation for his film, a slogan printed on a Brazilian's T-shirt ("Asian People, Stop Stealing Our Jobs") made him think of the fight between emerging economies to become the next "First World."[17]

The Brazilian media portrays Law as a criminal (this appears in the film in the form of a news item too) and paints the Brazilian authorities who sent him to prison as brave and efficient. In his feature, Yu presents a more complex image of the man and his family. Corrupt Brazilian officials and intermediaries feature in *Plastic City* as much as dubious businessmen of Asian origin do, foreclosing any possible identification between criminality and ethnicity. The sympathy that Yuda's character prompts in the audience emanates from his relationship with Kirín and Ocho. Even though Yuda thinks that Kirín has made mistakes, he does not hesitate to protect and guide him, from the moment when he rescues him in the jungle to the moment when, back in the jungle, he points his son to a possible direction for regeneration after the destruction of their empire in São Paulo by returning to Nature through death. The love the faithful Ocho feels for Yuda prevents her from accepting Kirín's advances, and Kirín does not rest until he sees his father out of jail, all of which are signs of respect and profound love.

In contrast to these sympathetic portrayals, Carvalho, the Brazilian intermediary between Yuda and the congressman and the police, appears as an evil character who is faithful only to himself. The officers who campaign against piracy appear in the background of a dialogue between two street peddlers who are afraid of losing their jobs (and this is not the only instance in which we see how the unemployment among the underprivileged is caused by anti-piracy campaigns run from above). Furthermore, the prison officers cannot distinguish between different types of Asians (when Kirín is in jail), which for an Asian audience is a highly negative trait. In terms of narrative space, Carvalho, the official representatives and the police occupy little space in the narrative when compared to Yuda's gang members.

Yuda is not, however, the protagonist of the film—Kirín is. In terms of characterization, Kirín is a handsome and stylish Japanese man, faithful to his friends, troubled with romantic relationships, and impulsive. The first image of him is that of a god up on a roof, "preaching" and throwing money to the peddlers who work for him, his arms outstretched in a resemblance to the famous statue of Christ the Redeemer. The attraction of, and admiration for, the character, which is conveyed by the upward movement of the camera and the low angle shot, is maintained in other parts of the film—particularly in the fight with the rival gang of Mr. Taiwan, where Kirín appears as an attractive Japanese yakuza. The tattoos that he wears, though, are more in the service of producing a modern and sexy image of Kirín than in suggesting yakuza ghettoization (his Brazilian girlfriend is also tattooed, for instance). Yu exploits Odagiri's grungy, gothic style outside the screen.

Besides this, instead of simply criminalizing the illicit activities of characters like Kirín and his father, Yu provides a historical perspective in the preamble of the film. In this scene, we view the jungle with the following intertitle: "Oiapoque, Brazil's Northern Border 1984. A gold mining region notorious for land disputes." Oiapoque is in reality a region marked by prostitution, attacks against indigenous people, a high prevalence of AIDS, and illegal gold mining. The polyrhythmic montage of the soundscape in this scene characteristic of magic realist films[18] includes shootings, and among the images of a visual montage we can see the blue disc in Brazil's national flag spanned by a band with the Brazilian motto "Ordem e Progresso" ("Order and Progress"), which starkly contrasts with the apparent lack of order or social justice shown and heard on the screen.

All this is reminiscent of the violent European conquest of the continent and its colonization based on slavery and mining for gold, which fuelled industrial capitalism. Once slavery was officially abolished and the European owners of mines found it increasingly difficult to buy slaves, Chinese indentured workers were sent to replace them. By setting the opening scene in the border between the remains of European colonialism in Latin America (the French Guiana) and Brazil, Yu dynamizes all these known historical references in the viewer's mind. And by starting with the persecution of Asian characters, Yu questions the discourse of the illegality of activities such as the sale of pirated DVDs and brand-name products that are characteristic of late capitalism and the scapegoating of the Asians.

LA SALADA

La salada is also based on real phenomena involving Asian migrants to Argentina who have been negatively reported in the media. The film is mainly concerned with the personal problems of a Korean family and two young migrants, a Taiwanese and a Bolivian, who find work in one of the biggest black markets in Latin America called La salada. The flows which Appadurai considers characteristic of globalization literally materialize in this film in images of bridges and a river. The real La salada market has a fascinating history. Established in 1991 by a group of mostly Bolivians—one of the groups of migrants considered less cultured by the Argentines, many of whom regard themselves as superior to most of their surrounding neighbors owing to their European descent[19]—this market continued to grow throughout the 1990s, but it wasn't until the 2001 crisis of the *corralito* when La salada flourished, partly thanks to the search of the middle classes for cheaper markets. If up to 2001 Argentina still had any dreams of being "the European country of Latin America" and of competing with Brazil, this was a moment of truth and realization of economic decline that persists until today, and the market La salada is an emblem of this change. The market has at times been mired in controversy for selling "productos truchos" (fake or pirated products) and for exploiting the workers who produce some of the goods to be sold in the market. A denunciation of wrongdoing at the market by unions has been echoed at some Argentine media outlets and the European Union.

Migrants who own businesses in this film do not seem exploitative. Intimate dialogues and interactions among characters, complex business transactions due to the migrants' linguistic limitations and the extensive use of various native languages other than Spanish (Korean, Quechua and Mandarin) construct a vision "from within" that counteracts the negative portrayals of migrants by unreflective groups and mass media. This allows the film's viewers to enter the world of the migrants, perceive their difficulties in adjusting to a difficult environment as well as to admire their strategies for survival. The film lacks Korean stereotypes such as those identified by Roxana Santamaría, Gabriela Itzcovich and Yunyoung Verónica Kim,[20] with the exception of the tendency to self-ghettoization, owing to the director's Taiwanese origin and the Asian background of some members of the crew. For this reason, it has received support from the *Instituto Nacional contra la Discriminación, la Xenofobia y el Racismo* (National Institute against Discrimination, Xenofobia, and Racism). In connection to this, the sale of counterfeit goods and the hiring of Bolivians also appear in a non-critical light, in contrast to criminalizing mainstream opinions.

Moreover, in the extrafilmic realm, for the Asian actors this film was an opportunity for overcoming stereotyping. The Korean actor Chang Kim Sung had worked for several television productions until he was hired to play the role of Walter, the loyal assistant to the director of a company, in the TV series *Graduados* that earned him a Tato Award in 2012.[21] Playing a male leading role in an Argentine film like *La salada* in 2014 meant a quantitative career leap for an Asian actor twelve years after his first appearance on TV, a career path similar to that of Ignacio Huang, who was relatively unknown before his roles in *Un cuento chino* and *La salada*. Therefore, the rise of Korean actors and actresses on the Argentine screens parallels the rise of the Korean communities in Argentine society, a fact that has not always been welcomed without fear. As one journalist wrote in 2012, "television is a world. This expression has never been as true as now. The small screen has turned into a real sample book of actors, conductors, panelists, juries, participants, and even extras from foreign countries. It is not a novelty because, historically, there have been foreign faces and accents on TV. This trend is, however, reaching its maximum level today."[22] Carolina Mera has noted that the upward social mobility of the Asian migrants generates this kind of anxiety among sectors of the traditional middle class.[23]

Aside from focusing on professionals who hold foreign passports rather than on non-Caucasian professionals who hold Argentine citizenship, the title of the article and the caption of the accompanying video are disparaging and exaggerated in their depiction of the migrant threat. In the article title, "Una TV sin fronteras: los extranjeros coparon las pantallas" (A TV without borders: foreigners occupied all the screens), the colloquial verb "copar" has negative connotations when it means "sweep the board" or "take all," as it does here. The video caption similarly reads "La TV se llenó de extranjeros" (The television was filled with foreigners/was taken by foreigners). Both headings induce the erroneous impression of an Argentine TV dominated by foreigners who are not yet incorporated into the Argentine national imaginary.

These are all signs that even a migrant country like Argentina is undergoing a process of social restructuring. As Commisso explains, migration in Argentina is hardly a new phenomenon, but there are differences between historical migratory waves and the current wave produced by globalization, although she does not delve into the nature of these differences. Junyoung Verónica Kim has noted that, in Argentina (as elsewhere), migrants are being used as scapegoats for the negative effects of an unbridled capitalist model applied in the country for decades. Instead of posing deep questions about the validity of this model, Koreans and Bolivians are seen as stealing the jobs and opportunities of deserving Argentines. What is evident is that these migrants pose a threat to the maintenance of the myth of Argentina as a "white" and "European" country.

In the midst of these pervasive prejudices and uncertainties in the social arena, *La salada*'s narrative focus on migration from the perspective of an Argentine-Taiwanese director, its use of Argentine public funds, and its role as a representative of Argentine cinema at film festivals all point to the need to reconstruct the notion of Argentine nationality in order to integrate these new forms of being Argentine without renouncing to hybridity. By integrating the new migrant waves and their hybrid identities into the notion of Argentine-ness without requiring assimilation or acculturation that was required in the past, *La salada* is furthermore regenerating the myth of Argentine as a hospitable country for migrants. I will now turn my attention to the examination of class differences in the films.

LA SALADA AND *PLASTIC CITY* ON CLASS

Technically, the films also position the viewer from the migrants' point of view or offer a sympathetic image of them. Subjective shots of the Tai-wainese character in *La salada* (Huang) are frequent, and there is a recurrent shot of the bridge from what the audience imagines is the inside of the market which seems to subvert the point of view of the media (instead of being seen from outside, the market vendors survey the outside from the market) (Figure 6.1). *La salada* is shot mainly in interiors—the market, private homes, and entertainment venues. There are no establishing shots of the market so that viewers are afforded a glimpse at the market's dimensions, unlike in *Plastic City*, which not only starts with a scene that provides a historical background to the narrative (the Oiapoque scene) but also aerial views of São Paulo and establishing shots of the Liberdade district (the Japanese area). There are also travelling scenes in which the streets of São Paulo are shown, all of which provide a clear context for the complex narrative.

In opposition to this, *La salada* is concerned with the minor problems of its characters about expanding the business and finding a partner. The market appears in separate scenes without a sense of connectivity and instead

Figure 6.1 **Seeing the Bridge *from* the Market.** *Source: La salada.*

presents images that are fragmented, as if the market had been compartmentalized to serve as background for different scenes. The contrast between the total picture of São Paulo in *Plastic City* and the fragmented view of the market area in *La salada* (after all, it is a film divided into three strands) finds its correlation in the superficial versus deep portrayal of class relations in each of the films.

Relations between employers and employees are presented as harmonious in *La salada*. There is no sign of exploitation inside the textile workshops, the restaurants, or the stalls. There is an illustrative scene of this approach with Mr. Kim and Bruno. Mr. Kim's fraternization with his Bolivian employee (Bruno) in the film goes against common perceptions in society that view the Koreans as exploitative of the Bolivians and Argentines working in dire conditions in Korean-run factories. The cinematography constructs the relationship between Mr. Kim and Bruno as affective with two-shots at moments in the narrative when there is a strong bond between them (Figure 6.2).

It is important to note that *La salada*'s "proposal" of Argentine ethnic regeneration is tied to the film's unproblematic view of the transformation of class structure provoked by recent migration. Employers are patient and understanding, there are no conflicts, and the middle-class Korean shares beers with the poor Bolivian worker at the karaoke lounge as he does with his Korean friend. Linguistic and social barriers are easily overcome and—it is implied—hard work will inevitably lead to upward mobility. By presenting this view, *La salada* is in line with the rejection of "the political imperative (what to do)"[24] by New Argentine Cinema and other cinemas of the region in the sense that social conflicts have been displaced to the

Figure 6.2   Mr. Kim with his Employee Bruno. *Source: La salada.*

Figure 6.3   Street Peddlers. *Source: Plastic City.*

private realm: what matters in *La salada*, a place marked in the media as a locus of social conflict due to globalization, is whether Huang will manage to conquer Angie or whether Mr. Kim's precautions to keep his daughter out of Luciano's sight will work. In this sense, this is a postmodern film in the Jamesonian sense.

Yu Lik-wai in *Plastic City* provides scaffolding similar to that of *La salada*, opposing the limitations of the media reports that inspired him to make the movie *Plastic City*; however, class mobility and class relations are treated differently in this film. Street peddlers of different ages, races, and genders devastated by the negative effects that the hypocritical crackdown on piracy have on their livelihoods are widely shown (Figure 6.3). Global and local exploitation are connected in this multi-layered film.

IMPLICATIONS OF FOLLOWING AESTHETIC CONVENTIONS OR STRETCHING THE LIMITS

The key for understanding the profound differences between *La salada* and *Plastic City* lies in their formal analysis and national/global conception. *La salada* is an art-house comedy mainly set in a market and the home of the protagonists whereas *Plastic City* is a thriller filmed in locations as diverse as the Amazon jungle, the border between the French Guiana and Brazil (Oiapoque, archival footage), shopping malls in the Liberdade district of São Paulo, busy streets, night clubs, a jail, derelict towers, and bridges, and flyovers where homeless people sleep and street gangs gather.

What has been said of the market La salada—that "[it is a] true representative of the new global economy," a symbol of what is left after the deregulation of markets and the deindustrialization of the country[25]—is equally applicable to the shopping malls and the streets of São Paulo in *Plastic City*. The spaces of Buenos Aires (*La salada*) host interclass relations in the twenty-first century in a city still reeling from the effects of the 2001 crisis, which prompted a sharp decline of the middle classes and an increase in the unemployed and underemployed in the informal economy. In the case of São Paulo, we can observe signs of transformation in a city that, since the 1980s, has been shifting from a developmental model of progress—where the state fulfilled a strong regulatory and productive role—into a neoliberal governmentality, where the state abandons protectionist import controls in favor of free trade and withdraws from privatized spaces like the shopping malls of *Plastic City*.[26]

It is obvious from this description that these spaces provide more than a mere setting for the narratives. Internationally distributed Latin American films set on locations where interclass relations can be controlled include the successful *7 cajas* (*7 Boxes*, Juan Carlos Maneglia and Carla Schembori, 2012) and *El abrazo partido* (*Lost Embrace*, Daniel Burman, 2004). Moreover, these spaces allow for a unique opportunity for social extension. It is no coincidence that *La salada*, *Plastic City*, *7 cajas*, and *El abrazo partido* are polyglot films where Spanish and Portuguese are spoken alongside Quechua, Mandarin, or Korean. The ethnic groups appearing in these films (Jewish, Chinese, Korean, Bolivian, native Latin American) rarely occupied center stage on national screens before these films' release. These innovations alter the generic conventions of the films so that, in addition to the audience expectations for a comedy or a thriller, new expectations appear regarding a multilingual and multicultural content and a tendency toward an episodic structure (in *La salada*) with several subplots connected through the common spaces of shopping malls and markets.

These similarities notwithstanding, *La salada* and *Plastic City* differ in their degree of aesthetic freedom and global reach. Juan Martín Hsu closely follows the trends of New Argentine Cinema while Yu Lik-wai's mixing of Latin American and Asian referents is highly idiosyncratic. Perhaps for these reasons, Yu's experimentation was not understood by critics at the Venice Film Festival where it premiered—as a result, this work lost the film festival recognition that was vital for the future of Yu's art-house production. In what follows, I compare these two different paths and the consequences that they have on class figuration.

●

LA SALADA'S AESTHETICS

Hsu was born in Buenos Aires and graduated in Image and Sound at the University of Buenos Aires (UBA). The addition of this Argentine director of Taiwanese origin to the group of New Argentine Cinema filmmakers is justified by his formal education, *La salada*'s aesthetics, and Hsu's metacinematic reflexivity in the form of exaggerated intertextual references to Fabián Bielinsky's *Nueve reinas* (*Nine Queens*, 2002) and Martín Rejtman's *Rapado* (1992).

The term New Argentine Cinema refers to a movement whose origins have been traced to the return of director and instructor Alejandro Agresti to Argentina in the 1990s. He had been in the Netherlands before that and was instrumental in getting the Hubert Bals Fund support for director Martín Rejtman who, in 1992, produced the film *Rapado*.[27] At times, the intertextual references to *Nueve reinas* and *Rapado* in *La salada* occupy the full frame and even though they are narratively justified and form part of the diegesis (the character Huang is watching those films), the frequency and length of these references presents a metacinematic reflection that interrupts the flow of *La salada*'s story. Aesthetic affiliation and self-referentiality seem to gain prominence over the stories being narrated. This aesthetic affiliation is strengthened with what Jens Andermann terms the "performances of showing and seeing" characteristic of New Argentine Cinema whereby characters observe attentively what surrounds them."[28] In *La salada*, Huang's observations focus the audience's attention to the market and the flow of vendors and customers shot on location.

New Argentine Cinema productions started to be collectively perceived as a new cinema upon the recognition given to two films in the late 1990s: *Pizza, birra, fasso* (Bruno Stagnaro and Adrián Caetano, 1998) at the Mar del Plata Film Festival in 1997, and *Mundo grúa* (*Crane World*, Pablo Trapero, 1999) at the BAFICI (Independent Film Festival of Buenos Aires) in 1999. One of the main changes introduced by these new filmmakers is a new "oralidad," in Rodrigo Moreno's words. Moreno, the director of *El custodio* (*The Bodyguard*, 2006), also a filmmaker and teacher of this generation, observes that "a movement of new directors appeared, those of my generation, whose first challenge was to create a language similar to the one used in daily life, in reality."[29]

Hsu presented the script for his film at the script workshop PROA, where he modified it in four months under the direction of Rodrigo Moreno. Initially, Hsu presented a complex script with many interweaving stories and a strong focus on the market, but as a result of this work with PROA and production constraints encountered during the filming process (it was difficult to control the crowds inside the market—as is obvious in some scenes—and the budget was limited), it was trimmed to three personal trajectories.

In this market, people from all classes and ethnic groups interact. The inclusion of Korean, Bolivian, Taiwanese, and Caucasian Argentine characters speaking Spanish, Korean, Mandarin, and Quechua in Hsu's film constitutes a novelty in the Argentine film scene where, despite being a film "industry" of a country of migrants, there is a scarcity of narratives of immigrants, particularly of immigrants who are not of European descent. The same scarcity applies to theatre and literature, with a few exceptions such as the work in theatre by Ignacio Huang and the novels by Washington Cucurto and Ariel Magnus. *La salada*'s contribution to "social extension" categorizes this film as "realist" in Raymond Williams' definition[30] at the same time that its new *oralidad* and the abandonment of the abstract narratives of post-dictatorship Argentina that Moreno had observed clearly link it to New Argentine Cinema. Other conventions followed by Hsu include loose narratives, lack of preachy dialogues (see, for instance, the first scene), and an innovative use of sound. *La salada* fills a gap in Argentine cinema identified by Gonzalo Aguilar: the themes of food and family are scarce because immigration "has continually been rendered invisible."[31] Food connects people in *La salada* when a Korean priest shows his friendship to Mr. Kim by giving him a herbal tea that is served by his daughter on many occasions throughout the film, Huang invites the girl he likes to eat pizza, Korean friends and relatives converse while eating at Korean restaurants, and Yungjin meets Luciano in a restaurant.

PLASTIC CITY'S AESTHETICS

Contrasting the neat classification of *La salada* within the canon of the New Argentine Cinema (if the idea of a canon is applicable here), *Plastic City* is a hybrid on a number of levels. Aesthetically, its explicit artistic references are derived from Murcof (a Mexican musician), Cassio Vasconcellos (a Brazilian photographer, also working as a consultant in *Plastic City*), Chinese swordplay films, and popular Japanese yakuza films such as those by Kinji Fukasuku or Takeshi Kitano, where stylized sword fights, sex in nightclubs, and tattoos are trademarks. All these references also exist in conjunction with the acknowledged appropriation of Suzuki Seijun's "synergy of action and psychology."[32] In an interview conducted by the press during a presentation of *Plastic City*, Yu Lik-wai clarified that he did not intend to use a social realist aesthetic to deal with the trade of illegal fake goods; instead, he preferred to use a more surrealist aesthetic approach where symbols and dreams are prominent.

Critics attending the premiere of the 65th Venice Film Festival in 2008 disliked *Plastic City*, and the few reviews published shortly afterwards attacked it mostly for its incongruent mixture of linear and non-linear styles, incomprehensible script,[33] and the shallowness of its characters. Additionally, Brazilian critics did not like certain liberties taken in the film, like the use of a helicopter to travel from São Paulo to the Amazonian jungle, and the presence of a white tiger in these latitudes. Others in Hong Kong found "exhilarating" the mixture of "'Infernal Affairs'-style intrigue with rough-and-tumble, in-your-face 'City of God' action."[34] *Cidade de Deus* is often used in the reviews, even though the only elements that *Plastic City* appropriates from *Cidade de Deus* are images of the favela and Brazilian youth gangs of secondary importance in the film.

The film also contains important magic realist elements. Both as a thriller and as a magic realist film (in the sense Jameson attributes to the term) the film relies on intricacy of plot to create apprehension and awe. As mentioned in the chapter on *Los bastardos*, history plays an important part in the style of magic realism, particularly "historical raw material in which disjunction is structurally present."[35] The disjuncture between classic capitalism (reflected in colonialism and the notion of empire) and late capitalism (reflected in globalization) is explicit in *Plastic City* in the contrast between the search for gold in Oiapoque and the sale in São Paulo of counterfeit goods made in China and Vietnam. Besides this, the use of past violence as it appears at the beginning of *Plastic City* is similar to the depictions of traumatic historical events in García Márquez's *One Hundred Years of Solitude* (for instance, violent repressions that are not acknowledged by authorities in real life appear in the novel). The traumas force both the writer and the filmmaker to find unconventional ways of expressing these events because a conventional, rational, style is no longer adequate to express irrational and disproportionate violence. *Plastic City*'s apocalyptic tone is also present in Yu's better received feature released a year later, *All Tomorrow's Parties* (2009)—this tone is one of the director's trademarks and therefore might not be a product of magic realist influences, but there are other elements in *Plastic City* that follow magic realist conventions.

The initial scene when Kirín's parents are killed is shot in a magic realist style (note the use of intense colors, equal treatment of natural, and magical elements, defamiliarization of common things, and discontinuous narrative): the jungle first appears red, then it displays intense, bright yellow patches that punctuate the frame in accordance with the firing of shots, and a little later its vegetation exhibits various hues of intense greens. In combination with this, we see fragments of a documentary (*Oiapoque-L'Oyapoque: Do outro lado do rio*, Lucas Bambozzi, 1999) and hear a hybrid soundscape combining the music of Murcof with the sounds of the jungle, gunshots, and a radio. At the end of the film, a peaceful white tiger appears unproblematically, looks at Yuda intensely, and summons him. Yuda understands the tiger and takes his own life. In the same place, the tiger, snakes, and trees appear to bleed, which provides an even more intense sense of magic that is unproblematically presented. While it could be argued that the visions are provoked by Yuda's use of drugs and constitute no particular magic realist intention, the relationship between History and Nature in this film nevertheless confirms this aesthetic affiliation.

In his analysis of *La casa de agua* (Jacobo Penzo, 1984), Jameson classifies this film as magic realist and compares it to other features that, like
Penzo's work, engage the ideologemes of History and Nature. In *La casa*,
the protagonist's historical destiny will lead him into political persecution and
his natural destiny will lead him to his death as a result of leprosy. While the
political persecution in the film has the potential to energize the spectators
toward political action, the inevitability of death caused by leprosy can only
lead to a private stoicism. Jameson argues that in certain bourgeois literature
there is a slippage of both kinds of destinies that constitutes a "dangerous
source of depolitization" and suggests that this does not happen in *La casa*
because in this film there is an unresolvable contradiction between both destinies at a formal level (reflected in the intensities of the bodies, images of
the poet screaming in pain, and the use of intense colors like those of the salt
plates) that "libidinally intensifies the remnants in the present of what had
been surgically excised of its other narrative temporalities."[36]

The same can be said of *Plastic City*. In the first part of the film, there is
a moment when Yuda starts to have serious problems with his businesses in
which he looks out to sea and ponders his chances of losing his empire. At
the end of the film, Yuda returns to Nature and stoically accepts his natural
destiny: death. The trees bleed and the blood runs into the river. A poem of
Buddhist, Borgesian, and Blakeian resonances follows:

. . . Every grain of sand is a world
Every particle is a universe . . .

The image of a rough sea similar to the one Yuda had contemplated when
he was pondering his chances of maintaining the empire reappears, but this
time the sea is closer and Yuda is no longer in the frame. The sound of the
waves remains in the background, almost covered by Murcof's music in the
foreground, which is significant because the latter has been used at critical
moments in the film charged with lyrical overtones. Kirín appears in the following shot, looking at a starkly different image of the sea, this time seen
from a distance. Kirín himself is framed by trees as in a painting, positioned
between the viewer and the sea.

To interpret this, I need to engage both Yu's use of the sea in other films
and Brazilian cinema's imagery of the sea. In Yu's 2003 *All Tomorrow's
Parties* (明日天涯) the sea also appears at the end of the film. After all the
destruction and disillusion experienced by the protagonist, the sea represents
hope and the light after darkness. The same can be said of the sea for Kirín
in *Plastic City*: after all the destruction that he has seen, the sea represents a
new beginning. But in addition to this reference to his own oeuvre, Yu Lik-
wai engages Brazilian art and history. The director was asked in an interview

whether *Plastic City*'s Brazil was a real Brazil or a Brazil of the mind, to which he replied,

> Sao Paulo is so "real" that it's sometimes vertiginous! I consider the film as a modern fable. In this Mestizo city, there are no facts, only fairy tales. I always have some vague sense of an imminent Utopia, and inexplicable longing for "somewhere else." In one way, Brazil is a Utopian society. Generations of immigrants have come to its virgin land to fashion a new world and a new god for themselves. If Utopia is a glorious dream of the future, then Plastic City is a pensive elegy for our future world.[37]

In Brazilian cinema, utopia—"the impossible dream of an ideal society, whose very perfection makes it unfeasible" in Nagib's terms[38] and "another word for the socialist project" in Jameson's[39]—evolves in two waves when it is expressed with maritime imagery, according to Nagib. Firstly, there is a revolutionary utopia of the 1960s represented in its rise by Rocha's *Deus e o diabo na terra do sol* (*God and the Devil in the Land of the Sun*, 1964) and in its fall (i.e., via its disbelief in the revolutionary project) by Rocha's *Terra em tramse* (*Land in Anguish*, 1967). Secondly, there is the globalized utopia of *Terra estrangeira* (*Foreign Land,* Walter Salles and Daniela Thomas, 1995) and the cinematic utopia of *Abril despedaçado* (*Behind the Sun*, Walter Salles, 2001), which according to Nagib is a reflection of both Rocha's first social utopia and the individual utopia of Truffaut's *Les quatre cents coups* (*The 400 Blows*, 1959). Following these matrices, the sea varies slightly in meaning in each film but often, as we see in *Midnight* and *Cidade de Deus*, "the access to the maritime paradise remains a privilege of the upper classes."[40]

In *Plastic City*, Yu Lik-wai reinterprets this tradition from a global film making perspective rather than from Latin American film history. His film is an attempt at visually articulating the contradiction between History and Nature. The juxtaposition of two different images of the sea at the end correspond to simultaneous and antithetical messages: The first image suggests to a certain extent a Buddhist acceptance of the destiny that Yuda has created for himself whereas, in the second, there is no ideological confusion between Nature and History of the sort that would invite one to resign in the face of the precariousness brought about by globalization. The sea is the destiny that Kirín must refuse in order to accept his destiny in History, which means his full integration in the Brazilian and the global social imaginary of characters like him and the growing neoliberal precariat. This antithesis "open[s] up a concrete perspective on the real future."[41]

The problematic question of the "national" in Brazil has been discussed by Stam, Vieira, and Xavier.[42] Yu Lik-wai deals with the integration of new Asian immigrants and the global precariat (the street peddlers in Brazil as well as the factory workers in China) into this transnational imagined community. In this sense, *Plastic City* constitutes an example of a "transnational allegory" that confirms the possibility of a "Third World *national* allegory . . . in the new *transnational* setting" that Sheldon Lu had questioned.[43]

Although this message is not explicit, it is further expressed in parts of the film when Kirín mentions to his workers how prices are low because Asians work as slaves. It is also visually expressed with recurrent images of hawkers occupying the full frame (when Yuda's empire is crumbling, the focus is not only on Yuda's family and close gang members, but also on all the workers who lose their jobs because of the anti-piracy campaign). The global flow of money (which can be allegorically interpreted as China's investment in Latin America) is highlighted by the emphasis on the color and texture of both money (the notes that Kirín throws from the roof) and gold (the nuggets that his mother kept in her hands). Comments from the film's producer, Chow Keung, point in the same direction: "Yu Lik-wai is a person who can observe these flows and how the Chinese survive because of the gaps left in different places in the world. The Chinese take advantage of these gaps to make their living."[44] As in a magic realist film made by Latin American filmmaker Rui Guerra (*Eréndira*), this film is "evocative and suggestive rather than didactic . . . rooted in cultural values rather than in any obvious political agenda,"[45] but it still calls to mind the problems faced by the precariat of the world.

Yu Lik-wai's experiment is nurtured by a wide range of artistic traditions with the aim of producing global art, whereas Juan Martín Hsu's film, at a more limited level of experimentation, enhances New Argentine Cinema's profile. The recourse to a circular narrative structure in *Plastic City* also differs significantly from *La salada*'s circularity. While in *Plastic City* an engagement with personal and global history opens questions about social restructuring at a global level, in *La salada* circularity is a stylistic device that produces a bourgeois narrative closure. I will finish this chapter by comparing these films' modes of production.

DIFFERENT FIGURATIONS AND DIFFERENT MODES OF PRODUCTION

A prize from the INCAA (the Argentine Film Institute) to produce his first feature (*La salada*) was a springboard for further co-production with Sudestada Cine (an Argentine producer specializing in art-house films) and Nephilim Producciones (a studio located in Madrid). The project was finished with the prizes "Cine en construcción" obtained at the 61st San Sebastian Film Festival in 2013 and Postproduction Prize Alba Cultura "Nuestra América Primera Copia" of the Festival Internacional del Nuevo Cine Latino Americano de la Habana in 2013. A characteristic feature of New Argentine Cinema is the fragmentation of production, which tends to include both international funding (particularly from Europe and North America) and governmental funding (from the INCAA, in accordance with the cinema law of 1994). Due to their small budgets, independent films in Argentina are generally shot across extended periods of time, but despite all the difficulties involved, new Argentine filmmakers such as Lucrecia Martel, Lisandro Alonso and Pablo Trapero have still managed to attract nearly as much global attention as "the three amigos" in Mexico (González Iñárritu, Cuarón, and del Toro) and as much as the Mexican global auteur Carlos Reygadas. There are also a number of new Argentine filmmakers who started to film feature films in the mid-1990s yet who managed to film continuously throughout the eighteen or so years since they began, despite the major crisis that Argentina experienced in 2001–02. International film festivals and institutions like the Hubert Bals Fund of the Rotterdam Film Festival, Sundance, Fonds Sud Cinéma of the French Government and the intergovernmental Ibermedia group became important for the realization of these projects, although funding from the INCAA still constitutes the main source of funding for many projects. Juan Martín Hsu took advantage of all those opportunities, but the public contribution of the Argentine state was essential for the completion of his project.

Yu Lik-wai's production methods are different from Hsu's. He was born in Hong Kong, but he has made most of his films in the PRC as the cinematographer of Jia Zhangke. This film in particular, *Plastic City*, is a Hong Kong-Brazil-France-Japan co-production. Since most Latin American co-productions "are carried out with European countries, and to a lesser extent with other countries in the region,"[46] this co-production between such distant areas of the world and different cultures is highly unusual. In fact, he may well be the second Chinese filmmaker not residing in Latin America to film a fiction film in the region after Wong Kar-Wai.[47] In this co-production, Brazil invested 60 percent of the budget even though the project originated in Hong Kong and was originally Yu Lik-wai's idea. The Hong Kong Production Company, Xtream Pictures, was set up in 2003 by Yu Lik-wai, Chow Keung, (*Plastic City*'s producer), and Jia Zhangke, the increasingly prestigious and critically acclaimed independent Chinese filmmaker of films such as *The World* and *A Touch of Sin*. Yu Lik-wai's work as a director has also been recognized at Cannes. His first drama feature, *Love Will Tear Us Apart*, was part of the Official Selection at the 52nd Cannes Film Festival, and *All Tomorrow's Parties* was selected at the same festival in the category of *Un Certain Regard* at the 56th event. The ties between Yu Lik-wai, Jia Zhangke, and Chow Keung originate from the IFVA, the visual arts festival in Hong Kong that was directed by Chow Keung in its first two occurrences. Both Jia Zhangke and Yu Lik-wai presented their first shorts in 1996 at this festival.

Yu's and Keung's association with the Brazilian producer Gullane is highly innovative and involved a great deal of risk. Instead of relying on the Hong Kong ADC for the funding, he mainly relied on private sources of funding. Unfortunately, *Plastic City* did not achieve the film festival recognition that was needed for success and fell into obscurity.

The treatment of global flows in regard to content and visual innovation is more complicated in *Los bastardos* (studied in chapter 5) and *Plastic City* than in *La salada* because the varied composition of institutions and actors in the production of the former two features involves a higher degree of reflection and a lived experience of what globalization entails (among the other reasons already examined). The directors who were more attuned to how filmmaking processes are affected by globalization (Escalante; Yu) were able to play with these complexities in their own works more successfully, and their political "intervention in the global future" is clearer than in the case of nationally circumscribed filmmaker like Hsu.

Finally, we may return to Appadurai's observation on culture: "It is in culture that ideas of the future, as much as those about the past, are embedded and nurtured."[48] Indeed, these films envision a continuation of the struggle to maintain or improve our social positions through class struggle or consumption from below. At any rate, the state is no longer an effective player in this fight and the struggle has inevitably acquired a global character, regardless of whether we remain in our original birthplace, oblivious to globalization or move across continents to take advantage of its fissures—like Yuda in *Plastic City*.

NOTES

1. Jörn Dosch, points out that the colonization of the Philippines by Spain was the first event to complete a global chain connecting Europe, the Americas, and Asia. Asian-Latin American connections continue to be important in the contemporary phase of globalization. Jörn Dosch, "Introduction. The Three-Phase Encounter of Two Continents," in *Asia and Latin America: Political, Economic and Multilateral Relations*, eds. Jörn Dosch and Olaf Jacob (London: Routledge, 2010), 1.

2. It is useful to remember that, historically, the recognition of the contribution of Chinese Immigrants to Latin American nation building encountered strong resistance in some Latin American nations. Kathleen López, "In Search of Legitimacy: Chinese Immigrants and Latin American Nation Building," in *Immigration and National Identities in Latin America*, eds. Nicola Foote and Michael Goebel (Gainesville: The University Press of Florida, 2014).

3. Many of these discourses are tinged with a threatening tone about the power of the Chinese to control Latin American economies. The journalists Juan Pablo Cardenal and Heriberto Araújo, who have followed Chinese investors around the world, have warned about the possible negative effects of the increasing Chinese investment worldwide (see *China's Silent Army: The Pioneers, Traders, Fixers and Workers*

Who Are Remaking the World in Beijing's Image). Official statements on both the Chinese and the Latin American sides usually emphasize the mutual benefits of the relationship and the construction of a different world order.

4. This publication is illustrative of the difficulties of finding experts on Asian-Latin American cultural interconnections: Julia Strauss and Ariel C. Armony, eds., *From the Great Wall to the New World: China and Latin America in the 21st Century* (Cambridge: Cambridge University Press, 2012).

5. A specialist in BRIC cinema, for instance, foresees an increase in this type of co-productions. Tatu-Ilari Laukkanen, "The Contemporary Cinema of the BRIC Countries and the Politics of Change" (PhD thesis, The University of Hong Kong, 2016), 742.

6. Sheldon Hsiao-peng Lu, ed., *Transnational Chinese Cinemas: Identity, Nationhood, Gender* (Honolulu: University of Hawai'i Press, 1997), 18, 105.

7. The ethnicity of the Cuban actor playing Chan Li-Po, Evaristo Samón Domínguez by his real name, is difficult to ascertain in a place like Cuba where hybridity is the norm, but he was not readily identified with the Chinese. This is a typical case of Caucasians standing for "the other."

8. In another Argentine film (*El Custodio*, 2006) there is a scene in a Chinese restaurant where we do see Chinese waiters and customers having a conflict with the family of the protagonist.

9. Natalia Milanesio, *Workers Go Shopping in Argentina: The Rise of Popular Consumer Culture* (Albuquerque: University of New Mexico Press, 2013), 229.

10. Gonzalo Aguilar, *New Argentine Film: Other Worlds* (New York: Palgrave Macmillan, 2008), 63, 65.

11. Joseph E. Stiglitz, *Globalization and Its Discontents* (New York: Norton, 2003), 9.

12. Arjun Appadurai, *Globalization* (Durham: Duke University Press, 2001), 6.

13. Pedro N. Mizukami, Oona Castro, Luiz Fernando Moncao, and Ronaldo Lemos, "Chapter 5: Brazil," in *Media Piracy in Emerging Economies*, ed. Joe Karaganis (New York: Social Sciences Research Council, 2011), 223.

14. Mizukami et al., "Chapter 5: Brazil," 261–62.

15. Muzikami et al. refer to Law Kin Chong as "Chong," but his surname is Law. The first word in Chinese names is the surname. Mizukami et al., "Chapter 5: Brazil," 262.

16. Rodrigo Bertolotto, "Chineses reclamam de perseguição em SP devido á fama de Law Kin Chong," *UOL*, December 4, 2007.

17. "*Plastic City*: Press Kit," 7.

18. Robert Stam, João Luiz Vieira, and Ismail Xavier, "The Shape of Brazilian Cinema in the Postmodern Age," in *Brazilian Cinema*, eds. Randal Johnson and Robert Stam, (New York: Columbia University Press, 1995), 440.

19. Roxana Santamaría and Gabriela Itzcovich, "Percepciones y prejuicios hacia inmigrantes coreanos y paraguayos residentes en la Argentina," in *Relaciones interculturales: Experiencias y representación social de los migrantes*, eds. Néstor Cohen and Carolina Mera (Buenos Aires: Antropofagia, 2005), 34.

20. Santamaría and Itzcovich, "Percepciones y prejuicios;" Yunyoung Verónica Kim, "Desarticulando el 'mito blanco': Inmigración coreana en Buenos Aires e

imaginarios nacionales," *Revista de crítica literaria latinoamericana* 71 (2010): 169–93.

21. This is the annual prize of the Cámara Argentina de Productoras Independientes de Televisión (CAPIT), Association of Independent Television Producers of Argentina.

22. Sandra Commisso, "Una TV sin fronteras: Los extranjeros coparon la pantalla," *Clarín,* November 29, 2012.

23. Carolina Mera, *La inmigración coreana en Buenos Aires. Multiculturalismo en el espacio urbano* (Buenos Aires: Eudeba, 1998).

24. Aguilar, *New Argentine Film,* 16.

25. Natalia Milanesio, *Workers Go Shopping in Argentina: The Rise of Popular Consumer Culture* (Albuquerque: University of New Mexico Press, 2013), 228.

26. Teresa P. R. Caldeira, "From Modernism to Neoliberalism in São Paulo."

27. Aguilar, *New Argentine Film,* 11–12.

28. Jens Andermann, *New Argentine Cinema* (London: I. B. Tauris, 2012), xvii.

29. Rodrigo Moreno, Telephone interview, August 23, 2014.

30. Raymond Williams, "A Lecture on Realism," *Screen* 18, no. 1 (1977): 61–74.

31. Aguilar, *New Argentine Film,* 197.

32. "*Plastic City*: Press Kit," 7.

33. Derel Elley, "Review: 'Plastic City,'" *Variety* August 30, 2008; James Wegg, "Plastic City (Dang Kou): Too Many Threads to Weave the Fabric," *James Wegg Review (JWR)* October 1, 2008.

34. Justice Lai, "Movie Review: Plastic City," *HK Magazine* September 8, 2008.

35. Jameson, "On Magic Realism," 311.

36. Jameson, "On Magic Realism," 308, 323.

37. "*Plastic City*: Press Kit," 7.

38. Lúcia Nagib, *Brazil on Screen. Cinema Novo, New Cinema, Utopia* (London: I. B. Tauris, 2007), 9.

39. Fredric Jameson, "Third-World Literature in the Era of Multinational Capitalism," *Social Text* 15 (1986), 80.

40. Nagib, *Brazil on Screen,* 30.

41. Jameson, "Third-World Literature," 77.

42. Robert Stam, João Luiz Vieira, and Ismail Xavier, "The Shape of Brazilian Cinema in the Postmodern Age," in *Brazilian Cinema,* Expanded ed., eds. Randal Johnson and Robert Stam, 393–96.

43. Sheldon Hsiao-peng Lu, ed., *Transnational Chinese Cinemas,* 105.

44. Keung Chow, Personal interview, May 11, 2013.

45. Stam, Vieira, and Xavier, "The Shape of Brazilian Cinema in the Postmodern Age," 441.

46. Jorge Mario Martínez Piva, Ramón Padilla Pérez, Claudia Schatan Pérez, and Verónica Vega Montoya, *The Mexican Film Industry and Its Participation in the Global Value Chain* (Mexico D.F.: UN, CEPAL, 2011), 20.

47. "*Plastic City*: Press Kit," 8.

48. Arjun Appadurai, *The Future as Cultural Fact: Essays on the Global Condition* (London: Verso, 2013), 181.

Conclusion

A considerable number of contemporary Latin American films from the five nations selected as well as the film scholarship centered around them give weight to the argument of the dissolution of class in contemporary societies. Carlos Reygadas' approach to filmmaking in Mexico as exemplified in *Post Tenebras Lux* and Carlos Aguilar's contention of the abandonment of *el pueblo* in most of contemporary Argentine filmmaking are just two paradigmatic examples of this belief in filmmaking and film scholarship respectively. Despite the widespread impression that class struggle has largely disappeared from the screen as an explicit theme,[1] not solely Venezuelan films but also nationally and globally sanctioned Mexican, Brazilian, Cuban and Argentine productions are enactments of the social contradictions associated to class relations in the texts and the entire filmmaking process, from the access to resources as spectators and producers to the films' circulation after postproduction. As Erik Olin Wright has noted in sociological studies, the contemporary belief in the dissolution of classes is but one of the beliefs. "Others believe class remains one of the fundamental forms of social inequality and social power,"[2] and make it explicitly visible in their films, although the aesthetics and politics of contemporary texts differ markedly from 1960s to 1970s paradigmatic films such as *La hora de los hornos* (Fernando Solanas, 1968), *Deus e o diabo na terra do Sol* (Glauber Rocha, 1964), and *De cierta manera* (Sara Gómez, 1977).[3]

Some scholars such as Ivana Bentes and Ana Ros have unsuccessfully attempted to describe the distinctive materializations of class in cinema of the first decade of the twenty-first century. Bentes, for instance, posits "[t]he inefficiency of modernity's totalizing political discourse," where "modernity's totalizing political discourse" stands for Marxism within the parameters of post-Marxist literature, but is unable to find a more satisfactory theory for the

accurate description of the films' devices whereby class relations are imagined as violent struggles. In her view,

> the surge of a new, Latin American "neorealism" that would include films such
> as *Amores Perros* (Alejandro González Iñárritu, 2000) and *O invasor* (*The Tres-
> passer*—Beto Brant, 2002), interest us here in what could be considered their
> affirmative, positive aspects. Our analysis reads the new brutality as a line of
> dialogue with the aesthetics of hunger and violence inherited from the sixties, as
> we have argued elsewhere (Bentes, 2003). Not merely as "continuity," impos-
> sible in the face of a new historical context, but rather as an extemporaneous
> dialogue: as a Latin American contribution to the construction of a vital and
> affirmative form of thinking about poverty, an aesthetics of confrontation and
> violence, which displaces or relativizes the myths of cordiality in the name of a
> new kind of virulence.[4]

A similar failure to theorize new forms of enacting class relations on films
combined with what appears to be skepticism toward Marxism is found in
Ana Ros' analysis of *Cama adentro* (*Live-in Maid*, Jorge Gaggero, 2004).
According to Ros,

> Gaggero's film challenges the kind of reading that equates every element in fic-
> tion with an element in "structural reality," according to abstract notions about
> how society works (such as "class"). By "challenging" I do not mean disregard-
> ing abstract notions per se. On the contrary, I mean that instead of establishing
> a link between abstraction and fiction to illuminate both fiction and the social
> conflicts addressed in fiction, *Live-in Maid* takes a step further and also illumi-
> nates theory by showing its limits.[5]

It becomes clear from these quotes that using class as a critical tool in
film studies often results in intuitions. A key reference for understanding this
structure of feeling[6] is what Jean-François Lyotard diagnosed as the crisis of
knowledge created by the end of grand narratives, that is, the end of sciences
that make recourse to metanarratives such as "the liberation of men" or "revolution," among others. Lyotard states that, instead of relying on these grand
narratives, Wittgensteinian language games that are not based on preexisting
legitimating narratives dominate our contemporary academic discourses. The
latter are governed by rules that carry with them their own legitimation.[7]
Fredric Jameson interprets Lyotard's diagnosis of epistemological concerns
and its interrelated view of a fully communicational society (where the social
bond would not be explained in terms of class as was understood earlier)
as the cultural logic of late capitalism, and refutes Lyotard's contentions by
arguing that "classical capitalism" still retains its explanatory power for the
"multinational and media societies of today."[8]

With this book, I have tried to accomplish two main objectives both within Latin American film and cultural studies: (1) to reignite the attention to class, and (2) to problematize the approaches to class. The first objective is closely tied to contemporary socio-political developments in line with a reawakening of class discourses in the society at large that have made Karl Marx popular again (the unexpectedly large attendances to seminars on Marx across the globe, new editions of publications on/by Marx, and the release of biopics of this philosopher are symptomatic of the contemporary search for Marxist answers to the increasing precariousness of life). The successive crises unfolding since 2008 which have brought to the spotlight the faults of neoliberalism in the industrialized world and some Latin American countries like Mexico, and the Turn-to-the-Left experienced in some large nations in Latin America inevitably left a mark on the screen, and these "effects" need to be systematically observed and examined. Emerging research interest in these effects such as those by Marc Zimmerman and Luis Ochoa Bilbao, Mabel Moraña and Jens Andermann are still insufficient and thus the present study's comparative focus on the enactment of class on films produced in strongly neoliberal and twenty-first-century socialist countries fills a gap in Latin American film scholarship. In addition to this, this book constitutes a unique contribution to the study of the cinematic presentation of other social developments characteristic of the twenty-first century such the surprising return of populism and the intensification of global migratory flows and co-productions within the Global South and the BRICS.

Secondly, when we look at class, we need to understand that this is a term subject to various conceptualizations and narrations. In some cases, finding correspondences between narratives and well-known conceptualizations of how class works proves easy while other narratives produce figurations of social changes yet to be conceptualized. I will illustrate this difference with a selection of the close textual analyses in previous chapters. The Venezuelan film *La clase* presents a classic "class struggle" between the proletariat and the bourgeoisie within an established Marxist theoretical approach that, incidentally, does not accurately reflect the complexity of class relations in contemporary Venezuela (neo-Marxists would provide a more nuanced description of the Venezuelan conjuncture by taking into account subjective perceptions as well as ownership of the means of production[9]). In contrast, the figuration of class formation in the Venezuelan film *Macuro* as being constructed through discourse according to the establishment of equivalences between social demands better represents a contemporary social logic. The latter social dynamics has been famously theorized by Ernesto Laclau and is widely known and used to interpret social movements in the twenty-first century in Latin America and elsewhere. A third example are instances of textualizations of class relations in the political unconscious that are yet to be fully conceptualized in other fields, and are analyzed here in the chapters concerned with the globalization of class on screen. The fictions in these chapters imagine the shifting field of class locations and relations in a world now completely immersed in globalization where the national framework has become almost irrelevant. In sum, this volume has attempted to map out the main approaches to class figurations and their study in the cinemas of the five nations concerned bearing in mind that this is just the beginning of a necessary systematic approach to a challenging and ever-changing subject.

Even though this book's protean approach permits the application of various theoretical frameworks to class analyses, it fully endorses Fredric Jameson's view of the need to establish a hierarchy among them.[10] This methodology enables the researcher to unveil the ideological underpinnings of the intended "neutral" or non-ideological approach to filmmaking of presumably depoliticized films (one of the most commonly observed approaches in scholarly discourses on contemporary filmmaking) without overriding it. Positing the priority of the political interpretation of texts offers the hermeneutical advantage of overcoming the indeterminacy inherent in the mere description of a film's politics. Ultimately, this approach demands that the researcher take a stance on processes unfolding in filmmaking such as "chronicling" extreme social inequality and developments in film reception toward the increasing inaccessibilty of the working class and the lumpen proletariat to cinemas due to high ticket prices and the "gated" architecture of the multiplexes where cinema theaters are located. These facts, as has been amply demonstrated, determine the accommodation of films to the tastes of the wealthiest spectators who are middle and upper-middle-class consumers. The observation of this phenomenon in some of the countries in this study should be cause for alarm among scholars but the criticism against these pernicious phenomena favored by neoliberalism among film and cultural researchers has not reached by far the levels that the rejection against Bolivarian cinema has provoked. However, the (limited) film reception initiatives in Venezuela toward social extension point to the effectiveness of community-oriented approaches to reverse the neoliberal ghettoization of film spectatorship in Latin America. If, as Wright points out, "Marxist class analysis is ultimately about the conditions and process of social change,"[11] and Jameson's method is committed to change, a neutral description and interpretation of the neoliberalization of cinema by specialists does not suffice.

A further reflection on this aspect of film and cultural scholarship is motivated by Jeffrey Middents' study of the interplay of criticism alongside filmmaking in the articulation of Peruvian national cinema.[12] Latin American film scholars have shaped our understanding of class relations on the screen alongside filmmakers. The near celebratory tone of some studies on the cinema of neoliberalism contrasts with the strong denunciatory tone against the aforementioned FVC productions, and this contradiction as well as the imbalance in anglophone scholarship's attention to each of these cinemas (if such generalizations as neoliberal cinema and FVC cinema are productive) point toward the involvement of scholars and critics in validating certain practices and censuring/critiquing others. This professional practice contributes to some extent to the wide distribution and study of narratives where the lower classes figure as individuals serving the upper-middle classes such as *Que horas ela volta?* (Anne Muylaert, 2015) while narratives filmed from a lower-class perspective like the Venezuelan *1, 2 y 3 mujeres* (Andrea Herrera Catalá, Andrea Ríos, Anabel Rodríguez Ríos, 2008) remain unnoticed and nearly invisible. This does not mean to say that scholarly attention is responsible for the deserved success of *Que horas ela volta?* and the absence of *1, 2 y 3 mujeres* from the international arena, nor does it mean in the least that scholarly attention to films determines a production's success. The high production value of *Que horas ela volta?*, Muylaert's talent and capacity to engage with audiences' worldwide, and her long experience in television are no doubt the most important factors responsible for the film's success. Similarly, *1, 2 y 3 mujeres* episodic structure, low budget, and poor distribution might be the main causes for the film's invisibility.

AESTHETICS AS AN ISOLABLE EXTRA-SOCIAL PHENOMENON

The significant correlation of class dissolution with a heightened attention to aesthetics tends to occur in global art films validated by juries at prestigious international film festivals and critics. Aesthetic innovation is favored at the expense of clear politics understood as the correspondence with recognizable phenomena in the political economy. Not all acclaimed contemporary filmmakers, however, emphasize the centrality of aesthetics in figurations of class relations or class differences, as the wide range of case studies examined here demonstrate. This book draws on the work of Raymond Williams to register the tendency to treat aesthetics as an "isolable extra-social phenomenon"[13]—the eternal debated question of the independence of art from economics—in a number of well-known films dealing with social problems. Comparing the politics of experimental films where aesthetic innovation plays a prominent role such as *Post Tenebras Lux* (Carlos Reygadas, 2012) and *Plastic City* (Yu Lik-wai, 2008) sheds light on the former's noncommittal attitude (apparent in the film's depiction of class relations as immobile class differences) and the latter's socially committed ideology. Before proceeding, it must be clarified that, the concept of ideology is important in Marxist thinking about culture but not exclusive of this tradition.[14] Within the field of film studies, John Hess' definition of it as "a relatively systematic body of ideas, attitudes, values, and perceptions, as well as, actual modes of thinking (usually unconscious) typical of a given class or group of people in a specific time and place"[15] makes clear that ideology is not individual. Against some narrow interpretations of Marxist cultural analysis that try to demonstrate that a film's ideology is directly caused by certain economic conditions (i.e., that the base determines the superstructure), Hess, among others, interprets the base and the superstructure as a whole, as an integrated structure rather than separate entities, a view to which this book subscribes.

Having made this clarification, a further proof of the link between the primacy of the aesthetic and the impetus toward depoliticization is evident in *La salada*'s strong focus on intertextual references aimed at unequivocally inserting the film within the New Argentine Cinema aesthetics when dealing with migration and job precariousness. This approach to filmmaking indicates that this is viewed as a movement where aesthetics has somehow been isolated from the social problem, as some specialists in New Argentine Cinema seem to mean in their descriptions. In examining this phenomenon with regard to *el pueblo*, Gonzalo Aguilar points out that,

> antes que partir de la política como un dato exterior en el que sostener una imagen, estas películas—al negarse a la categoría que había dominado el cine de los años sesenta—introducen lo político en la imagen, como fuerza y como interrogante. Antes que una apertura del cine a la política, lo que se piensa en el espacio del cine es la posibilidad misma de una acción política. ¿Cómo fundar desde la imagen lo político si a la salida del cine ya no hay ningún pueblo esperando?[16]

In Aguilar's words, contemporary cinema questions the possibility of political action rather than embedding a pro-filmic reality in the image. Aguilar questions the possibility of a politics of the image if there is no *pueblo* outside the cinema. *La salada* adopts this New Argentine Cinema attitude toward filmmaking and, in contrast to *Plastic City*, presents a harmonious relationship between employers and employees based on common sentimental problems of all human beings even though *La salada* is set in a typical mega-market emerging as a result of globalization and neoliberalism in different Latin American countries which is key for understanding global class locations and conflicts produced by global flows of people and objects. Hsu comfortably glides through the terrain established by a non-committed film movement that has received ample international recognition.

A particular Latin American manifestation of the discussion over the autonomy of culture from the political and the economic revolves around magic realism. Two Nobel prize winners for Literature, Gabriel García Márquez and Mario Vargas Llosa hold opposing views. García Márquez stresses how magic realism arises from the need to convey the excesses of reality. For him, magic realism poses a deep relationship between art and the socio-political conjunctures from where it emanates, not just as an inspiration, but also as an intervention.[17] Contrary to this view, Vargas Llosa advocates a kind of radical separation between literature and history. For him, while imagining Latin America as the land of *lo real maravilloso* (magic realism) is acceptable in literature, the fields of history and economics require a different level of rigor, as they should follow a scientific method of interpretation.[18] The films *Los bastardos* and *Plastic City* prove the persistence of magic realism to vigorously combine aesthetics and politics in the new millennium.

CLASS RELATIONS AS THEME AND PRACTICE

In my attempt at mapping the geography of class relations in the contemporary cinemas of Venezuela, Cuba, Mexico, Brazil, and Argentina, a wide range of factors were taken into account including the texts' figurations alongside legislation, film development policies of public institutions or supranational organizations and independent or major producers that provide funding or prestige, infrastructure development, production, and consumption. Chuck Kleinhans, aware of the successful elaboration of gender and race as critical concepts in matters of film representation and reception, drew a roadmap for a similar development in class studies. The critical conceptualization of class could include reception studies with a focus on class in the same way that female spectatorship models were developed.[19] The present study took into account secondary literature on reception studies related to class but the establishment of measures to increase the access of the lower classes to filmmaking production, distribution, and exhibition and the analysis of reception in connection to social class are areas in need of further study.

The awareness of the construction of class at all stages of production was already present to a certain extent in NLAC, where theorizations about aesthetics and exhibition in relation to the audience were common.[20] For NLAC, class was a theme and, most importantly, an attempt to change dominant distribution and exhibition patterns and to democratize the film production scene by offering more opportunities to the underprivileged. Although contemporary cinema retains the thematic concern with class, in most cinemas there are no public or private initiatives to engage all sectors of the population in filmmaking regardless of their class nor are there schemes to guarantee access for all to cinemas that could counter observed trends toward audience segregation driven by the market observed in Mexico,[21] Argentina and Brazil. Close analysis of all the films under study revealed class dynamics in relation to the socio-political situation of each nation, but the results did not show a strict division of class ideologies along national lines. What remains clear, however, is the effect that extra-textual global dynamics exert on the films' ideologies of class (audience tastes shaped by Hollywood and its conservative class ideology, treatment of aesthetics according to what is acceptable by international fora of Eurocentric critics and filmmakers, total rejection of revolutionary rhetoric, etc.).

If the means of producing films are not in the hands of the working class or the underprivileged who know their own world "inside out" (as Borges writes)[22] and there are no systematic initiatives to democratize the filmmaking practice, a situation whereby upper-middle-class and middle-class filmmakers will hold the power of audiovisual and narrative imagination of social relations is likely to continue. Initiatives (research and otherwise) aimed at raising awareness ("un despertar de conciencias") about these dynamics and systematic measures destined to reverse them are urgently needed, and existing counter-neoliberal practices should be celebrated.

NOTES

1. See more on the survival of the term in Javier Trímboli, "The Survival of Words: Revolution and Class Struggle," *Journal of Latin American Cultural Studies* 27, no. 1 (2018): 63–81.

2. Erik Olin Wright, ed., *Approaches to Class Analysis* (N.p.: Cambridge University Press, 2005), i.

3. Glauber Rocha's cinema of ecstasy has been differentiated from the dialectical cinema of Fernando Solanas and Sara Gómez, at the same time that Glauber Rocha and Fernando Solanas have been distinguished as two opposing forms of enacting *el pueblo*, but their contextualization within public spheres where discourses around *el pueblo* shared a relatively uniform understanding of the term distinguishes these three films as a group from contemporary films produced in conjunctures where the effects of decades of advanced capitalism and the resurgence of "populist" movements across the globe give the masses, the people, and the multitude different and much more heterogeneous meanings. For more on the differences between Rocha and Solanas, see Gonzalo Aguilar, *Más allá del pueblo*, 184, 186–87.

4. Ivana Bentes, "Global Periphery: Aesthetic and Cultural Margins in Brazilian Audiovisual Forms," in *New Argentine and Brazilian Cinema*, eds. Jens Andermann and Álvaro Fernández Bravo (New York: Palgrave Macmillan, 2013), 107.

5. Ana Ros, "Leaving and Letting Go as Possible Ways of Living Together in Jorge Gaggero's *Cama Adentro/Live-in Maid*," in *New Trends in Argentine and Brazilian Cinema*, eds. Cacilda Rêgo and Carolina Rocha, 99.

6. This term, coined by Raymond Williams, refers to "meanings and values as they are actively lived and felt" in a generation. Raymond Williams, *Marxism and Literature* (Oxford: Oxford University Press, 2009), 132.

7. Jean-François Lyotard, *The Postmodern Condition: A Report on Knowledge* (Manchester: Manchester University Press, 1984), 10.

8. Fredric Jameson, "Foreword," in *The Postmodern Condition: A Report on Knowledge*, ed. Jean-François Lyotard (Manchester: Manchester University Press, 1984), viii.

9. The author of the book *Barrio Rising: Urban Popular Politics and the Making of Modern Venezuela* (2015), Alejandro Velasco, has noted the shifting allegiances of slum residents in Venezuela which might be indicative of people's subjective perceptions of their own class. Pablo Stefanoni, "Venezuela, ¿por qué no bajan de los cerros? Entrevista a Alejandro Velasco," *Nueva Sociedad. Democracia y política en América Latina*, June 2017.

10. See Fredric Jameson, *The Political Unconscious: Narrative as a Socially Symbolic Act* (London: Routledge, 2002), 16. Since the 1980s, when postmodernism became the cultural dominant, Marxism is generally regarded outmoded.

11. Wright, ed., *Approaches to Class Analysis*, 20.

12. Jeffrey Middents, *Writing National Cinema: Film Journals and Film Culture in Peru* (Hanover, NH: Dartmouth College Press, 2009), 4.

13. Williams, *Marxism and Literature*, 153.

14. Williams, *Marxism and Literature*, 55.

15. John Hess, "Film and Ideology," *Jump Cut* 17 (1978): n.p.

16. Aguilar, *Más allá del pueblo*, 191.

17. Gabriel García Márquez, "The Solitude of Latin America. Gabriel García Márquez, Nobel Lecture," *Nobelprize.org. The Official Web Site of the Nobel Prize*, Nobel Foundation, December 8, 1982.

18. Mario Vargas Llosa, *Sueño y realidad de América Latina* (Barcelona: Arcadia, 2010), 24–25.

19. Chuck Kleinhans, "Class in Action," in *The Hidden Foundation*, eds. David E. James and Rick Berg, 256–58.

20. See, for instance, Julio García Espinosa's reflections in Michael Chanan, *Cuban Cinema*, 305, and Glauber Rocha's manifesto "Down with Populism," in *Twenty-five Years of The New Latin American Cinema*, ed. Michael Chanan (London: BFI and Channel Four, 1983).

21. See, for instance, Mexico's case in Misha MacLaird, *Aesthetics and Politics in the Mexican Film Industry* (New York: Palgrave Macmillan, 2013), 2.

22. See chapter 2.

References

FILMOGRAPHY

1, 2 y 3 mujeres [*1, 2 and 3 Women*]. Dir. Andrea Herrera Catalá, Andrea Ríos and Anabel Rodríguez Ríos. Venezuela, 2008. Amazonia Films. DVD.

7 cajas [*7 Boxes*]. Dir. Juan Carlos Maneglia and Carla Schombori Paraguay, 2012. Film.

El abrazo partido [*Lost Embrace*]. Dir. Daniel Burman. Argentina, 2004. New Yorker, 2005. DVD.

Abril despedaçado [*Behind the Sun*]. Dir. Walter Salles. Brazil, 2001. Buena Vista, 2002. DVD.

Alicia en el pueblo de Maravillas [*Alice in Wondertown*]. Dir. Daniel Díaz Torres. Cuba, 1991. Film.

All Tomorrow's Parties [*Ming ri tian ya*, 明日天涯]. Dir. Yu Lik-wai. China, 2009. Ying yi zhi, 2010. DVD.

Amarrados [*Tied Up*]. Dir. Amat Escalante. Mexico, 2002. Film.

Amores perros. Dir. Alejandro González Iñárritu. Mexico, 2000. Studio Home Entertainment, 2001. DVD.

The Avengers. Dir. Joss Whedon. USA, 2012. Warner Home, 2010. DVD.

Aventurera. Dir. Alberto Gout. Mexico, 1950. Film.

Los bastardos [*The Bastards*]. Dir. Amat Escalante. Mexico, 2008. Kino, 2009. DVD.

La batalla de Chile [*The Battle of Chile*]. Dir. Patricio Guzmán. Chile-Cuba, 1975–1979. Icarus Films, 2009. DVD.

Battleship Potemkin. Dir. Sergei Eisenstein. Soviet Union, 1925. Film.

Bolívar eterno, ciudadano de la libertad [*Eternal Bolívar, Citizen of Freedom*]. Efterpi Charalambidis. Venezuela, 2006. Film.

Caín adolescente [*Adolescent Cain*]. Dir. Román Chalbaud. Venezuela, 1959. Film.

Cama adentro [*Live-in Maid*]. Dir. Jorge Gaggero. Argentina, 2004. Koch Lorber, 2007. DVD.

155

CAP: dos intentos [*CAP: Two Attempts*]. Dir. Carlos Oteyza. Venezuela, 2016. Film.

Carandiru. Dir. Héctor Babenco. Brazil, 2003. Sony Pictures Classics, 2004. DVD.

La casa de agua [*The House of Water*]. Dir. Jacobo Penzo. Venezuela, 1984. Film.

Cidade de Deus [*City of God*]. Dir. Fernando Meirelles and Kátia Lund. Brazil, 2002. Film.

La ciénaga [*The Swamp*]. Dir. Lucrecia Martel. Argentina, 2001. Home Vision, 2005. DVD.

La clase [*The Class*]. Dir. José Antonio Varela. Venezuela, 2007. Fundación Villa del Cine, n.d. DVD.

Comando X. Dir. José Antonio Varela, 2008. Fundación Villa del Cine, n.d. DVD.

Conducta [*Behavior*]. Dir. Ernesto Daranas. Cuba, 2014. Film.

El crimen del Padre Amaro [*The Crime of Father Amaro*]. Dir. Carlos Carrera. Mexico, 2002. Columbia TriStar, 2003. DVD.

Un cuento chino [*A Chinese Take-Away*]. Dir. Sebastián Borensztein. Argentina, 2011. Film.

El custodio [*The Bodyguard*]. Dir. Rodrigo Moreno. Argentina, 2006. Film.

De cierta manera [*One Way or Another*]. Dir. Sara Gómez. Cuba, 1977. Film.

De nadie [*No One*]. Dir. Tin Dirdamal. Mexico, 2005. Laguna, 2007. DVD.

Desde allá [*From Afar*]. Dir. Lorenzo Vigas. Venezuela, 2015. Film.

Deus e o diabo na terra do sol [*God and the Devil in the Land of the Sun/Black God, White Devil*]. Dir. Glauber Rocha. Brazil, 1964. Versátil, 2003. DVD.

Los dioses rotos [*Fallen Gods*]. Dir. Ernesto Daranas Serrano. Cuba, 2008. ICAIC, 2008. DVD.

Doméstica [*Housemaids*]. Dir. Gabriel Mascaro. Brazil, 2012. Film.

Doña Bárbara. Dir. Fernando de Fuentes and Miguel M. Delgado. Mexico, 1943. Film.

Las elegidas [*The Chosen Ones*]. Dir. David Pablos. Mexico, 2015. Film.

Eréndira. Dir. Rui Guerra. France-Mexico-West Germany, 1983. Film.

Fresa y chocolate [*Strawberry and Chocolate*]. Dir. Tomás Gutiérrez Alea and Juan Carlos Tabío. Cuba, 1993. Film.

Funny Games. Dir. Michael Haneke. USA-France-UK-Austria-Germany-Italy, 2007. Film.

Gaijin: Os caminhos da liberdade [*Gaijin: A Brazilian Odyssey*]. Dir. Tizuka Yamasaki, Brazil, 1980. Film.

Godard on Television: 1960–1999. Dir. Michel Royer. France, 1999. Film.

Graduados [*Graduates*]. Dir. Miguel Colom. Argentina, 2012. Telefe series.

Los guantes mágicos [*The Magic Gloves*]. Dir. Martín Rejtman. Argentina, 2003. Gijef, 2005. DVD.

Habanastation [*Havanastation*]. Dir. Ian Padrón. Cuba, 2011. Global Films, 2011. DVD.

Hands of Stone. Dir. Jonathan Jakubowicz. Panama-USA, 2016. Film.

Happy Together. Dir. Wong Kar-Wai. Hong Kong-Japan-South Korea, 1997. Film.

Hasta cierto punto [*Up to a Point*]. Dir. Tomás Gutiérrez Alea. Cuba, 1983. DVD.

Heli. Dir. Amat Escalante. Mexico, 2013. Cai Chang, 2014. DVD.

Historia del miedo [*History of Fear*]. Dir. Benjamín Naishtat. Argentina, 2014. Film.

Homicidio culposo. Dir. César Bolívar. Venezuela, 1983. Film.

La hora de los hornos [*The Hour of Furnaces*]. Dir. Fernando Solanas and Octavio Getino. Argentina, 1968. Cinesur, 2007. DVD.

El infierno [*El Narco/Hell*]. Dir. Luis Estrada. Mexico, 2010. Film.

O invasor [*The Trespasser*]. Dir. Beto Brant. Brazil, 2002. Film.

La jaula de oro [*The Golden Dream*]. Dir. Diego Quemada-Díez. Guatemala-Spain-Mexico, 2013. Deltmac (Taiwan), 2014. DVD.

Kiss of the Spider Woman. Dir. Héctor Babenco. Brazil-USA, 1985. City Lights, 2008. DVD.

Lake Tahoe. Dir. Fernando Eimbcke. Mexico, 2008. Film Movement, 2009. DVD.

Libertador Morales, el Justiciero [*Libertador Morales, the Justice Maker*]. Dir. Efterpi Charalambidis. Venezuela, 2009. Film.

Lucía. Dir. Humberto Solás. Cuba, 1968. Film.

Macuro, la fuerza de un pueblo [*Macuro, the Strength of the People*]. Dir. Hernán Jabes. Venezuela, 2008. Fundación Villa del Cinc, n.d. DVD.

O mecanismo [*The Mechanism*]. Dir. José Padilha. 2018. Netflix series.

Memoria del saqueo [*Memory of Plunder*]. Dir. Fernando Solanas. Argentina, 2004. DVD.

Memorias del subdesarrollo [*Memories of Underdevelopment*]. Dir. Tomás Gutiérrez Alea. Cuba, 1968. Film.

Miss Bala. Dir. Gerardo Naranjo. Mexico-USA, 2011. Film.

Mundo grúa [*Crane World*]. Dir. Pablo Trapero. Argentina, 1999. Facets Video, 2004. DVD.

La nana [*The Maid*]. Dir. Sebastián Silva. Chile-Mexico, 2009. Film.

El Norte. Dir. Gregory Nava. USA, 1983. Film.

Nosotros los Nobles [*The Noble Family*]. Dir. Gary Alazraki. Mexico, 2013. Warner, 2013. DVD.

Nosotros, los pobres [*We, the Poor*]. Dir. Ismael Rodríguez. Mexico, 1948. Warner, 2007. DVD.

Nueve reinas [*Nine Queens*]. Dir. Fabián Bielinsky. Argentina, 2002. Film.

Oiapoque-L'Oyapoque: Do outro lado do rio. Dir. Lucas Bambozzi. Brazil, 1999. Film.

Los olvidados [*The Young and the Damned*]. Dir. Luis Buñuel. Mexico, 1950. Films sans frontières, 2001. DVD.

Ônibus 174 [*Bus 174*]. Dir. José Padilha and Felipe Lacerda. Brazil, 2002. Film.

Orfeu. Dir. Carlos Diegues. Brazil, 1999. Film.

El otro Francisco [*The Other Francisco*]. Dir. Sergio Giral, 1974. Film.

Papita, maní y tostón. Dir. Luis Carlos Hueck. Venezuela, 2013. Film.

Pelo malo [*Bad Hair*]. Dir. Mariana Rondón. Venezuela, 2014. Film.

Pixote. Dir. Héctor Babenco. Brazil, 1981. Film.

Pizza, birra, fasso. Dir. Bruno Stagnaro and Adrián Caetano. Argentina, 1998. Facets, 2005. DVD.

Plastic City [*Dangkou*, 荡寇]. Dir. Yu Lik-wai, Nelson (余力爲). Brazil-Hong Kong, 2008. Kam, 2009. DVD.

Por primera vez [*For the First Time*]. Dir. Octavio Cortázar. Cuba, 1967. Film.

Post Tenebras Lux. Dir. Carlos Reygadas. Mexico, 2012. Verve, n.d. DVD.

Puente Llaguno, claves de una masacre [*Llaguno Bridge, Keys to a Massacre*]. Dir. Ángel Palacios. Venezuela, 2004. Film.

Les quatre cents coups [*The 400 Blows*]. Dir. François Truffaut. France, 1959. Fox Lorber, 1999. DVD.

Que horas ela volta? [*The Second Mother*]. Dir. Anna Muylaert. Brazil, 2015. Oscilloscope Laboratories, 2016. DVD.

Rapado. Dir. Martín Rejtman. Argentina, 1992. Transeuropa, 2005. DVD.

Redes. Dir. Emilio Gómez Muriel and Fred Zinnemann. Mexico, 1936. *Martin Scorsese's World Cinema Project No. 1*. Criterion Collection, 2013. DVD.

Réimon [*Reimon*]. Dir. Rodrigo Moreno. Argentina, 2014. Film.

La región salvaje [*The Untamed*]. Dir. Amat Escalante. Mexico-Denmark-France-Germany-Norway-Switzerland, 2016 Film.

The Revolution Will Not Be Televised [*La revolución no será transmitida*]. Dir. Kim Bartley and Donnacha O'Briain. Ireland-UK, 2003. Ministerio de Comunicación e Información (Venezuela), 2002. DVD.

RoboCop. Dir. José Padilha. USA, 2014. Film.

La salada. Dir. Juan Martín Hsu. Argentina, 2014. Film.

Salt of the Earth. Dir. Herbert J. Biberman. USA, 1954. Alpha, 2004. DVD.

Sangre [*Blood*]. Dir. Amat Escalante. Mexico, 2005. Videomax, 2007. DVD.

Santa y Andrés [*Santa and Andrés*]. Dir. Carlos Lechuga. Cuba, 2016. Film.

Secuestro express [*Express Kidnapping*]. Dir. Jonathan Jakubowicz. Venezuela, 2005. Intercontinental, n.d. DVD.

La serpiente roja [*The Red Snake*]. Dir. Ernesto Caparrós. Cuba, 1937. Film.

Silvia Prieto. Dir. Martín Rejtman. Argentina, 1999. Film.

O som ao redor [*Neighbouring Sounds*]. Dir. Kleber Mendonça Filho. Brazil, 2012. Cinema Guild, 2013. DVD.

Stellet Licht [*Silent Light*]. Dir. Carlos Reygadas. Mexico, 2007. Film.

Strike. Dir. Sergei Eisenstein. Soviet Union, 1925. Film.

Terra em transe [*Land in Anguish*]. Dir. Glauber Rocha. Brazil, 1967. Film.

Terra estrangeira [*Foreign Land*]. Dir. Walter Salles and Daniela Thomas. Brazil, 1995. Film.

Tocar y luchar [*To Play and to Fight*]. Dir. Alberto Arvelo. Venezuela, 2006. Film.

A Touch of Sin. Dir. Jia Zhangke. China, 2013. Film.

Tropa de elite [*Elite Squad*]. Dir. José Padilha. Brazil, 2007. CN Entertainment, 2007. DVD.

Tropa de elite 2: O inimigo agora é outro [*Elite Squad 2/Elite Squad: The Enemy Within*]. Dir. José Padilha. Brazil, 2010. New Video, 2011. DVD.

El violín [*The violin*]. Dir. Francisco Vargas. Mexico, 2005. Film.

BIBLIOGRAPHY

Acosta, José Miguel, et al. *Panorama histórico del cine en Venezuela*. Caracas: Fundación Cinemateca Nacional, 1997.

Aguilar, Gonzalo. *Más allá del pueblo. Imágenes, indicios y políticas del cine*. Buenos Aires: Fondo de Cultura Económica, 2015.

———. *New Argentine Film: Other Worlds*. New York: Palgrave Macmillan, 2008.

Althusser, Louis. *On the Reproduction of Capitalism: Ideology and Ideological State Apparatuses*. London: Verso, 2014.

Andermann, Jens. *New Argentine Cinema*. London: I.B. Tauris, 2012.

———. "Turn of the Tide? Cultural Critique and the New Right." *Journal of Latin American Cultural Studies* 27, no. 1 (2018): 1–3.

Andermann, Jens, and Álvaro Fernández Bravo, eds. *New Argentine and Brazilian Cinema: Reality Effects*. New York: Palgrave Macmillan, 2013.

Andrews, George Reid. "Racial Inequality in Brazil and the United States, 1990–2010." *Journal of Social History* 47, no. 4 (2014): 829–54.

Appadurai, Arjun. *The Future as Cultural Fact: Essays on the Global Condition*. London: Verso, 2013.

———, ed. *Globalization*. Durham: Duke University Press, 2001.

Ayala Blanco, Jorge. *La fugacidad del cine mexicano*. México, DF: Océano, 2001.

Barnard, Timothy. "Popular Cinema and Populist Politics." In Vol. 2 of *New Latin American Cinema*, edited by Michael T. Martin, 443–55. Detroit: Wayne State University Press, 1997.

Barthes, Roland. *Writing Degree Zero*. New York: Hill and Wang, 1977.

Beasley-Murray, Jon, Maxwell A. Cameron, and Eric Hershberg. "America's Left Turns: An Introduction." *Third World Quarterly* 30, no. 2 (2009): 319–30.

Beers, Mayra. "Murder in San Isidro: Crime and Culture during the Second Cuban Republic." *Cuban Studies* 34 (2003): 97–129.

Bentes, Ivana. "The Aesthetics of Violence in Brazilian Film." In *City of God in Several Voices*, edited by Else R.P. Vieira, 82–92. Nottingham: CCCP, 2005.

———. "Global Periphery: Aesthetic and Cultural Margins in Brazilian Audiovisual Forms." In *New Argentine and Brazilian Cinema*, edited by Jens Andermann and Álvaro Fernández Bravo, 103–17. New York: Palgrave Macmillan, 2013.

Bernardet, Jean Claude. "Trajectory of an Oscillation." In *Brazilian Cinema*, edited by Randal Johnson and Robert Stam, 281–89. New York: Columbia University Press, 1995.

Blaser, Liliane. "Instituto de formación cinematográfica Cotrain: Diez años aprendiendo a enseñar." *Objeto Visual* 4 (1997): 9–15.

Borges, Jorge Luis. *Collected Fictions*. New York : Viking, 1998.

Bourdieu, Pierre. *Distinction. A Social Critique of the Judgement of Taste*. London: Routledge, 2010.

Brading, Ryan. *Populism in Venezuela*. New York: Routledge, 2013.

Brazil. ANCINE, Agência Nacional do Cinema. *Informe de acompanhamento de mercado. SADIS agregado 2010. Informe Anual*. 2010.

————. *Informe de acompanhamento do mercado. Filmes e bilheterias. Resultados de 2011*. 2011.

Britto García, Luis. *Dictadura mediática en Venezuela. Investigación de unos medios por encima de toda sospecha*. Caracas: Ediciones Correo del Orinoco, 2012.

————. *El imperio contracultural: del rock a la postmodernidad*. La Habana: Editorial Arte y Cultura, 2005.

Burton, Julianne (see also Burton-Carvajal, Julianne), ed. *The Social Documentary in Latin America*. Pittsburgh: University of Pittsburgh Press, 1990.

Burton-Carvajal, Julianne (see also Burton, Julianne). "South American Cinema." In *World Cinema: Critical Approaches*, edited by John Hill and Pamela Church Gibson, 194–210. New York: Oxford University Press, 2000.

Burucúa, Constanza, and Carolina Sitnisky, eds. *The Precarious in the Cinemas of the Americas*. Cham: Palgrave Macmillan, 2018.

Buscombe, Edward. "Sound and Color." *Jump Cut* 17 (1978): 23–25.

Caldeira, Teresa P. R. *City of Walls: Crime, Segregation and Citizenship in São Paulo*. Berkeley: University of California Press, 2000.

————. "From Modernism to Neoliberalism in São Paulo: Reconfiguring the City and Its Citizens." In *Other Cities, Other Worlds: Urban Imaginaries in a Globalizing Age*, edited by Andreas Huyssen, 51–77. Durham: Duke University Press, 2008.

Calle, Luis de la, and Luis Rubio. "Clasemedieros." *Nexos* (May 2010). http://www.nexos.com.mx/?p=13742.

Capriles, María Cristina. "La investigación y la formación cinematográfica en Venezuela insertas en el sistema educativo venezolano." Paper presented at II Simposio de Investigación y Formación Cinematográfica, CNAC, Centro Nacional Autónomo de Cinematografía, Caracas, July 2012.

Cardenal, Juan Pablo, and Heriberto Araújo. *China's Silent Army: The Pioneers, Traders, Fixers and Workers Who Are Remaking the World in Beijing's Image*. London: Allen Lane, 2013.

Castañeda, Jorge. "Latin America's Left Turn." *Foreign Affairs* 85, no. 3 (2006): 28–43.

————. *Mañana Forever?: Mexico and the Mexicans*. New York: Vintage, 2011.

Castillo, José. "Carlos Reygadas." *Bomb* 111 (2010): 70–77.

Caulfield, Norman. *NAFTA and Labor in North America*. Urbana: University of Illinois Press, 2010.

Chacón Mora, Gonzalo. "Imagining the Malandro: Anti-politics and the representation of the Malandro in Venezuelan Cinema." Paper presented at The Aesthetics of Politics and the Politics of Aesthetics in Contemporary Venezuela Conference, University of Cambridge, September 2014.

Chanan, Michael. *Cuban Cinema*. Minneapolis: University of Minnesota Press, 2004.

————, ed. *Twenty-Five Years of the New Latin American Cinema*. London: BFI, 1983.

Chávez Frías, Hugo, and Marta Harnecker. *Understanding the Venezuelan Revolution: Hugo Chávez Talks to Marta Harnecker*. New York: Monthly Review, 2005.

Cicalo, André. "Nerds and Barbarians: Race and Class Encounters through Affirmative Action in a Brazilian University." *Journal of Latin American Studies* 44, no. 2 (2012): 235–60.

Davis, Mike. *Planet of Slums*. London: Verso, 2006.

Deleuze, Gilles. *Cinema 2: The Time-Image*. London: Continuum, 2005.

Deleyto, Celestino, and María del Mar Azcona. *Alejandro González Iñárritu*. Urbana: University of Illinois, 2010.

Delgado, Kevin M. "Spiritual Capital: Foreign Patronage and the Trafficking of Santería." In *Cuba and the Special Period: Culture and Ideology in the 1990's*, edited by Ariana Hernández-Reguant, 51−66. New York: Palgrave Macmillan, 2009.

De Luca, Tiago. *Realism of the Senses in World Cinema: The Experience of Physical Reality*. London: I.B. Tauris, 2014.

Derné, Steve. *Globalization on the Ground: Media and the Transformation of Culture, Class, and Gender in India*. Los Angeles: Sage, 2008.

Duno-Gottberg, Luis. "The Role of the State in Cuba and Venezuela." In *The Routledge Companion to Latin American Cinema*, edited by Marvin D'Lugo, Ana M. López and Laura Podalsky, 49−52. London: Routledge, 2018.

———. "Social Images of Anti-Apocalypse: Bikers and the Representation of Popular Politics in Venezuela." *A contra corriente* 6, no. 2 (2009): 144−72.

Dussel, Enrique. "Philosophy of Liberation, the Postmodern Debate, and Latin American Studies." In *Coloniality at Large: Latin America and the Postcolonial Debate*, edited by Mabel Moraña, Enrique Dussel, and Carlos A. Jáuregui, 335−49. Durham: Duke University Press, 2008

Echeverría, Esteban. *El matadero*. Buenos Aires: Centro Editor de América Latina, 1966.

Ellner, Steve. *Rethinking Venezuelan Politics: Class, Conflict, and the Chávez Phenomenon*. Colorado: Lynne Rienner, 2008.

———. "Venezuela's Social-Based Democratic Model: Innovations and Limitations." *Journal of Latin American Studies* 43 (2011): 421−49.

Elsaesser, Thomas. *European Cinema: Face to Face with Hollywood*. Amsterdam: Amsterdam University Press, 2005.

Falicov, Tamara. "Hollywood's Presence in Latin America: Production Participation to Distribution Dominance." In *The International Encyclopedia of Media Studies*, edited by Angharad N. Valdivia. Vol. 2: *Media Production*, edited by Vicki Mayer, 255−76. Chichester: Wiley-Blackwell, 2013.

Fanon, Franz. *The Wretched of the Earth*. Harmondsworth: Penguin, 1967.

Farrell, Michele Leigh. "Narrating Precariousness in Cuba beyond Havana and the ICAIC: The Case of Televisión Serrana's Ariagna Fajardo and *¿A dónde vamos?*" In *The Precarious in the Cinemas of the Americas*, edited by Constanza Burucúa and Carolina Sitnisky, 101—120. Palgrave Macmillan, 2018.

———. "Redefining Cuban Film and the Imagined Community: A Close-up on Nuevo realizador Aram Vidal." *Delaware Review of Latin American Studies* 15, no. 2 (2014). http://udspace.udel.edu/handle/19716/19668.

Faux, Geoffrey P. *The Global Class War: How America's Bipartisan Elite Lost Our Future--and What It Will Take to Win It Back*. Hoboken, NJ: Wiley, 2006.

Fernandes, Sujatha. *Who Can Stop the Drums? Urban Social Movements in Chávez's Venezuela*. Durham: Duke University Press, 2010.

Ferreira, Francisco H.G., Julian Messina, Jamele Rigolini, Luis-Felipe López-Calva, María Ana Lugo, and Renos Vakis. *Economic Mobility and the Rise of the Latin American Middle Class*. Washington, DC: World Bank, 2013.

Fletcher, Bill Jr. "Right-Wing Populism: The Herpes in the System of Racial Capitalism." Keynote address at How Class Works Conference, SUNY-Stonybrook, June 2010.

Foster, David William. "Films by Day and Films by Night in São Paulo." In *Latin American Cinemas: Local Views and Transnational Connections*, edited by Nayibe Bermúdez Barrios, 101–23. Calgary: University of Calgary Press, 2011.

Foucault, Michel. *Discipline and Punish: The Birth of the Prison*. New York: Vintage, 1995.

———. "Of Other Spaces." *Diacritics* 16, no. 1 (1986): 22–27.

French, John D. "Understanding the Politics of Latin America's Plural Lefts (Chávez/Lula): Social Democracy, Populism and Convergence on the Path to a Post-Neoliberal World." *Third World Quarterly* 30, no. 2 (2009): 349–70.

Frens-String, Joshua, and Alejandro Velasco. "Right Turn." *NACLA Report on the Americas* 48, no. 4 (2016): 301–02.

Gabriel, Teshome H. 1982. *Third Cinema in the Third World: The Aesthetics of Liberation*. Michigan: UMI Research Press, 1982.

Gallegos, Rómulo. *Doña Bárbara*. Madrid: Siruela, 2010.

García Borrero, Juan Antonio. *Cine cubano, la pupila insomne.* https://cinecubanola pupilainsomne.wordpress.com/.

García Canclini, Néstor. *Imaginined Globalization*. Durham and London: Duke University Press, 2014.

———. "Will There Be Latin American Cinema in the Year 2000? Visual Culture in a Postnational Era." In *Framing Latin American Cinema: Contemporary Critical Perspectives*, edited by Ann Marie Stock, 246–58. Minneapolis: University of Minnesota Press, 1997.

García Márquez, Gabriel. "The Solitude of Latin America. Gabriel García Márquez, Nobel Lecture." Nobel Prize acceptance speech. *Nobelprize.org: The Official Web Site of the Nobel Prize*. Nobel Foundation, December 8, 1982.

Geoghegan, Thomas. *Only One Thing Can Save Us: Why America Needs a New Kind of Labor Movement*. New York: New Press, 2014.

Getino, Octavio. *Cine iberoamericano. Los desafíos del nuevo siglo*. Buenos Aires: CICCUS, 2007.

Gomes, Paulo Emílio Salles. *Cinema: Trajetória no subdesenvolvimento*. São Paulo: Paz e Terra, 1996.

Guneratne, Anthony R., and Wimal Dissanayake, eds. *Rethinking Third Cinema*. New York: Routledge, 2003.

Gutiérrez Alea, Tomás. *The Viewer's Dialectic*. Part 1. Translated by Julia Lesage. *Jump Cut* 29 (1984): 18–21.

———. *The Viewer's Dialectic*. Part 2. Translated by Julia Lesage. *Jump Cut* 30 (1985): 48–53.

———. *The Viewer's Dialectic*. Part 3. Translated by Julia Lesage. *Jump Cut* 32 (1987): 57–60.

Haddu, Miriam. *Contemporary Mexican Cinema 1989–1999: History, Space and Identity*. New York: The Edwin Mellen Press, 2007.

Hall, Stuart. "Cultural Studies and the Politics of Internationalization: An Interview with Stuart Hall by Kuan-Hsing Chen." In *Stuart Hall: Critical Dialogues in*

Cultural Studies, edited by David Morley and Kuan-Hsing Chen, 393–409. London: Routledge, 1996.

———. "The Meaning of New Times." In *Stuart Hall: Critical Dialogues in Cultural Studies*, edited by David Morley and Kuan-Hsing Chen, 222–36. London: Routledge, 1996.

Hannerz, Ulf. *Transnational Connections: Culture, People, Places*. London: Routledge, 1996.

Harvey, David. *A Brief History of Neoliberalism*. New York: Oxford University Press, 2005.

———. "Introduction." In *The Communist Manifesto*, edited by Karl Marx and Friedrich Engels, 1–30. London: Pluto Press, 2008.

Heise, Tatiana Signorelli. *Remaking Brazil: Contested National Identities in Contemporary Brazilian Cinema*. Cardiff: University of Wales Press, 2012.

Herlinghaus, Hermann. "Affectivity Beyond 'Bare Life': On the Non-Tragic Return of Violence in Latin American Film." In *A Companion to Latin American Literature and Culture*, edited by Sara Castro-Klaren, 584–601. Malden, MA: Blackwell, 2008.

Herrera Montero, Lucía. "Memorias, cuerpos y narraciones en el espacio de la prisión. *Carandiru* de Héctor Babenco." In *Miradas al margen: Cine y subalternidad en América Latina y el Caribe*, edited by Luis Duno-Gottberg, 181–99. Caracas: Fundación Cinemateca Nacional, 2008.

Hess, John. "Film and Ideology." *Jump Cut* 17 (1978): 14–16.

———. "No Mas Habermas, or … Rethinking Cuban Cinema in the 1990s." *Screen* 40, no. 2 (1999): 203–07.

Higbee, Will, and Song Hwee Lim. "Concepts of Transnational Cinema: Towards a Critical Transnationalism in Film Studies." *Transnational Cinemas* 1, no. 1 (2010): 7–21.

Higson, Andrew. "The Limiting Imagination of National Cinema." In *Cinema & Nation*, edited by Mette Hjort and Scott MacKenzie, 63–74. London: Routledge, 2000.

Hodges, Robert C. "The Making and Unmaking of *Salt of the Earth*: A Cautionary Tale." PhD thesis, University of Kentucky, 1997.

Holmes, Amanda. "Landscape and the Artist's Frame in Lucrecia Martel's La ciénaga/*The Swamp* and *La niña santa*/*The Holy Girl*." In *New Trends in Argentine and Brazilian Cinema*, edited by Cacilda Rêgo and Carolina Rocha, 131–46. Bristol: Intellect, 2011.

Hopenhayn, Martín. "¿Integrarse o subordinarse? Nuevos cruces entre política y cultura." In *Cultura, Política y Sociedad. Perspectivas latinoamericanas*, edited by Daniel Mato, 17–40. Buenos Aires: CLACSO, 2005.

Jabor, Arnaldo. "Preface." In *City of God in Several Voices: Brazilian Social Cinema as Action*, edited by Else R.P. Vieira, iii–iv. Nottingham: CCCP, 2005.

James, David E., and Rick Berg, eds. *The Hidden Foundation: Cinema and the Question of Class*. Minneapolis: University of Minnesota Press, 1996.

Jameson, Fredric. "The Aesthetics of Singularity." *NLR* 92 (2015): 101–32.

———. "Class and Allegory in Contemporary Mass Culture: Dog Day Afternoon as a Political Film." *College English* 38, no. 8 (1977): 843–59.

————. "Foreword." In *The Postmodern Condition: A Report on Knowledge*, edited by Jean-François Lyotard, xii–xxi. Manchester: Manchester University Press, 1984.

————. "On Magic Realism in Film." *Critical Inquiry* 12, no. 2 (1986): 301–25.

————. *The Political Unconscious: Narrative as a Socially Symbolic Act*. London: Routledge, 2002.

————. "Postmodernism, or the Cultural Logic of Late Capitalism." *NLR* 146 (1984): 53–92.

————. *Postmodernism or the Cultural Logic of Late Capitalism*. Durham: Duke University Press, 1991.

————. *Representing Capital: A Commentary on Volume One*. London: Verso, 2011.

Janoschka, Michael, and Axel Borsdorf. "Condominios Fechados and Barrios Privados: The Rise of Private Residential Neighbourhoods in Latin America." In *Private Cities: Global and Local Perspectives*, edited by Georg Glasze, Chris Webster, and Klaus Frantz, 92–108. London: Routledge, 2006.

Janoschka, Michael, Jorge Sequera, and Luis Salinas. "Gentrification in Spain and Latin America: A Critical Dialogue." *International Journal of Urban and Regional Research* 38, no. 4 (July 2014): 1234–65.

Johns, Christina Jacqueline. *The Origins of Violence in Mexican Society*. Westport: Praeger, 1995.

Johnson, Randal, and Robert Stam, eds. *Brazilian Cinema*. Expanded ed. New York: Columbia University Press, 1995.

Johnson, Randal. "Television and the Transformation of the Star System in Brazil." In *A Companion to Latin American Cinema*, edited by Maria M. Delgado, Stephen M. Hart, and Randal Johnson, 21–35. Malden: John Wiley & Sons, 2017.

Kapur, Jyostna, and Keith B. Wagner, eds. *Neoliberalism and Global Cinema: Capital, Culture, and Marxist Critique*. New York: Routledge, 2011.

Karush, Matthew B. *Culture of Class. Radio and Cinema in the Making of a Divided Argentina, 1920–1946*. Durham: Duke University Press, 2012.

Kim, Yunyoung Verónica. "Desarticulando el 'mito blanco': Inmigración coreana en Buenos Aires e imaginarios nacionales." *Revista de crítica literaria latinoamericana* 71 (2010): 169–93.

Kleinhans, Chuck. "Class in Action." In *The Hidden Foundation: Cinema and the Question of Class*, edited by David E. James and Rick Berg, 240–63. Minneapolis: University of Minnesota Press, 1996.

Kolb-Neuhaus, Roberto. "Silvestre Revueltas's *Redes*: Composing for Film or Filming for Music?" *The Journal of Film Music* 2, nos. 2–4 (2009): 127–44.

Kracauer, Siegfried. *From Caligari to Hitler: A Psychological History of the German Film*. Princeton: Princeton University Press, 2004.

Krstić, Igor. *Slums on Screen: World Cinema and the Planet of Slums*. Edinburgh: Edinburgh University Press, 2016.

Laclau, Ernesto. *On Populist Reason*. London: Verso, 2005.

Lapsley, Robert, and Michael Westlake. *Film Theory: An Introduction*. Manchester: Manchester University Press, 2006.

Lawrenson, Edward, and Bernardo Pérez Soler. "Pup Fiction." *Sight and Sound* 11, no. 5 (2001): 3, 28–30.

Leen, Catherine. "City of Fear: Reimagining Buenos Aires in Contemporary Argentine Cinema." *Bulletin of Latin American Research* 27, no. 4 (2008): 465–82.

Lima, Bruna Della Torre De Carvalho. "Criticism and Condescension: The Triumph of the Poor in *The Second Mother.*" *Latin American Perspectives* 211, no. 6 (November 2016): 141–43.

López, Ana M. "*The Battle of Chile*: Documentary, Political Process, and Representation." In *The Social Documentary in Latin America*, edited by Julianne Burton, 267–87. Pittsburgh: University of Pittsburgh Press, 1990.

López, Ana M., and Dolores Tierney. "In Focus: Latin American Film Research in the Twenty-First Century Introduction." *Cinema Journal* 54, no. 1 (2014): 112–14.

López, Kathleen. "In Search of Legitimacy: Chinese Immigrants and Latin American Nation Building." In *Immigration and National Identities in Latin America*, edited by Nicola Foote and Michael Goebel, 182—204. Gainesville: The University Press of Florida, 2014.

Lu, Sheldon Hsiao-peng, ed. *Transnational Chinese Cinemas: Identity, Nationhood, Gender.* Honolulu: University of Hawai'i Press, 1997.

Lukács, Georg. *The Meaning of Contemporary Realism.* London: Merlin Press, 1963.

Lusnich, Ana Laura, and Javier Cossalter, eds, *Actas del II Simposio Iberoamericano de estudios comparados sobre cine y audiovisual: perspectivas interdisciplinarias. Debates del cine y la historia.* Proc. of RICiLa (Red de Investigadores sobre Cine Latinoamericano) Conference: December 5–7, 2012, Biblioteca del Congreso de la Nación Argentina. Buenos Aires: Facultad de Filosofía y Letras. UBA, 2013.

Lyotard, Jean-François. *The Postmodern Condition: A Report on Knowledge.* Manchester: Manchester University Press, 1984.

Maciel, David R. "Pochos and Other Extremes in Mexican Cinema; or, El cine mexicano se va de bracero, 1922–1963." In *Chicanos and Film: Representation and Resistance*, edited by Chon A. Noriega, 94–113. Minneapolis: University of Minnesota Press, 1992.

MacLaird, Misha. *Aesthetics and Politics in the Mexican Film Industry.* New York: Palgrave Macmillan, 2013.

Manza, Jeff. "Class." In *Oxford Bibliographies in Sociology*, edited by Lynette Spillman. Oxford University Press, 2014. http://www.oxfordbibliographies.com.

Maricato, Ermínia. "The Statute of the Peripheral City." In *The City Statute of Brazil: A Commentary*, edited by Celso Santos Carvalho and Anaclaudia Rossbach, 5–22. São Paulo: Cities Alliance and Ministry of Cities, 2010. http://documents.worldbank.org/curated/en/781901468014398230/The-City-Statute-of-Brazil-a-commentary.

Marsh, Leslie L. "Reordering (Social) Sensibilities: Balancing Realisms in *Neighbouring Sounds.*" *Studies in Spanish & Latin American Cinemas* 12, no. 2 (2015): 139–57.

———. "Women's Filmmaking and Comedy in Brazil: Anna Muylaert's *Durval Discos* (2002) and *É Proibido Fumar* (2009). In *Latin American Women Filmmakers:*

Production, Politics, Poetics, edited by Deborah Martin and Deborah Shaw, 149–71. London: I. B. Tauris, 2017.

Martínez Piva, Jorge Mario, Ramón Padilla Pérez, Claudia Schatan Pérez, and Verónica Vega Montoya. *The Mexican Film Industry and Its Participation in the Global Value Chain*. Mexico, DF: UN, CEPAL, 2011. PDF file. Serie Estudios y Perspectivas CEPAL 122.

Marx, Karl, and Friedrich Engels. *The Communist Manifesto*. London: Pluto Press, 2008.

Massey, Doreen. "Politics and Space/Time." *NLR* 1, no. 196 (November–December 1992): 65–84.

Mayobre, José Antonio. "Venezuela and the Media: The New Paradigm." In *Latin Politics, Global Media*, edited by Elisabeth Fox and Silvio Waisbord, 176–95. Austin: University of Texas Press, 2002.

Medeiros, Luiz Antônio de. *A CPI da pirataria: os segredos do contrabando e da falsificação no Brasil*. São Paulo: Geração Editorial, 2005.

Mejía Arango, Juan Luis. "Apuntes sobre las políticas culturales en América Latina, 1987–2009." *Pensamiento Iberoamericano* 4, 2ª etapa.1 (2009): 105–30.

Mera, Carolina. *La inmigración coreana en Buenos Aires. Multiculturalismo en el espacio urbano*. Buenos Aires: Eudeba, 1998.

Mercer, John, and Martin Shingler. *Melodrama: Genre, Style, Sensibility*. London: Wallflower, 2004.

Middents, Jeffrey. *Writing National Cinema: Film Journals and Film Culture in Peru*. Hanover, NH: Dartmouth College Press, 2009.

Milanesio, Natalia. *Workers Go Shopping in Argentina: The Rise of Popular Consumer Culture*. Albuquerque: University of New Mexico Press, 2013.

Mignolo, Walter. "Epistemic Disobedience and the Decolonial Option: A Manifesto." *TRANSMODERNITY: Journal of Peripheral Cultural Production of the Luso-Hispanic World*, 1, no. 2 (2011). https://escholarship.org/uc/item/62j3w283.

Mizukami, Pedro N., Oona Castro, Luiz Fernando Moncao, and Ronaldo Lemos. "Chapter 5: Brazil." In *Media Piracy in Emerging Economies*, edited by Joe Karaganis, 219–304. New York: Social Sciences Research Council, 2011.

Moraña, Mabel, ed. *Cultura y cambio social en América Latina*. Madrid: Iberoamericana; Vervuert, 2008.

Morley, David, and Kuan-Hsing Chen, eds. *Stuart Hall: Critical Dialogues in Cultural Studies*. London: Routledge, 1996.

Mota da Silva, Denise. *Vizinhos distantes. Circulação cinematográfica no Mercosul*. São Paulo: Annablume, 2007.

Mraz, John. *Looking for Mexico: Modern Visual Culture and National Identity*. Durham: Duke University Press, 2009.

Mulvey, Laura. "Visual Pleasure and Narrative Cinema." *Screen* 16, no. 3 (1975): 6–18.

Nagib, Lúcia. *Brazil on Screen. Cinema Novo, New Cinema, Utopia*. London: I.B. Tauris, 2007.

———. *O cinema da retomada. Depoimentos de 90 cineastas dos anos 90*. São Paulo: Editora 34, 2002.

———. *World Cinema and the Ethics of Realism*. New York: Continuum, 2011.

Nair, Parvati, and Julián Daniel Gutiérrez-Albilla. *Hispanic and Lusophone Women Filmmakers: Theory, Practice and Difference*. Manchester: Manchester University Press, 2013.

Navarro, Vinicius. "Local Filmmaking in Brazil: Place, Politics, and Pernambuco's New Cinema." *Studies in Spanish and Latin American Cinemas* 14, no. 1 (2017): 59–75.

Neale, Stephen. *Cinema and Technology: Image, Sound, Colour*. London: McMillan, 1985.

Neri, Marcelo. *A nova classe média. O lado brilhante da base da pirâmide*. São Paulo: Saraiva, 2011.

Newman, Kathleen. "A Different Mexican Postcard: Fernando Eimbcke's *Lake Tahoe* (2008)." *Studies in Spanish & Latin American Cinemas* 12, no. 2 (2015): 159–74.

Page, Joanna. *Crisis and Capitalism in Contemporary Argentine Cinema*. Durham: Duke University Press, 2009.

Paranaguá, Paulo Antonio, ed. *Mexican Cinema*. London: BFI; IMCINE, 1995.

Pardo, Alejandro. *The Europe-Hollywood Coopetition: Cooperation and Competition in the Global Film Industry*. Pamplona: University of Navarra, 2007.

Peluffo, Ana. "Staging Class, Gender and Ethnicity in Lucrecia Martel's *La ciénaga/The Swamp*." In *New Trends in Argentine and Brazilian Cinema*, edited by Cacilda Rêgo and Carolina Rocha, 211–23. Bristol: Intellect, 2011.

Pérez, Gilberto. "Melodrama of the Spirited Woman: Aventurera." In *Latin American Melodrama: Passion, Pathos and Entertainment*, edited by Darlene J. Sadlier, 19–32. Urbana: University of Illinois Press, 2009.

Pick, Zuzana M. *The New Latin American Cinema: A Continental Project*. Austin: University of Texas Press, 1993.

Pinardi, Sandra. "Una política sin sujeto, una práctica del silencio." *Objeto Visual. Cuadernos de Investigación de la Cinemateca Nacional de Venezuela. Lecturas y miradas del cine venezolano* 13 (2007): 11–25.

Podalsky, Laura. "Landscapes of Subjectivity in Contemporary Mexican Cinema." *New Cinemas: Journal of Contemporary Film* 9, nos. 2 & 3 (2011): 161–82.

———. *The Politics of Affect and Emotion in Contemporary Latin American Cinema: Argentina, Brazil, Cuba and Mexico*. New York: Palgrave Macmillan, 2011.

———. "Unpacking Periodization." In *The Routledge Companion to Latin American Cinema*, edited by Marvin D'Lugo, Ana M. López, and Laura Podalsky, 62–74. Oxon: Routledge, 2018.

Ramonet, Ignacio. *La dictadura de la comunicación*. Madrid: Debate Editorial, 1998.

Rêgo, Cacilda, and Carolina Rocha, eds. *New Trends in Argentine and Brazilian Cinema*. Bristol: Intellect, 2011.

Rich, B. Ruby. "An/Other View of New Latin American Cinema." In *Feminisms in the Cinema*, edited by Laura Pietropaolo and Ada Testaferri, 168–90. Bloomington: Indiana University Press, 1995.

———. "Why Do Film Festivals Matter? (2003–2004)." In *The Film Festival Reader*, edited by Dina Iordanova, 157–65. St Andrews: St Andrews Film Studies, 2013.

Robin, Diana, and Ira Jaffe, eds. *Redirecting the Gaze: Gender, Theory and Cinema in the Third World*. Albany: State University of New York, 1999.

Rocha, Glauber. "Down with Populism!" in *Twenty-five Years of The New Latin American Cinema*, edited by Michael Chanan. London: BFI and Channel Four, 1983.

Ros, Ana. "Leaving and Letting Go as Possible Ways of Living Together in Jorge Gaggero's *Cama Adentro/Live-in Maid*." In *New Trends in Argentine and Brazilian Cinema*, edited by Cacilda Rêgo and Carolina Rocha, 97–116. Bristol: Intellect, 2011.

Ruétalo, Victoria. "Border-Crossings and Textual Gaps: A 'Globalized' Mode of Production in *Profundo Carmesí* and *Terra Estrangeira*." *Studies in Hispanic Cinemas* 5, nos. 1&2 (2008): 57–71.

Sánchez Prado, Ignacio M. *Screening Neoliberalism: Transforming Mexican Cinema 1988–2012*. Nashville: Vanderbilt University Press, 2014.

Sanoja Obediente, Mario, and Iraida Vargas-Arenas. *La revolución bolivariana. Historia, cultura y socialismo*. Caracas: Monte Ávila Editores Latinoamericana C.A., 2008.

Santamaría, Roxana, and Gabriela Itzcovich. "Percepciones y prejuicios hacia inmigrantes coreanos y paraguayos residentes en la Argentina." In *Relaciones interculturales: Experiencias y representación social de los migrantes*, edited by Néstor Cohen and Carolina Mera, 25–38. Buenos Aires: Antropofagia, 2005.

Sarmiento, Domingo Faustino. *Facundo: Civilización y Barbarie*. Madrid: Cátedra, 2016.

Schroeder Rodríguez, Paul A. "After New Latin American Cinema." *Cinema Journal*. 51, no. 2 (2012): 87–112.

Schwan, Anne, and Stephen Shapiro. *How to Read Foucault's Discipline and Punish*. London: Pluto Press, 2011.

Shaw, Deborah. *Contemporary Cinema of Latin America: Ten Key Films*. New York: Continuum, 2003.

———. "Intimacy and Distance-Domestic Servants in Latin American Women's Cinema: *La mujer sin cabeza* and *El niño pez/The Fish Child*. In *Latin American Women Filmmakers: Production, Politics, Poetics*, edited by Deborah Martin and Deborah Shaw, 123–48. London: I. B. Tauris, 2017.

Shaw, Lisa, and Stephanie Dennison. *Brazilian National Cinema*. London: Routledge, 2007.

———. *Latin American Cinema: Essays on Modernity, Gender and National Identity*. Jefferson: McFarland, 2005.

Shortell, Timothy. "Durkheim's Theory of Social Class." Course materials. Department of Sociology, Brooklyn College, CUNY, n.d.

Skeggs, Beverley. *Class, Self, Culture*. London: Routledge, 2004.

Smith, Paul Julian. "Transnational Cinemas: The Cases of Mexico, Argentina and Brazil." In *Theorizing World Cinema*, edited by Lúcia Nagib, Chris Perriam, and Rajinder Dudrah, 63–76. London: I.B. Tauris, 2012.

Soares, Luiz Eduardo, André Batista, and Rodrigo Pimentel. *Elite da Tropa*. Rio de Janeiro: Objetiva, 2006.

Stam, Robert. "The Carandiru Massacre: Across the Mediatic Spectrum." In *New Argentine and Brazilian Cinema*, edited by Jens Andermann and Álvaro Fernández Bravo, 139–56. New York: Palgrave Macmillan, 2013.

————. "Beyond Third Cinema: The Aesthetics of Hybridity." In *Rethinking Third Cinema*, edited by Anthony R. Guneratne and Wimal Dissanayake, 31–48. New York: Routledge, 2003.

Stam, Robert, and Louise Spence. "Colonialism, Racism and Representation: An Introduction." *Screen* 24, no. 2 (1983): 2–20.

Stam, Robert, João Luiz Vieira, and Ismail Xavier. "The Shape of Brazilian Cinema in the Postmodern Age." In *Brazilian Cinema*, edited by Randal Johnson and Robert Stam, 387–472. New York: Columbia University Press, 1995.

Standing, Guy. *A Precariat Charter: From Denizens to Citizens*. London: Bloomsbury, 2014.

————. *The Precariat: The New Dangerous Class*. London: Bloomsbury Academic, 2011.

Stavrides, Stavros. "Heterotopias and the Experience of Porous Urban Space." In *Loose Space: Possibility and Diversity in Urban Life*, edited by Karen A. Franck and Quentin Stevens, 174–92. London: Routledge, 2007.

Stiglitz, Joseph E. *Globalization and Its Discontents*. New York: Norton, 2003.

Stock, Ann Marie, ed. *Framing Latin American Cinema: Contemporary Critical Perspectives*. Minneapolis: University of Minnesota Press, 1997.

Stocking, George W. Jr. *Victorian Anthropology*. New York: Free Press, 1987.

Stoneman, Rod. *Chávez. The Revolution Will Not Be Televised. A Case Study of Politics and the Media*. London: Wallflower Press, 2008.

Strauss, Julia C., and Ariel C. Armony, eds. *From the Great Wall to the New World: China and Latin America in the 21st Century*. Cambridge: Cambridge University Press, 2012.

Suárez Faillace, Belkis "La ciudad de *Caracas amor a muerte* y *Secuestro Express*." Paper presented at Jornadas de la Sección de Estudios Venezolanos, LASA, Caracas, June 2008.

Subero, Gustavo. *Queer Masculinities in Latin American Cinema: Male Bodies and Narrative Representations*. London: I.B. Tauris, 2014.

Sueiro Villanueva, Yolanda. *Inicios de la exhibición cinematográfica en Caracas (1896–1905)*. Caracas: Fondo Editorial Humanidades y Educación, UCV, 2007.

Tompkins, Cynthia. *Experimental Latin American Cinema: History and Aesthetics*. Austin: University of Texas Press, 2013.

Trímboli, Javier. "The Survival of Words: Revolution and Class Struggle." *Journal of Latin American Cultural Studies* 27, no. 1 (2018): 63–81.

Valencia Ramírez, Cristóbal. "Venezuela's Bolivarian Revolution: Who Are the Chavistas?" *Latin American Perspectives* 32, no. 3 (2005): 79–97.

Vargas Llosa, Mario. *Sueño y realidad de América Latina*. Barcelona: Arcadia, 2010.

Vázquez, Mercedes (see also Vázquez, María Mercedes and Vázquez Vázquez, María Mercedes). "*Secuestro express* and *La clase*: Politics of Realism in Contemporary Venezuelan Filmmaking." *Jump Cut*, 52.

Vázquez, María Mercedes. "Brazil at a Socio-Cinematic Crossroads: State Intervention on Screen." In *Brazil in Twenty-First Century Popular Media: Culture, Politics, and Nationalism on the World Stage*, edited by Naomi Pueo Wood, 113–138. Maryland: Lexington Books Press, 2014.

Vázquez Vázquez, María Mercedes. "The Question of Class in Contemporary Latin American Cinema." PhD thesis, The University of Hong Kong, 2015.

Venegas, Cristina. "Filmmaking with Foreigners." In *Cuba and the Special Period: Culture and Ideology in the 1990's*, edited by Ariana Hernández-Reguant, 37–50. New York: Palgrave Macmillan, 2009.

Vieira, Else R.P. *City of God in Several Voices: Brazilian Social Cinema as Action.* Nottingham: CCCP, 2005.

Villazana, Libia. "De una política cultural a una cultura politizada: La República Bolivariana de Venezuela y su revolución cultural en el sector audiovisual." In *E Pluribus Unum? National and Transnational Identities in the Americas = Identidades nacionales y transnacionales en las Américas*, edited by Josef Raab and Sebastian Thies: 161–73. Münster: LIT; Tempe, 2008.

———. "The Politics of the Audiovisual Cultural Revolution in Latin America and the Caribbean." In *Counter-Globalization and Socialism in the 21st Century: The Bolivarian Alliance for the Peoples of Our America*, edited by Thomas Mur: 188–202. New York: Routledge, 2013.

———. *Transnational Financial Structures in the Cinema of Latin America: Programa Ibermedia in Study*. Germany: VDM Verlag, 2009.

Waisbord, Silvio. "Media Populism: Neo-Populism in Latin America." In *The Media and Neo-Populism. A Contemporary Comparative Analysis*, edited by Gianpietro Mazzoleni, Bruce Horsfield, and Julianne Stewart: 197–216. Westport: Praeger, 2003.

Wayne, Mike, and Deirdre O'Neill. "Form, Politics and Culture: A Case Study of *The Take*, *The Revolution Will Not Be Televised* and *Listen to Venezuela*." In *Neoliberalism and Global Cinema: Capital, Culture, and Marxist Critique*, edited by Jyostna Kapur and Keith B. Wagner, 113–32. New York: Routledge, 2011.

Weber, Max. *Economy and Society*. Berkeley: University of California Press, 1978.

Weininger, Elliot B. "Foundations of Pierre Bourdieu's Class Analysis." In *Approaches to Class*, edited by Erik Olin Wright, 82–118. N.p.: Cambridge University Press, 2005.

Weintraub, Jeff, and Krishan Kumar, eds. *Public and Private in Thought and Practice: Perspectives on a Grand Dichotomy*. Chicago: University of Chicago Press, 1997.

Weisbrot, Mark, Stephan Lefebvre, and Joseph Sammut. *Did Nafta Help Mexico? An Assessment after 20 Years*. PDF file. Washington D.C.: Centre for Economic and Policy Research (CEPR), 2014.

Williams, Raymond. *Culture and Materialism: Selected Essays*. 1980. London: Verso, 2005.

———. "A Lecture on Realism." *Screen* 18, no. 1 (1977): 61–74.

———. *Marxism and Literature*. Oxford: Oxford University Press, 2009.

Wilson, Jason. "Writing for the Future: Echeverría's "El Matadero" and Its Secret Rewriting by Jorge Luis Borges and Adolfo Bioy Casares as "La fiesta del monstruo." *Forum for Modern Language Studies* 43, no. 1 (2007): 81–92.

The World Bank. "New World Bank Report Finds 50 Percent Increase in Middle Class in Latin America and the Caribbean over Last Decade." The World Bank, November 13, 2012.

Wright, Erik Olin, ed. *Approaches to Class Analysis.* N.p.: Cambridge University Press, 2005.

———. "Class, State and Ideology: An Introduction to Social Science in the Marxist Tradition." *Course Materials of Sociology 621.* Department of Sociology. University of Wisconsin, Madison, 2013.

Yau, Esther C. M. "Compromised Liberation: The Politics of Class in Chinese Cinema of the Early 1950s." In *The Hidden* Foundation: *Cinema and the Question of Class,* edited by David E. James and Rick Berg, 138–71. Minneapolis: University of Minnesota Press, 1996.

Zimmerman, Marc, and Ochoa Bilbao, Luis, eds. *Giros culturales en la marea rosa de América Latina.* Puebla: LACASA, 2012.

Žižek, Slavoj. *In Defense of Lost Causes.* London: Verso, 2008.

Zweig, Noah. "Villa Del Cine (Cinema City): Constructing Bolivarian Citizens for the Twenty-First Century." *Situations* 4, no. 1 (2011): 133–49.

Index

About the Author

María Mercedes Vázquez Vázquez is a lecturer and honorary assistant professor at the University of Hong Kong. Her publications include book chapters and articles on Venezuelan, Brazilian, and Mexican cinemas and an annotated bibliography on Latin American cinema (OUP). She teaches Latin American and European cinema, Spanish, Hispanic Culture, and Literature. She heads the research subcommittee of the Committee on Gender, Equality and Diversity of the Faculty of Arts, and curates HKU's Latin American film series.